Lecture Notes in Computer Science 8155

Commenced Publication in 1973
Founding and Former Series Editors:
Gerhard Goos, Juris Hartmanis, and Jan van Leeuwen

Jarkko Kari   Martin Kutrib
Andreas Malcher (Eds.)

Cellular Automata and Discrete Complex Systems

19th International Workshop, AUTOMATA 2013
Gießen, Germany, September 17-19, 2013
Proceedings

 Springer

Volume Editors

Jarkko Kari
University of Turku
Department of Mathematics
20014 Turku, Finland
E-mail: jkari@utu.fi

Martin Kutrib
Andreas Malcher
Universität Gießen
Institut für Informatik
Arndtstraße 2
35392 Gießen, Germany
E-mail: {kutrib, malcher}@informatik.uni-giessen.de

ISSN 0302-9743   e-ISSN 1611-3349
ISBN 978-3-642-40866-3   e-ISBN 978-3-642-40867-0
DOI 10.1007/978-3-642-40867-0
Springer Heidelberg New York Dordrecht London

Library of Congress Control Number: 2013947368

CR Subject Classification (1998): F.1.1, F.2.2, I.6, C.2, E.3, D.4.6

LNCS Sublibrary: SL 1 – Theoretical Computer Science and General Issues

Typesetting: Camera-ready by author, data conversion by Scientific Publishing Services, Chennai, India

Printed on acid-free paper

Springer is part of Springer Science+Business Media (www.springer.com)

Preface

The 19th International Workshop on Cellular Automata and Discrete Complex Systems (AUTOMATA 2013) was organized by the Institut für Informatik of the Universität Giessen and took place at the campus of natural sciences. It was a three-day workshop starting September 17 and ending September 19, 2013. The Universität Giessen is one of the older universities in the German-speaking part of Europe. It was founded in 1607.

AUTOMATA 2013 continues a series of events established in 1995. The aims of the annual workshops are:

- To establish and maintain a permanent, international, multidisciplinary forum for the collaboration of researchers in the field of Cellular Automata (CA) and Discrete Complex Systems (DCS).
- To provide a platform for presenting and discussing new ideas and results.
- To support the development of theory and applications of CA and DCS (for example, parallel computing, physics, biology, social sciences, and others) as long as fundamental aspects and their relations are concerned.
- To identify and study within an inter- and multidisciplinary context, the important fundamental aspects, concepts, notions and problems concerning CA and DCS.

This volume contains the invited contributions and the accepted full papers of AUTOMATA 2013. We would like to thank the invited speakers

- Nazim Fatès (Inria Nancy Grand-Est, Nancy, France)
- Enrico Formenti (University of Nice Sophia Antipolis, Nice, France)
- Pedro de Oliveira (Mackenzie Presbyterian University, São Paulo, Brazil)

for accepting our invitations and presenting us several diverse perspectives on cellular automata.

There were 15 full and 11 exploratory papers submitted to AUTOMATA 2013 by a total of 47 authors from 17 different countries, from all over the world, Belgium, Brazil, Chile, China, Finland, France, Germany, India, Italy, Japan, Montenegro, Poland, Slovenia, Spain, Ukraine, United Kingdom, and USA. We would like to thank all authors for their contributions. From the 15 full papers submitted the Program Committee selected 8 papers on the basis of three referee reports each. Contributions in the exploratory category are not included in this volume. The submission and refereeing process was supported by the EasyChair conference management system. We warmly thank the members of the Program Committee for their excellent work in making this selection. We also thank the additional external reviewers for their careful evaluation. All these efforts were the basis for the success of the workshop. The collaboration with Springer for preparing this volume was very efficient and pleasant. We like to thank in particular Alfred Hofmann and Anna Kramer from Springer for their help.

We are also grateful to the additional members of the Organizing Committee consisting of Susanne Gretschel, Markus Holzer, Sebastian Jakobi, Katja Meckel, Julien Provillard, Heinz Rübeling, and Matthias Wendlandt for their support of the sessions and the accompanying events.

Finally, we are indebted to all participants for attending the workshop. We hope that this workshop will be a successful and fruitful meeting, will bear new ideas for investigations, and will bring together people for new scientific collaborations.

September 2013

Jarkko Kari
Martin Kutrib
Andreas Malcher

Organization

AUTOMATA 2013 was organized by the Institut für Informatik of the Universität Giessen, Germany. The conference took place at the campus of natural sciences.

Program Committee

Bruno Durand	Université Montpellier 2, France
Paola Flocchini	University of Ottawa, Canada
Anahí Gajardo	University of Concepcion, Chile
Eric Goles	Adolfo Ibáñez University, Chile
Pierre Guillon	University of Aix-Marseille, France
Rolf Hoffmann	Technical University Darmstadt, Germany
Jarkko Kari	University of Turku, Finland
Martin Kutrib	Universität Giessen, Germany
Danuta Makowiec	Gdansk University, Poland
Andreas Malcher	University of Giessen, Germany
Bruno Martin	University of Nice Sophia Antipolis, France
Genaro Martínez	University of the West of England, United Kingdom
Kenichi Morita	Hiroshima University, Japan
Hidenosuke Nishio	Kyoto University, Japan
Ferdinand Peper	National Institute of Information and Communications Technology, Japan
Victor Poupet	Université Montpellier 2, France
Kai Salomaa	Queen's University, Canada
Klaus Sutner	Carnegie Mellon University, USA
Véronique Terrier	University of Caen, France
Hiroshi Umeo	Osaka Electro-Communication University, Japan
Thomas Worsch	Karlsruhe Institute of Technology, Germany

External Referees

Jean-Charles Delvenne	Alexander Shen
Jean-Marie Le Bars	Guillaume Theyssier
Andrei Romashchenko	Jean-Baptiste Yunès
Ville Salo	

Organizing Committee

Susanne Gretschel

Markus Holzer

Sebastian Jakobi

Martin Kutrib

Andreas Malcher

Katja Meckel

Julien Provillard

Heinz Rübeling

Matthias Wendlandt

Sponsoring Institutions

Universität Giessen

Table of Contents

Conceptual Connections around Density Determination in Cellular Automata

Pedro P.B. de Oliveira

Universidade Presbiteriana Mackenzie, Faculdade de Computação e Informática,
Rua da Consolação 896, Consolação, 01302-907 São Paulo, SP – Brazil
pedrob@mackenzie.br

Abstract. A recurring and well studied benchmark problem in the context of computations with cellular automata is the attempt to determine which is the most frequent cell state in an arbitrary initial configuration. Although extremely simple in formulation, the problem has unveiled a rich web of conceptual connections which, at the same time, have enlarged and challenged our understanding about how to perform computations within cellular automata. Here, we outline such a conceptual web, and provide a personal assessment of some of its loose ends, with possibly fruitful paths to address them.

Keywords: Density classification task, DCT, global majority problem, emergent computation, cellular automata, number conserving rule.

1   Introduction

By looking up the cellular automata (CAs) literature in order to find out which are the most well studied computation performed by them, two tasks readily come out: the firing squad synchronisation problem and the density classification task, the latter outnumbered by the former. It is useful to compare the two.

In a simplified way, while the firing squad demands that a state synchronisation be achieved among the various cells of the entire lattice, density classification imposes that a decision be made, based upon information gathered over the entire lattice, namely, the more frequent cell state; in both cases, the effectiveness of the computation carried out is granted according to their reaching predefined global configurations, after sufficiently long time.

Crucial in these problems is the existence of trivial solutions by processes allowed global access to the entire lattice; this is naturally forbidden by a CA based solution, by definition, so as to enforce that the solution to a global problem be achieved by purely local means.

Notwithstanding such a necessary similarity, it is useful to identify differences between the two problems. While the firing squad can be solved by a single rule (with many examples already known, in fact), density classification cannot.

Also, while the CAs related to the former task have typically been obtained through stepwise and careful thought-out engineering, many times supplemented by formal methods, the CAs for the latter have been most effectively found by

J. Kari, M. Kutrib, and A. Malcher (Eds.): AUTOMATA 2013, LNCS 8155, pp. 1–14, 2013.
© Springer-Verlag Berlin Heidelberg 2013

search methods, mostly evolutionary, in the space of possible rules. Additionally, density classification is structurally much simpler than the firing squad, in that it has a much simpler definition; it is more general in terms of the notion it is based upon – that of a majority – which also appears in various other contexts in science; it is more abstract, insofar as the notion of majority provides a direct link to the formal language notion of context sensitivity; and also more flexible in terms of the variations it admits.

So, such a diverse combination of features renders density classification a paradigmatic testbed for studying computations in the context of cellular automata ([Mitchell, 1998]). As such, much have already been learned in its respect, which ended up unveiling a web of conceptual connections, far beyond its original motivation of a mere tool to help addressing the notion of fault tolerance in cellular automata. Nevertheless, very challenging questions have been opened up, several of them still in need of a response. It is about those conceptual connections and their current loose ends that this paper is about, even if in condensed form.

In the following section we define the problem, and in the next we examine what is known and what remains unknown so far about it. The subsequent section concludes, by providing a personal assessment of some open issues still challenging us, and possibly fruitful paths to address them. The presentation has a survey flavour, systematic but general, with various details omitted.

2   Density Classification

Cellular automata (CAs) consist of a grid-like regular lattice of cells, together with a state transition rule, the cells having an identical pattern of local connections to others, the lattice being subjected to some boundary condition, usually periodic ([Wolfram, 2002]; [Kari, 2005]). Each cell can take on one of k discrete states, assumedly varying from 0 to k-1, and the neighbourhood of a cell is defined as the cell, together with those connected to it. The rule yields the next state for every cell, as a function of its neighbourhood; at each time step, all cells synchronously have their states updated. The size of the neighbourhood is usually written as $2r+1$, where r is the radius (or range) of the automaton. The particular case of binary one-dimensional CAs with $r = 1$ yields the so-called elementary CA rules and its corresponding elementary space.

In order to refer to rules of any given space, their numbers are defined herein according to Wolframs standard lexicographic ordering of the state transitions, in that the rule number is the decimal representation of the state transition outputs, with the left-most output referring to the neighbourhood consisting of all cells in the state $k - 1$, with the remaining state transitions ordered in lexicographic order, down to the right-hand neighbourhood that consists of all cells in the 0-state.

In its standard and simplest formulation, the density classification task (DCT, for short) states that a binary, one-dimensional CA has to converge to a final configuration of all cells being in the 1-state, when an odd-sized initial configuration, in periodic boundary condition, has more 1s than 0s, and to a configuration of all 0s, otherwise; Figure 1 illustrates the two cases. This is essentially the case of *global majority* determination in the initial configuration, even though for historical reasons the reference to *density* has been used, in reference to the percentage of 1s (or 0s), in which case one may refer to the problem as the determination of $\rho > 1/2$.

While solving the DCT is a trivial task for any computational system with central control, this not the case for any fully distributed system, with local processing, as a cellular automaton. Solving the DCT has attracted attention in the literature in particular due to the hope that good results achieved by a specific technique for density decision could carry over to other cellular automata based problems; furthermore, on a broader sense, majority determination is paradigmatic in various areas of science, as a model of how global phenomena come about from locally constrained action ([Moreira, Mathur, Diermeier and Amaral, 2004]), also appearing in other contexts of computer science ([Flocchini, 2009]) and even the social sciences (for instance, [Lanchier and Neufer, 2013]).

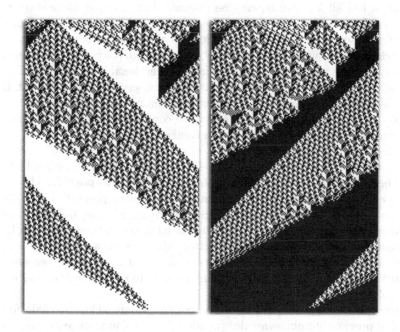

Fig. 1. Temporal evolution (with time running downward) of one of the best rules described in [Wolz and de Oliveira, 2008] in the one-dimensional DCT, from random initial configurations of size 149, with more 0s on the left, and more 1s on the right

3   What Is Known and What Is Not

3.1   Standard Formulation

The standard density classification task was defined as such in [Packard, 1988], but implicitly it had been around since 1978, after [Gacs, Kurdyumov and Levin, 1978]. But it was only in 1995 that the problem was proven to be impossible to solve, by [Land and Belew, 1995]. Later, [Chau, Siu and Yan, 1999] proved the impossibility of the k-ary version of DCT, and, building upon the proof of [Land and Belew, 1995], [Reynaga and Amthauer, 2003] could prove that two-dimensional DCT cannot be solved either. Apparently, no proof has been given of the impossibility of DCT in arbitrary lattice dimensions, but it is generally believed that this is indeed the case.

An alternative path leading to the unsolvability of DCT comes from its relation to the general properties of conservation and balancedness of a rule. A rule is *conservative* (or specifically number conservative, which is the case at issue) if it is able to preserve the sum modulo k of the states in all cells, throughout any temporal evolution; and a rule is said to be balanced when its k-ary representation has all k states equally represented. For example, elementary rule 184 (or its dynamically equivalent 226) is number conserving, regardless of the initial binary sequence in the lattice, since the number of cells in the 1-state is kept unchanged throughout the temporal evolution. So, [Capcarrère and Sipper, 2001] showed that the possibility of solving d-dimensional DCT (for any d integer) would require the rule to be able to be both conservative and balanced. But since [Fukś, 2000] had proven that conservation entails balancedness, solving d-dimensional DCT would require the rule to be conservative which, by definition of the standard formulation of DCT, is a contradiction.

The fact is that after the impossibility of solving the standard DCT formulation became established, research efforts shifted, in this context, towards looking for the best rule that could solve the problem as perfectly as possible. The DCT for one- and d-dimensional cellular automata shares many properties with other problems suitable for evolutionary algorithms. As such, using different search techniques, mostly evolutionary computation methods, various attempts have been made and, over time, better and better rules have been found. The search for one-dimensional, binary, radius 3 rules of size 149 turned out to become the standard benchmark setting used by many authors to document the abilities of their evolutionary search techniques.

Using sophisticated evolutionary techniques [Wolz and de Oliveira, 2008] found over 7000 previously unknown rules (in 3000 distinct equivalence classes) with efficacy >85.91%, and over 9500 rules with efficacy >85.50%, both figures obtained with evaluations against half a million initial configurations, randomly generated with binomial distribution of densities. The rule table symmetries that define dynamically equivalent rules play a significant role in guiding the search towards better rules. The (supposedly) best rule found, and its unique symmetric equivalent, score 88.99%. After so many extensive searches carried out, it seems likely that these two rules might indeed be the best imperfect rules for DCT; however, the challenge to prove this observation remains open.

As far as the standard two-dimensional DCT is concerned, [Bušić, Fatès, Mairesse and Marcovici, 2013] shows that the so-called Toom's rule, perfectly solves the two-dimensional DCT, but only with infinite two-dimensional lattice; with finite lattice sizes, as stated in [Fatès, 2012], the rule performs very badly. On a distinct slant, [Reynaga and Amthauer, 2003] performs an attempt to construct a two-dimensional generalisation of the GKL rule – after [Gacs, Kurdyumov and Levin, 1978], the first ever rule proposed for one-dimensional DCT, at the very inception of the problem – which did perform better than Toom's rule (as noted in [Fatès, 2012]), but lagged behind the best rule shown in [Oliveira and Siqueira, 2006] and even in [Morales, Crutchfield and Mitchell, 2000], both by evolutionary means.

[Wolz and de Oliveira, 2008] still seem to hold to this date the best results for two-dimensional DCT. While the best score reported with Moore neighbourhood in [Oliveira and Siqueira, 2006] was about 70%, on a sample of 10000 initial configurations of size 21 × 21, randomly generated with uniform distribution of densities, [Wolz and de Oliveira, 2008] reports on more than 1000 rules at the same level, the best one reaching 83.3% on a sample of 1 million initial configurations with uniform distribution of densities. Using von Neumann neighbourhood with radius 2, the performance of the best rules found were around 81.0%. Experiments were also performed with the three-dimensional DCT, and rules were found with von Neumann neighbourhood of radius 1, scoring around 76.0%, on lattice size 5 × 5 × 5.

From a different slant, also worth of mention is the result by [Gómez Soto and Fukś, 2011], indicating that the local majority rule alone progressively improves its performance in the d-dimensional DCT, as the dimensionality of space increases. This conjecture, drawn from computational experiments and theoretical arguments based on the mean-field approximation of CA rules, is yet to be proven, though.

3.2   Alternative Formulations

Non-periodic Boundary Condition. Notwithstanding the unsolvability of DCT in its standard formulation, the task can be perfectly solved if formulated differently. Accordingly, [Sipper, Capcarrère and Ronald, 1998] showed that elementary CA rule 184 alone can account for a solution, if periodic boundary is replaced by fixed background of 0-states; the related previous supposed solution in [Capcarrère, Sipper and Tomassini, 1996] involving rule 184 in periodic boundary condition is questionable, since it relies on global information.

Temporal Combination of Distinct Rules. On a different approach, [Fukś, 1997] showed that the standard DCT is solvable by the trivial combination of running, in sequence, elementary rules 184 and 232, which are, respectively, the conservative rule known as the traffic rule and the majority rule. More precisely, the author shows that the solution can achieved by running rule 184 for up to $\lfloor (N-2)/2 \rfloor$ time steps, N being the lattice size, followed by running rule 232 for additional $\lfloor (N-1)/2 \rfloor$ time steps; it is also remarked that in order to get a faster rule, with radius T, it would suffice to compose rules 184 and 232 with themselves T times, thus generating rules that can do in 1 time step what 184 and 232 do in T steps. The paper then sketches the argument that with generalised versions of the traffic and majority rules, it would be possible to classify any critical density $\rho_c = 1/n$, $n \geq 2$, n integer.

Following and extending this idea, [Chau, Yan, Wan and Siu, 1998] were able to provide a solution for any rational density ρ_c, which generalises the previous results. Pushing even further, [Chau, Siu and Yan, 1999] defined their *affinity* and *propagation* rules, extended from what the traffic and majority rules do in the previous solutions, and generalised the previous DCT solutions to the k-ary case. However, in a sense, these rules are effectively *classes* of rules since the rule radii are directly dependent not only on the number of states k (which is fine), but also on the lattice size N. This entails that, for each lattice size, different rules are effectively *instantiated*, thus rendering the approach somewhat questionable; after all, if one is allowed to use such an information, it would trivially suffice to construct specific majority rules with radius $N/2$. As hinted at in the paper, the generalisation of the idea to arbitrary densities was on course but, as far as I know, it has not come out; its generalisation to arbitrary dimensions has not been carried out either, apparently.

[Kanoh and Wu, 2003] then showed another standard DCT solution with 2 rules, and [Martins and de Oliveira, 2005] showed 2 further solutions with 2 rules and 24 solutions with 3 rules; in these latter cases, all the rules are elementary, and the rule combinations have been found by evolutionary searches in the space of possible combinations of a given size.

It is interesting that in the solution in [Chau, Siu and Yan, 1999] it becomes clear that the first rule to be applied (the *affinity* rule) has to be conservative, eventually providing a general explanation for the findings of [Fukś, 1997] and [Chau, Yan, Wan and Siu, 1998], and bringing back the issue of conservation to the context of density determination. In fact, from the algorithm [Boccara and Fukś, 1998] had provided to determine whether an arbitrary binary one-dimensional CA is conservative, the same authors provided a generalisation to the k-ary case ([Boccara and Fukś, 2002]). It is tempting to think that better k-ary solutions to DCT might exist out of the combination of the latter algorithm with the result by [Chau, Siu and Yan, 1999].

Spatial Arrangement of Different Rules. Analogously to the idea of successfully performing temporal combination of rules, one might ask about the possibility of performing density determination by employing non-uniform CAs – also known as hybrid or heterogeneous CAs – in which different cells in the lattice are ascribed different rules ([Dennunzio, Formenti and Provillard, 2012]). Although [Maiti, Munshi and Chaudhuri, 2006] clearly states that a solution to density classification is given by means of one-dimensional, binary CAs (of arbitrary radii), in periodic boundary condition, only an approximate solution is in fact shown, with the authors even performing the error analysis of the supposed solutions they derive; nevertheless, the technique employed therein, based upon the analysis of the so-called *rule vector graph* (RVG) of a CA is quite promising.

More recently, [Naskar and Das, 2012] showed how to construct a binary, non-uniform CA, with *null* boundary condition (i.e., fixed, on a background of 0s), with finite number N of cells, that will always converge to either of the two uniform configurations 0^N or 1^N and argue that such a *doubly quiescent cellular automaton* could be used for density classification; although this seems a sensible idea, the achievement is yet to be shown.

By adding the possibility of temporal rule combinations to a non-uniform CA, a variant [Sahoo, Choudhury, Pal, Kumar and Nayak, 2009] defined and named *programmable* cellular automaton, it was possible to derive exact solutions, not surprisingly though, for both standard one- and two-dimensional DCT.

My own experience with the standard DCT favours the impossibility of a solution, after extensive computational experiments showing that no solution does exist out of testing all possible combinations of elementary CA rules in lattices with 3, 5 and 7 cells, and that there is strong statistical evidence that this should also be the case for lattices with 9 and 11 cells [de Oliveira, Faria, Zanon and Leite, 2013]. All in all, as far as I am aware, no non-uniform solution to DCT is presently available, although no proof has been given that it cannot exist.

Rules with Memory. Another CA variant that has been used was to embed memory in the CA processing; with this additional feature, [Stone and Bull, 2009] provided empirical evidence that an evolutionary search for good rules in the standard DCT was facilitated. Analogously, [Alonso-Sanz and Bull, 2009] showed that a given two-dimensional rule embedded with memory outperformed the memoryless version in the two-dimensional DCT; more than that, the method in fact led to a rule which seems to be currently the best known solution, with performance around 90%, a figure that has to be taken with caution, since it was obtained on a small set of only 10000 initial configurations, 149 cells long, randomly generated with binomial distribution of densities. It remains to be shown whether the usage of memory can lead to a perfect solution.

Stochastic Rules. By relaxing the deterministic feature of the cell updates, we end up with a probabilistic CA. [Fukś, 2002] was the first to tackle DCT following this approach, by defining an elementary type CA, with synchronous update, where each state transition has a probability of leading to 0 or 1, except the neighbourhoods 000 and 111 which, respectively, always lead to 0 and 1. This rule can be described as if, for each cell independently, performing a shift to the left with probability p_1, a shift to the right also with probability p_1, or remaining in its original state with probability $1 - 2p_1$, for $p_1 \in (0, 1/2)$; in other words, the rule can be regarded as a probabilistic mixing of elementary rules 170 (the left-shift rule) and 240 (the right-shift rule).

Later, [Schüle, Ott and Stoop, 2009] provided another elementary probabilistic CA, also preserving deterministic state transitions for neighbourhoods 000 and 111, to 0 and 1, respectively, but in such a way that it can now be described as performing, for each cell independently, an XOR with probability $1 - p_2$, and the majority with probability p_2, for $p_2 \in (0, 1)$; this time the rule can be conceived of as a probabilistic mixing of elementary rules 150 (the XOR rule) and 232 (the majority rule).

Recently, [Fatès, 2013] discussed another elementary probabilistic CA (unveiled earlier, in a previous paper of the author). The approach in this case relies on a *more* deterministic CA than the two predecessors, in that six, out of the eight possible state transitions are deterministic, namely, 000→0, 001→0, 010→0, 011→1, 101→1 and 111→1. This rule, named the *traffic-majority* rule, comes from the fact that it equates to a description in terms of the application, for each cell independently, of elementary 184 (the traffic rule) with probability $1 - p_3$ and elementary rule 232 (the majority rule) with probability p_3, for $p_3 \in (0, 1)$. Key to this rule is the fact that, while those in [Fukś, 2002] and [Schüle, Ott and Stoop, 2009] are solutions in the statistical sense, the traffic-majority rule is shown to have the property that it can solve DCT with arbitrary precision, given sufficient time. But two remarks need to be made. First, that the highest the targetted performance, the longer it takes for convergence Second, that, given a lattice size, once the probability value p_3 is adjusted for a target performance, it does not necessarily carry over to other sizes; in fact, it is an open question to this date how to obtain the correct probability value p_3 of the rule, for a given lattice size. Notwithstanding the latter two difficulties, obtaining the rule is a quite remarkable result, in that it clearly shows that randomness can be helpful to perform a computation which would not be possible otherwise.

Based on the success of the previous approach, [Fatès, 2012] discussed whether it would be possible to devise a solution to the two-dimensional DCT from a generalisation of the latter. But the result was not satisfactory. In trying to achieve a better rule, a different stochastic rule was devised, but this time with asynchronous update, acting on pairs of cells. Such form of *interacting particle system* eventually led to a performance that seems to equal it to the good deterministic rule with memory shown in [Alonso-Sanz and Bull, 2009], as hinted at earlier.

[Bušić, Fatès, Mairesse and Marcovici, 2013] also shows solutions with stochastic CAs with synchronous update (the standard probabilistic CA) as well as with asynchronous update (an interacting particle system, as they define). In this respect, drawing on Toom's rule (which is deterministic), an asynchronous rule is defined that also solves two-dimensional DCT in infinite lattices. The paper also discusses possibilities of solving one-dimensional DCT on the infinite lattice size by means of three CA models, two deterministic and one probabilistic, all conjectured to do the job. The formal approach carried out therein is powerful, thus holding promise that it may also yield interesting results for finite lattices.

Different Update Schemes. In terms of deterministic asynchronous CAs for one-dimensional density classification, scarce efforts were made to find rules by evolutionary searches, with no success; for instance, [Tomassini and Venzi, 2002] evolved rules for three different updating schemes but only managed to find rules that could not even outperform some known synchronous, imperfect rules of the literature at the time. Furthermore, by showing that some elementary rules can behave as universal pattern generators, [Vielhaber, 2012] recently introduced the idea of computing by appropriately defining the update scheme of a CA, in a deterministic fashion; with this, it becomes tempting to see whether a DCT solution could be couched in this approach, even if this would be yet another formulation of the problem.

4 Towards Tying up Some of the Loose Ends: A Personal Assessment

The evolutionary search techniques described in [Wolz and de Oliveira, 2008], originally targeted to the standard, one-dimensional formulation of the DCT, ended up leading to unparalleled good results in all typical dimensions, to a point that, to this date, the best rules mentioned therein remain the best of their respective classes. Equally remarkable was that the same techniques have also been successfully applied to another task, the *parity problem*, where the objective is to determine the parity of the number of 1s in the initial configuration ([Betel, de Oliveira and Flocchini, 2013]). It is this kind of carrying-over of automatic design techniques that I believe will allow us to avail ourselves of more instances of CAs that perform predefined computational tasks. Because of this, just like the fruit-fly – *Drosophila Melanogaster* – has played a key historical role to the field of evolutionary biology, I believe that the DCT will prove to have a similar importance to evolutionary approaches in cellular automata.

In spite of all the efforts made throught the years, by different CA models and design approaches, there are still many open questions, as pointed at earlier, at specific parts of the text.

Among them, a crucial open question is the determination of which is (are) the best possible imperfect rule(s) for a given rule radius. One difficulty that the computational experiments have made evident is the lack a robust criterion to compare rule performances. Issues like the size of the lattice and the kind of sampling are critical for the corresponding scores; an illustrative discussion on these issues is provided in [Oliveira, Martins, Carvalho and Fynn, 2009]. A recent example is also symptomatic of this difficulty. In a very nice work [Kari and Le Gloannec, 2012] showed a very good rule for one-dimensional DCT (their ALTER1 rule, Wolfram number 3131836998858091454413790721636720149125) which, tested under 100 thousand initial configurations with binomial distribution of densities, scored best than the (possibly) best rule from [Wolz and de Oliveira, 2008], that they named WdO (the same rule used to generate Figure 1, actually); it is also mentioned that around 20 others had been found that also seemed better than WdO, but these are not unveiled. It turns out that ALTER1 had also been found (as well as their COE2) among the 3000 best rules from [Wolz and de Oliveira, 2008] but, due to the more strict testing performed therein (usually 500 thousand initial configuration as a baseline), ALTER1 had been placed in the seventh position among those 3000 rules, with a score of 88.71%, a contrast with the score reported in [Kari and Le Gloannec, 2012] of 89.66%. This is a crucial practical problem that requires a robust decision criterion, either empirical or formal. Indeed, in the absence of such a conceptual basis, even when various millions of initial configurations are employed, with distinct density distributions, the decision does not necessary get crystal clear.

Another essential difficulty is that we still lack a way to analyse what is required in a rule so that predefined computations be accomplished; and in the case of search techniques towards rules with a given characteristics, we still lack understanding of the general properties of the search space, so as to identify which pathways should be followed. In this respect, [Vèrel, Collard, Tomassini and Vanneschi, 2007] in a way goes about one such kind of analysis, even if mostly as an illustration only. And as far as rule properties is concerned, the success of [Wolz and de Oliveira, 2008] reinforces the fact the internal symmetries of a rule are key to a successful design. But we need more.

One promising such pathway is the exploration of the connections between DCT and conservative properties, a connection that has in a sense always permeated the conceptual developments around the problem, as can be seen previously in this paper.

In tune with the idea, [de Oliveira, 2004] had explored the possibility of devising a parameter related to the conservative properties of the CA evolution, as they might bear relevance to good rules for DCT. For that, an approach was conceived, related to the property of (number) conservation of a rule ([Boccara and Fukś, 2002]). Accordingly, in [de Oliveira, 2004] a parameter was defined aimed at providing an estimate of the *conservation degree* of any given rule, that is, a measure of the amount of number conservation entailed by the rule.

This idea was triggered from the rationale developed in [Fukś, 2000], that density classification requires conservation; however, the standard DCT formulation precludes conservative rules from being good DCT rules, because of the imposition that the entire lattice should converge to either 0s or 1s. So, the intuition in [de Oliveira, 2004] was that the conservative rules of a given search space might be considered 'beacons' that good DCT rules should be attracted to, but never reach. Following this idea and, given the absence of a way to generate the conservative rules of the radius 3 space, so as to put that intuition under test, [de Oliveira, 2004] defined a notion of conservation degree, based upon the conservation condition established in [Boccara and Fukś, 2002] and showed that good DCT rules were clearly correlated to high values of conservation degree. The rules used for this evaluation were those available for [de Oliveira, Bortot and Oliveira, 2006], which were in the range from about 80% to 86% efficacy. But while the correlation with the defined measure was clear, the interpretation of this quantity was not, that is, although it had been derived from the Boccara-Fukś conditions, the question arose as to whether the quantity was really measuring the supposed conservation degree of a rule. In fact, it was noticed that the quantity might yield distinct values for rules belonging to the same class of dynamical equivalence, which could not happen if the quantity definition was correct. In the attempt to 'fix' the definition and answer the question of the true meaning of the quantity, a careful analysis was carried out in [Schranko and de Oliveira, 2010], which led to the 'fixed' version of the quantity and to the conclusion that, even the new quantity could not really be considered a true measure of the conservation degree of a rule. Nevertheless, the new definition seems definitely associated with non-trivial conservative properties of a rule, its value possibly being correlated to the rule proximity to conservative rules in the space, so that, good DCT rules should have high value of the quantity, in tune with the original intuition. The detailed analysis of the very good rules in [Wolz and de Oliveira, 2008] in terms of their 'fixed' conservation degree should provide rich insights into the issue.

Quite significantly, [Kari and Le Gloannec, 2012] managed to enumerate all conservative rules with maximum internal conjugate-reflexion symmetry from the radius 3 space, and showed that the aforementioned rule WdO is in fact at Hamming distance 1 from one of the enumerated conservative rules, thus strongly pointing at the truthfulness of the original intuition. It should also be very fruitful to check such an observation for all 3000 very good rules from [Wolz and de Oliveira, 2008]. The intuition that led [Kari and Le Gloannec, 2012] onto the same pathway as [de Oliveira, 2004] of correlating DCT to conservation came from a different perspective, namely, the idea by the first author of conceiving a DCT rule that would had the same dynamical properties as the GKL rule, but that would render the proof of these properties simpler; it is very interesting that the rule had the notion of conservation at its core.

Finally, there is also a remarkable fact in the conceptual developments around DCT that brings to mind the relation between simplicity and formal elegance. Notice that while DCT cannot be solved by a single rule, no matter the size of its radius, it can be solved in the domain of the simple elementary rules, be it in the form of temporal combination of rules, or by blending elementary rules in stochastic fashion. It is an appealing challenge ahead to see whether the power of this simplicity can also be retained when doing spatial arrangements of rules, in non-uniform CAs, and whether it scales up to larger dimensions.

Acknowledgements. This paper outlines the ideas addressed in my invited talk at AUTOMATA 2013; I'm very thankful to its organisers for the kind invitation. My work on DCT has been carried out over the years thanks to grants provided by FAPESP – São Paulo Research Foundation, MackPesquisa – Fundo Mackenzie de Pesquisa, and Wolfram Research.

References

[Alonso-Sanz and Bull, 2009] Alonso-Sanz, R., Bull, L.: A very effective density classifier two-dimensional cellular automaton with memory. Journal of Physics A 42(48), 485101 (2009)

[Betel, de Oliveira and Flocchini, 2013] Betel, H., de Oliveira, P.P.B., Flocchini, P.: Solving the parity problem in one-dimensional cellular automata. Natural Computing 12 (2013)

[Boccara and Fuks, 1998] Boccara, N., Fukś, H.: Cellular automaton rules conserving the number of active sites. Journal of Physics A 31, 6007–6018 (1998)

[Boccara and Fukś, 2002] Boccara, N., Fukś, H.: Number-conserving cellular automaton rules. Fundamenta Informaticae 52, 1–13 (2002)

[Bušić, Fatès, Mairesse and Marcovici, 2013] Bušić, A., Fatès, N., Mairesse, J., Marcovici, I.: Density classification on infinite lattices and trees. Electronic Journal of Probability 18(51), 1–22 (2013)

[Dennunzio, Formenti and Provillard, 2012] Dennunzio, A., Formenti, E., Provillard, J.: Non-uniform cellular automata: Classes, dynamics, and decidability. Information and Computation 215, 32–46 (2012)

[de Oliveira, 2004] de Oliveira, P.P.B.: Where are the good CA rules for the density classification task? In: Proc. of the 2004 NKS Conference, Boston (April 2004), http://www.wolframscience.com/conference/2004/presentations/ HTMLLinks/index_49.html

[de Oliveira, Bortot and Oliveira, 2006] de Oliveira, P.P.B., Bortot, J.C., Oliveira, G.M.B.: The best currently known class of dynamically equivalent cellular automata rules for density classification. Neurocomputing 70(1-3), 35–43 (2006)

[de Oliveira, Faria, Zanon and Leite, 2013] de Oliveira, P.P.B., Faria, F., Zanon, R.M., Leite, R.M.: Computational evidence against the possibility of density determination with non-uniform arrangements of elementary rules (manuscript under preparation 2013)

[Fatès, 2012] Fatès, N.: A note on the density classification problem in two dimensions. In: Formenti, E. (ed.) Proc. of the 18th International Workshop on Cellular Automata and Discrete Complex Systems: Exploratory Papers Proceedings, pp. 11–18 (2012) Rapport de Recherche I3S - ISRN: I3S/RR-2012-04-FR

[Fatès, 2013] Fatès, N.A.: Stochastic cellular automata solutions to the density classification problem - When randomness helps computing. Theory of Computing Systems 53(2), 223–242 (2013)

[Flocchini, 2009] Flocchini, P.: Contamination and decontamination in majority-based systems. Journal of Cellular Automata 4(3), 183–200 (2009)

[Fukś, 1997] Fukś, H.: Solution of the density classification problem with two cellular automata rules. Physics Review E 55, 2081R–2084R (1997)

[Fukś, 2000] Fukś, H.: A class of cellular automata equivalent to deterministic particle systems. In: Feng, S., Lawniczak, A.T., Varadhan, S.R.S. (eds.) Hydrodynamic Limits and Related Topics, pp. 57–69. Amer. Math. Soc., Providence (2000)

[Fukś, 2002] Fukś, H.: Nondeterministic density classification with diffusive probabilistic cellular automata. Physical Review E 66(6), 066106 (2002)

[Gacs, Kurdyumov and Levin, 1978] Gacs, P., Kurdyumov, G.L., Levin, L.A.: One-dimensional uniform arrays that wash out finite islands. Problemy Peredachi Informatsii 14, 92–98 (1978)

[Lanchier and Neufer, 2013] Lanchier, N., Neufer, J.: Stochastic dynamics on hypergraphs and the spatial majority rule model. Journal of Statistical Physics 151(1-2), 21–45 (2013)

[Land and Belew, 1995] Land, M.W.S., Belew, R.K.: No two-state CA for density classification exists. Physical Review Letters 74(25), 5148 (1995)

[Kari, 2005] Kari, J.: Theory of cellular automata: A survey. Theoretical Computer Science 334, 3–33 (2005)

[Kari and Le Gloannec, 2012] Kari, J., Le Gloannec, B.: Modified traffic cellular automaton for the density classification task. Fundamenta Informaticae 116(1-4), 141–156 (2012)

[Maiti, Munshi and Chaudhuri, 2006] Maiti, N.S., Munshi, S., Pal Chaudhuri, P.: An analytical formulation for cellular automata (CA) based solution of density classification task (DCT). In: El Yacoubi, S., Chopard, B., Bandini, S. (eds.) ACRI 2006. LNCS, vol. 4173, pp. 147–156. Springer, Heidelberg (2006)

[Martins and de Oliveira, 2005] Martins, C.L.M., de Oliveira, P.P.B.: Evolving sequential combinations of elementary cellular automata rules. In: Capcarrère, M.S., Freitas, A.A., Bentley, P.J., Johnson, C.G., Timmis, J. (eds.) ECAL 2005. LNCS (LNAI), vol. 3630, pp. 461–470. Springer, Heidelberg (2005)

[Mitchell, 1998] Mitchell, M.: Computation in cellular automata: A selected review. In: Gramss, T., Bornholt, S., Gross, M., Mitchell, M., Pellizzari, T. (eds.) Non-Standard Computation, pp. 95–140. Wiley-VCH, Weinheim (1998)

[Morales, Crutchfield and Mitchell, 2000] Morales, F., Crutchfield, J., Mitchell, M.: Evolving two-dimensional cellular automata to perform density classification: a report on work in progress. Parallel Computing 27, 571–585 (2000)

[Moreira, Mathur, Diermeier and Amaral, 2004] Moreira, A.A., Mathur, A., Diermeier, D., Amaral, L.A.N.: Efficient system-wide coordination in noisy environments. Proc. of the National Academy of Sciences 101(33), 12085–12090 (2004)

[Naskar and Das, 2012] Naskar, N., Das, S.: Characterization of non-uniform cellular automata having only two point states - $0n$ and $1n$. In: Proc. of the 18th International Workshop on Cellular Automata and Discrete Complex Systems: Exploratory Papers Proceedings, pp. 29–37 (2012) Rapport de Recherche I3S - ISRN: I3S/RR-2012-04-FR

[Oliveira and Siqueira, 2006] Oliveira, G.M.B., Siqueira, S.R.C.: Parameter characterization of two-dimensional cellular automata rule space. Physica D 217(1), 1–6 (2006)

[Oliveira, Martins, Carvalho and Fynn, 2009] Oliveira, G.M.B., Martins, L.G.A., Carvalho, L.B., Fynn, E.: Some investigations about synchronization and density classification tasks in one-dimensional and two-dimensional cellular automata rule spaces. In: de Oliveira, P.P.B., Kari, J. (eds.) Proc. of Automata 2009: 15th International Workshop on Cellular Automata and Discrete Complex Systems, pp. 209–230. Luniver Press & Universidade Presbiteriana Mackenzie, So Paulo (2009)

[Packard, 1988] Packard, N.H.: Adaptation towards the edge of the chaos. In: Kelso, J.A.S., Mandell, A.J., Shlesinger, M.F. (eds.) Dynamic Patterns in Complex Systems, pp. 293–301. World Scientific, Singapore (1988)

[Reynaga and Amthauer, 2003] Reynaga, R., Amthauer, E.: Two-dimensional cellular automata of radius one for density classification task $\rho = 1/2$. Pattern Recognition Letters 24(15), 2849–2856 (2003)

[Sahoo, Choudhury, Pal, Kumar and Nayak, 2009] Sahoo, S., Choudhury, P.P., Pal, A., Nayak, B.K.: Solutions on 1D and 2D density classification problem using programmable cellular automata. arXiv:0902.2671 [nlin.CG], 14 pages (2009)

[Schranko and de Oliveira, 2010] Schranko, A., de Oliveira, P.P.B.: Towards the definition of conservation degree for one-dimensional cellular automata rules. Journal of Cellular Automata 5(4-5), 383–401 (2010)

[Gómez Soto and Fukś, 2011] Gómez Soto, -.M., Fukś, H.: Performance of the majority voting rule in solving the density classification problem in high dimension. J. Phys. A: Math. Theor 44, art. no. 444101 (2011)

[Stone and Bull, 2009] Stone, C., Bull, L.: Evolution of cellular automata with memory: The density classification task. BioSystems 97(2), 108–116 (2009)

[Tomassini and Venzi, 2002] Tomassini, M., Venzi, M.: Evolving robust asynchronous cellular automata for the density task. Complex Systems 13(3), 185–204 (2002)

[Vèrel, Collard, Tomassini and Vanneschi, 2007] Vèrel, S., Collard, P., Tomassini, M., Vanneschi, L.: Fitness landscape of the cellular automata majority problem: View from the Olympus. Theoretical Computer Science 378, 54–77 (2007)

[Vielhaber, 2012] Vielhaber, M.: Computing by Temporal Order: Asynchronous Cellular Automata. In: Formenti, E. (ed.) Proc. of the 18th International Workshop on Cellular Automata and Discrete Complex Systems: Electronic Proc. in Theoretical Computer Science, vol. 90, pp. 166–176 (2012)

[Wolfram, 2002] Wolfram, S.: A New Kind of Science. Wolfram Media (2002)

[Wolz and de Oliveira, 2008] Wolz, D., de Oliveira, P.P.B.: Very effective evolutionary techniques for searching cellular automata rule spaces. Journal of Cellular Automata 3(4), 289–312 (2008)

A Guided Tour of Asynchronous Cellular Automata

Nazim Fatès

Inria Nancy Grand-Est, LORIA UMR 7503,
54 600, Villers-lès-Nancy, France
nazim.fates@loria.fr

Abstract. Research on asynchronous cellular automata has received a great amount of attention these last years and has turned to a thriving field. We survey the recent research that has been carried out on this topic and present a wide state of the art where computing and modelling issues are both represented.

1 Introduction

Research on asynchronous cellular automata has gained momentum in the last decade as it can be seen from the increase in the number of publications dedicated to this topic or the organisation of scientific meetings dedicated to this topic.

Cellular automata are discrete dynamical systems that were initially constructed by von Neumann and Ulam to study self-reproduction from a logical and mechanistic point of view [95]. The interest of cellular automata stems from the simplicity of their structure: they are constituted of a collection of simple automata, the *cells*, that are spatially arranged on a grid and which evolve according to a *local rule* which gives the new state of a cell according to its previous state and the previous states of its neighbours. Classically, cellular automata are updated synchronously, that is, all cells change their state simultaneously at discrete time steps and the global state of the system at a given time is obtained from the information gained on the state of the system at the previous time. This hypothesis has many advantages: with this type of updating, the system is deterministic and simple to define. The use of a common shared time allows one to simulate such systems very easily and, in some cases, to derive analytical results on the behaviour of the rule. There are however some reasons why this hypothesis of perfect synchrony could be questioned:

- When cellular automata represent a model of a natural system, one should examine if there is a need of a global clock that synchronises the transitions of the model. In particular, is this clock an external phenomenon (e.g., the daily varying light of the sun) or is it an effect that emerges from the numerous interactions between the components?
- When cellular automata are considered as a model of a massively parallel computing device, then, operating such a device without having to distribute the signal of a clock could have many advantages such as an increase in the speed of computations, economy of energy, simplicity of design, etc.

J. Kari, M. Kutrib, and A. Malcher (Eds.): AUTOMATA 2013, LNCS 8155, pp. 15–30, 2013.
© Springer-Verlag Berlin Heidelberg 2013

These statements however do not unequivocally plead for the use of the asynchronous models as opposed to their synchronous counterparts. Indeed, as soon as the question of asynchrony is raised, numerous other questions have to be answered ; for instance: What type of asynchronism should be used? What are the properties of the system that are acquired or lost when turned from synchronous to asynchronous ? How should we study the new system (analytically, experimentally, etc.) ?

The purpose of this short review is to introduce the readers to the wide landscape of asynchronism in cellular automata. As a first version destined to the audience of AUTOMATA'13, and like all guided tours, it is not meant to be exhaustive nor fully objective, but rather to introduce some entry points and discussions on this wide topic. The author of the present text will be grateful to all indications or corrections that will be given to him. Interested readers are encouraged to check for updated versions of this text[1].

2   Early Works

Nakamura was one of the first authors to investigate the computation abilities of asynchronous cellular automata (ACA) [61]. He described several techniques to construct universal ACA and showed how to simulate a given q-state deterministic CA with an ACA of the same neighbourhood whose state space is extended to $3q^2$ states (see also Toffoli [90] and Nehaniv [63]).

The construction relies on the idea that if a cell is updated, it will then wait the neighbouring cells to "catch up" and makes the next transition only when all its neighbours are up to date ; additionally, it keeps its old state available for the neighbouring cells in order for them to perform the "right" transitions. This construction was later improved by the use of only $q^2 + 2q$ states by Lee, Peper et al. [50,67].

Priese wrote a note where he considers (two-dimensional) cellular automata as a particular case of asynchronous rewriting systems (semi-Thue-systems) and widens the scope by considering also the case where more than one cell may be re-written at a time (the overlapping problem) [69]. He uses his construction to show how to build asynchronous circuits which are equivalent to asynchronous concurrent Petri nets.

Following this path, Zielonka examined how asynchronous CA could be used to describe the situations of concurrency that arise in distributed systems [19]. Pighizzini clarified the computing abilities of Zielonska's models [68] and the problem of how to determinise non-deterministic Büchi asynchronous cellular automata was solved by Muscholl [60]. Droste generalised to pomsets the original notion of Zielonska's asynchronous mappings [25]; these questions was later re-investigated by Kuske [26,45,46].

Readers wishing to learn more on the universality of asynchronous CA may refer to the study by Takada et al., in which many important arguments and useful references can be found [88].

---

[1] See http://hal.inria.fr/hal-00845623 or visit the author's web page.

3   Numerical Simulations and Experimental Studies

At the same time when the systematic exploration of complete cellular spaces (such as Elementary Cellular Automata) were carried out, authors have examined the effect of asynchronism by the means of numerical simulation. Ingerson and Buvel carried out a pioneering work were they could show that the behaviour of simple rules could be overwhelmed by simple modifications [14]. Most importantly, they questioned to which extent was the behaviour of a rule the consequence of the local rule and to which extent it was due to the updating scheme.

Bersini and Detours explored the difference between the Game of Life and closely related models with various updating schemes [10]. They observed a "stabilising effect" of asynchronous updating. Their views were based on small-size experiments, with grids no larger than 20*20 cells. With such lattice sizes, they were able to observe that the Game of Life with asynchronous updating may "freeze" on some fixed-point pattern that has a labyrinth aspect.

Schönfisch and de Roos gave a decisive impulse to the research on ACA by comparing various updating schemes and by exhibiting clear examples to show that the effect of these schemes could alter significantly the behaviour of a CA [81]. They distinguish time-driven and step-driven updating methods, depending on whether the updating of a cell is triggered by the determination of an event given by a continuous time proper to each cell or by a global clock which would send signals to all or part of the cells.

Note that it may be believed at first sight that "time-driven" methods provide a more realistic simulation framework since the updating signal is not artificially shared among cells. As shown by the authors themselves, this is not true since it is easy to build a "step-driven" method that emulates a "time-driven" method: as the update is sequential, the only relevant information for the evolution of the updating is the order of updating, and a correspondence between the two schemes can thus be established. Moreover, as various authors tend to believe, even the hypothesis of sequentiality of events which states that no two updating events can happen at the same time is not necessarily realistic. Indeed, this hypothesis would be relevant only in the case where the transitions between states are instantaneous. As this hypothesis is far from being valid in many cases (especially in biological systems), a certain "degree of synchrony" between cells should thus be assumed. As this degree is difficult to measure, the problem is not so much about choosing the "right" model of updating but rather to estimate the robustness of model, that is, the degree to which it is sensitive or not to changes of its updating scheme.

This idea lead Fatès and Morvan to examine how the 256 Elementary cellular automata (ECA) reacted to an updating where the degree of synchrony was varied [33]. This updating scheme they used, named simply α-asynchronism[2]

---

[2] Note that the terms α-asynchronism and α-synchronism have been both used and are both relevant: the confusion comes from the fact that α is the name of the scheme and the synchrony rate. We use here the term α-asynchronism, as it is the form that was first proposed and which has been adopted by various authors such as Regnault, Correia, Worsch, Fukś, etc.

consists in updating each cell with probability α, the *synchrony rate*, and leaving the state of the cells unchanged otherwise. In order to quantify the observations, the authors used the value of the asymptotic density as a means to estimate changes in the behaviour of the system. This parameter was considered as a first approximation to detect changes in the behaviour: a strong variation of the asymptotic density indicates that the system has undergone a transformation while an absence of variation does not say anything on the stability of the system as other modifications than the density may occur.

Despite its simplicity, this approach revealed that no direct relationship between the asynchronous behaviour and the "complexity" of the synchronous behaviour (Wolfram classes) existed. Four qualitative responses to variations were remarked:

1. continuous variation of the behaviour (e.g. ECA 232),
2. discontinuity around $\alpha = 1$ (e.g. ECA 2 or 110),
3. phase transition for a critical value $\alpha_c < 1$ (e.g. ECA 50),
4. non-regular behaviour (e.g. ECA 184).

An interesting development on the work of asynchronism concerns how it mixes with traditional noise. Early references that address this question are a paper by Gharavi and Anantharam, where they study a well-known result of Toom [39], and the work of Kanada, which tackles ECA rules [44]. Mamei et al. also considered this question for studying "complex decentralised pervasive computing systems" that are models as two-dimensional binary CA [56]. The most recent development is by Silva and Correia, who have given a detailed account on robust or sensitive some ECA can be to asynchronism combined with noise [83].

The case of asynchronous CA simulated on a non-regular topology was tackled by Baetens et al., who examined an asynchronous updating with cells linked by the frontiers of a Voronoi tessellation [5].

4   Phase Transitions

Blok and Bergersen showed that the Game of Life was subject to a phase transition when it was updated asynchronously [11]. They used *alpha*-asynchronism and showed the existence of a transition from a "static" behaviour, where the system would settle on fixed points, to a "living" behaviour where the system evolves by forming labyrinth-like patterns. These authors identified that the change of behaviour was a second-order phase transition that belongs to the directed percolation universality class.

Fatès identified that directed percolation was also the "signature" displayed by seven of the minimal ECA rules [27]. A special rule, namely ECA 178, was shown to belong to the PC/DP2 universality class, a class very similar to DP but where the each state 0 and 1 play a symmetric role.

The phase transition occurring in the Game of life was also re-examined in detail, especially by studying how this phenomenon was affected by random perturbations of the topology of the CA [28,29]. The main finding was that this phase transition was strongly dependent on the regularity of the grid and that it was progressively "washed out" as links between cells were progressively removed.

Another puzzling phenomenon was remarked [33]: two systems, started from different initial conditions, but evolving with the same updating sequence, could rapidly "coalesce" into the same state. This is not particularly surprising per se except in the case where this coalescence phenomenon occurs even before the system stabilises on a fixed point. Rouquier and Morvan studied systematically the coalescence phenomenon for the 256 ECA [75]. Their study revealed that it was possible to observe that some ECA would always coalesce, while other would never coalesce, and that there existed some rules which displayed a phase transition between a coalescing and non-coalescing behaviour, depending on the synchrony rate.

5 Analytical Results

Compared to the experimental work devoted to asynchronous CA, analytical results are relatively rare, but they are gaining momentum as more probabilistic techniques are being developed.

One of the first analytical results of a systematic classification were given by analysing the ECA with two quiescent states under fully asynchronous dynamics [34], that is when only one cell is updated randomly at each time step. These results were later extended by Regnault et al. tackling the case of α-asynchronous updating [35] and by Chassaing and Gerin, who examined what was continuous limit of the processes when the grid was made infinite [17].

Fatès and Gerin also examined how to classify the two-dimensional totalistic CA with fully asynchronous updating [32]. They proposed a partial classification of the 64 rules and an analysis of the convergence of some well-known rules. Among the interesting phenomena remarked, they exhibited a list of rules, which showed an "erratic" behaviour: the question was to determine if these rules were exhibiting a non-converging behaviour or a "metastable" behaviour, that is, if a (long) random sequence of updates could drive the system to a stable state. By using techniques from automatic planning, Hoffmann et al. could solve this problem for one rule and showed that it converged to a fixed point in (at most) exponential time [41]. (See also the tutorial paper presented in the same proceedings [31]).

Links between the notions of asynchrony and reversibility were examined by Das et al. [79,21]. Wacker and Worsch also examined the question of reversibility of ACA [96], but took a different point of view. This question is mainly open at the moment and is currently explored by various angles.

Concerning the analysis of phase transition phenomena, Regnault carried out a pioneering work by analysing in detail how the asynchronous minority rule displayed various types of behaviour, depending on whether the von Neumann and Moore neighbourhood was used [73] or even when more general graphs were considered [76]. Two different complementary views exist on phase transitions: the most common way of describing a phase transition is to establish that for an *infinite* system, a qualitative difference of behaviour occurs for an infinitesimal variation of the control parameter. This second approach was adopted by Regnault who could (partially) prove that for *finite systems*, this phase transition corresponds to a variation of the convergence time from a linear to a polynomial function of the system's size [72].

Fukś and Skelton analysed three simple α-asynchronous rules [37]. They considered infinite systems with an initial Bernoulli measure as an initial condition and determined how the asymptotic density varies as a function of the initial density (that is, the parameter of the Bernoulli measure). Such results are generally rather difficult to obtain for the deterministic ECA.

6   Definitions of ACA and Their Mathematical Properties

Gács was one of the first authors to investigate the question of whether the evolution of an asynchronous system could be independent of the order of updating [38]. He showed that although this property was undecidable, there existed a sufficient condition to verify this independence.

These question was re-examined by Mortveit, Macauley et al., who studied in which cases repetitions of sequential updates on Elementary Cellular Automata could produce a set of periodic points that would be independent of the updating order [54,55,53]. They obtained a list of 104 ECA which display such an independence and, interestingly, proposed a new representation of ECA that differs from the classical Wolfram code and that could prove useful for future analysis of asynchronous systems. (Another alternative notation is presented in Ref. [34]).

The possibility to simulate asynchronous rules by a universal asynchronous simulator was examined by Worsch [97], who proved that there was an α-synchronous host that could simulate any α-asynchronous guest that would be updated with the same synchrony rate. This result can be even generalised to other types of asynchronism such as fully asynchronous updating or to an even wider variety of updating called "purely asynchronous updating".

Manzoni examined how the dynamical properties of CA, such as injectivity, surjectivity, permutivity, etc., could be re-defined and studied in the asynchronous updating context [57]. An extended definition of asynchronous CA based on the use of probability measures was proposed by Formenti et al. [24]. Dennunzio et al. have proposed an original way to simulate a universal Turing machine by the means of a fully asynchronous CA [23]. They introduce the notion of "scattered strict simulation" in which they tolerate that only a subset of cells is used to perform the simulation. They find that asynchrony induces a quadratic slowdown compared to the speed of the simulated Turing machine.

Regarding the various possibilities to define asynchronous updating schemes, Bandini et al. presented a formal description and analysis of various schemes and tested their effects on one-dimensional binary rules where the local function depends only on two neighbours (also called "radius-1/2" rules) [6].

Finally, we want to mention the extension of asynchronism proposed by Bouré et al.: while most approaches of asynchronism studied so far are based on the dichotomy updated / not updated, this approach named β- and γ-synchronism, models imperfect communication of states between neighbours [13]. The main finding of the authors is that if many previously observed phenomena, such as the existence of phase transitions that depend on the synchrony rate, are reproduced, some unexpected phenomena also arise such as the conservation of additional quantities (ECA 50) and the unexpected disappearance of some phase transitions. This underlines the necessity to continue to propose various perturbations of the "classical" CA in order to examine how their properties are dependent on various hypotheses such as a perfect updating.

7   Computing with ACA

Tomassini and Venzi [91], Capcarrere [15] and Nehaniv [62] have studied how interesting asynchronous cellular automata may be used to solve problems such as the density classification or the global synchronisation. Readers interested in this issue are referred to a study by Vanneschi and Mauri, in which an enlightening discussion on these various contributions is found and where the authors present findings of robust and generic rules [93].

Suzudo examined the use of genetic algorithms to find mass-conservative ACA that would generate non-trivial patterns [86,87]. He classified these patterns into three categories: checkerboards, stripes and sand-like. Although in this work asynchronism is mainly used to ensure mass conservation, it appears also as a useful means of generating regular patterns out of randomness, a task that is known to be very difficult in the synchronous setting (see e.g. [30]).

Another major field of research on asynchronous CA was developed by Peper, Lee and their collaborators. In their constructions, asynchronous computations are realised with particles that follow Brownian movements and which interact through special "gates" [3,2,49]. These constructions result in delay-insensitive circuits that are Turing universal (see e.g. [47,51] and references therein). Recently, Schneider and Worsch presented a 3-state CA that uses Moore neighbourhood which can simulate any delay-insensitive circuit [80]. It is also worth mentioning that these techniques also allowed the design of asynchronous models of self-reproduction [48].

In an original line of thought, Vielhaber has designed a formal framework in which computations are made by a proper use of the order of updating [94]. In particular, he showed that ECA 57 with periodic boundary conditions was a rule especially adapted for such a purpose.

8   Modelling with ACA

We are now close to end this guided tour and it is time to mention the work devoted to modelling physical or artificial systems with asynchronous cellular automata. While this part could be much more developed, we will keep it as short as possible and mention only a few entry points to the topic. The reason is that there is a huge number of works which employ asynchronous cellular automata, often without even mentioning the fact explicitly. We will thus try to concentrate only on some papers where the question of the updating is explicitly mentioned.

A good example is given by Huberman and Glance, who challenged the validity of the simulations of spatially-extended models of the Prisoner's dilemma on the basis that asynchronous and synchronous updating lead to drastically opposed conclusions [43]. This question was re-examined by Newth and Cornforth [64], and Grilo and Correia [40], who used α-asynchronous updating to explore a wide range of degrees of synchrony. Saif and Gade also investigated this issue and found that there was a first order transition between a regime with an all-defector state to a mixed state [78]. All these works share in common the conclusion that many of the previously observed equilibrium states are mere artifacts of a synchronous updating on a regular lattice.

Another interesting biological example is given by Messinger et al., who investigated the link between emergence of synchrony and the simultaneous opening and closing stomatal arrays in plants [58].

In physics, Radicchi et al. [70] studied how simulations of an Ising spin system would be dependent on the synchrony rate and also detected phase transitions. (Note that contrary to the previously seen cases [27,73,29], the update rule is here stochastic). Like Correia et al., the authors emphasise the fact that neither totally synchronous nor totally asynchronous updating is fully relevant for modelling natural systems.

Ruxton and Saravia have discussed the importance of the ordering in the context of ecological modelling, studying a stochastic model of colonisation of an environment by a species [77]. They argue in favour of adapting the updating scheme to the physical reality of the system that is modelled. The authors also emphasise the need to describe precisely the updating scheme that is used in order facilitate the reproducibility of the experiments. An idea that is also developed by Caron-Lormier et al. at the same time [16].

On the simulation side, Overeinder and Sloot were among the first to examine how to deal with the simulation on ACA on distributed systems [66]. Bandman and other authors studied how to simulate chemical systems with asynchronous CA [8,82]. Hoseini et al. made an implementation of asynchronous CA with FPGAs [42]. They propose a particular design of the FPGA in order to construct a "conformal computer", that is, a computer made of physical cells "arrayed on large thin flexible substrates or sheets. Sheets may be cut, joined, bent, and stacked to conform to the physical and computational needs of an application" [42].

On the applications side, we mention the work of Bandini et al., who used asynchronous CA with memory for the design of an illumination facility [7] and the work or Minoofam et al., who applied asynchronous CA for producing calligraphic patterns in the Arabic language (Kufic style) [59].

9   Asynchronism in Similar Models

We end this guided tour on an opening on the issue of asynchrony in the models of computation that have a structure similar to cellular automata. In fact, this topic is again so wide that it will not be possible to fully cover it and we will be obliged to indicate only a few recent papers and entry points to the topic.

One first proposition to link the updating in multi-agent systems and cellular automata was made by Cornforth et al., but the models they studied are in fact standard asynchronous cellular automata [20]. The question of how to "translate" a multi-agent system with sequential updating into a synchronous CA was tackled by Spicher et al. [84]. In order to model the displacement of the agents, they proposed to operate with "transactional cellular automata" where the movements of particles occur with the help of synchronous communications between neighbouring cells. One positive effect of turning to the synchronous CA is to remove the spurious effects that could be linked to a particular updating order (the authors give the example of a model of Diffusion-Limited-Aggregation).

The link between large-scale multi-agent systems and asynchronous cellular automata was also examined by Tošić [92]. This author argues that the structure of cellular automata needs to be modified in several aspects, among which it should be made asynchronous, in order to serve as a basis for modelling large groups of interacting agents.

An alternative approach to model (discrete) multi-agent systems was proposed by Chevrier and Fatès, who studied the dynamics of a simple multi-turmite systems, also known as multiple Langton's ants. Their formalism, inspired by cellular automata, captures the possibility to have *synchronous* interacting agents [18]. The difficulty relies in describing how to solving conflicts that occur when two or more agents simultaneously want to modify the environment. The solution relies on a framework invented by Ferber and Muller called influence-reaction [36]. Belgacem and Fatès later extended this work by considering a wider range of updating procedures and discovered some phenomena (e.g., gliders) that resisted variations in the updating choices [9].

Bouré et al. designed a first version of an asynchronous Lattice-Gas Cellular Automaton (LGCA) [12]. Their proposition can be seen as a bridge between cell-based updating and agent-based updating. In this model, movements of particles are defined explicitly, like in multi-agents, but the updating is made cell by cell, like in classical cellular automata. Various responses to asynchrony are observed depending on the patterns on which the system stabilises: stripes or clusters are robust while checkerboards, a somewhat paradoxical pattern, are shown not be robust. This construction needs however to be completed as there is to date no agreement on what an asynchronous LGCA should be, in particular on how to respect the locality of the model in the asynchronous setting.

The effect of asynchronous updating in genetic regulatory networks has also been investigated by many authors, for instance, Aracena et al. [4], Sené et al. [22], and Noual [65]. These authors examine the robustness of the system under the variation of updating schemes and this perturbation is coupled with various topological modifications of the network such as adding or removing links in the graph or changing boundary conditions. The question of the effect of a synchronous updating in neural networks has been discussed by Taouali et al. [89]. In particular, the authors introduce an interesting distinction between the use of (a)synchronous updating at the modelling level and at the implementation level.

To end this tour, we mention that various works studied the differences between synchronous and asynchronous updating in coupled map lattices [52,74,1]. Similarly, the effects of the updating in the Asymmetric Exclusion Process (ASEP) have been studied by Rajewsky et al. [71].

References

1. Abramson, G., Zanette, D.H.: Globally coupled maps with asynchronous updating. Physical Review E 58, 4454–4460 (1998), http://link.aps.org/doi/10.1103/PhysRevE.58.4454
2. Adachi, S., Peper, F., Lee, J.: Computation by asynchronously updating cellular automata. Journal of Statistical Physics 114(1-2), 261–289 (2004)
3. Adachi, S., Peper, F., Lee, J.: Universality of hexagonal asynchronous totalistic cellular automata. In: Sloot, P.M.A., Chopard, B., Hoekstra, A.G. (eds.) ACRI 2004. LNCS, vol. 3305, pp. 91–100. Springer, Heidelberg (2004), http://dx.doi.org/10.1007/978-3-540-30479-1_10
4. Aracena, J., Goles, E., Moreira, A., Salinas, L.: On the robustness of update schedules in boolean networks. Biosystems 97(1), 1–8 (2009), http://www.sciencedirect.com/science/article/pii/S0303264709000471
5. Baetens, J.M., Van der Weeën, P., De Baets, B.: Effect of asynchronous updating on the stability of cellular automata. Chaos, Solitons & Fractals 45(4), 383–394 (2012), http://dx.doi.org/10.1016/j.chaos.2012.01.002
6. Bandini, S., Bonomi, A., Vizzari, G.: An analysis of different types and effects of asynchronicity in cellular automata update schemes. Natural Computing 11(2), 277–287 (2012), http://dx.doi.org/10.1007/s11047-012-9310-4
7. Bandini, S., Bonomi, A., Vizzari, G., Acconci, V.: An asynchronous cellular automata-based adaptive illumination facility. In: Serra, R., Cucchiara, R. (eds.) AI*IA 2009. LNCS, vol. 5883, pp. 405–415. Springer, Heidelberg (2009), http://dx.doi.org/10.1007/978-3-642-10291-2_41
8. Bandman, O.: Parallel composition of asynchronous cellular automata simulating reaction diffusion processes. In: Bandini, S., Manzoni, S., Umeo, H., Vizzari, G. (eds.) ACRI 2010. LNCS, vol. 6350, pp. 395–398. Springer, Heidelberg (2010), http://dx.doi.org/10.1007/978-3-642-15979-4_41
9. Belgacem, S., Fatès, N.: Robustness of multi-agent models: the example of collaboration between turmites with synchronous and asynchronous updating. Complex Systems 21(3), 165–182 (2012), http://www.complex-systems.com/abstracts/v21_i03_a01.html
10. Bersini, H., Detours, V.: Asynchrony induces stability in cellular automata based models. In: Brooks, R.A., Maes, P. (eds.) Proceedings of the 4th International Workshop on the Synthesis and Simulation of Living Systems (Artificial Life IV), pp. 382–387. MIT Press (1994)
11. Blok, H.J., Bergersen, B.: Synchronous versus asynchronous updating in the "game of life". Physical Review E 59, 3876–3879 (1999)

12. Bouré, O., Fatès, N., Chevrier, V.: First steps on asynchronous lattice-gas models with an application to a swarming rule. In: Sirakoulis, G.C., Bandini, S. (eds.) ACRI 2012. LNCS, vol. 7495, pp. 633–642. Springer, Heidelberg (2012), http://dx.doi.org/10.1007/978-3-642-33350-7_65

13. Bouré, O., Fatès, N., Chevrier, V.: Probing robustness of cellular automata through variations of asynchronous updating. Natural Computing 11, 553–564 (2012), http://dx.doi.org/10.1007/s11047-012-9340-y

14. Buvel, R.L., Ingerson, T.E.: Structure in asynchronous cellular automata. Physica D 1, 59–68 (1984)

15. Capcarrère, M.S.: Evolution of asynchronous cellular automata. In: Guervós, J.J.M., Adamidis, P., Beyer, H.G., Schwefel, H.P., Fernández-Villacañas, J.L. (eds.) PPSN VII. LNCS, vol. 2439, pp. 903–912. Springer, Heidelberg (2002), http://dx.doi.org/10.1007/3-540-45712-7_87

16. Worsch, T.: (intrinsically?) universal asynchronous CA. In: Sirakoulis, G.C., Bandini, S. (eds.) Proceedings of ACRI 2012. pp. 689–698. Lecture Notes in Computer Science, Springer (2012), http://dx.doi.org/10.1007/978-3-642-33350-7_70

17. Chassaing, P., Gerin, L.: Asynchronous cellular automata and brownian motion. In: DMTCS Proceedings of AofA 2007, vol. AH, pp. 385–402 (2007), http://www.dmtcs.org/dmtcs-ojs/index.php/proceedings/article/viewArticle/dmAH0129

18. Chevrier, V., Fatès, N.: How important are updating schemes in multi-agent systems? an illustration on a multi-turmite model. In: Proceedings of AAMAS 2010, pp. 533–540. International Foundation for Autonomous Agents and Multiagent Systems, Richland (2010), http://doi.acm.org/10.1145/1838206.1838282

19. Cori, R., Métivier, Y., Zielonka, W.: Asynchronous mappings and asynchronous cellular automata. Information and Computation 106(2), 159–202 (1993), http://dx.doi.org/10.1006/inco.1993.1052

20. Cornforth, D., Green, D.G., Newth, D.: Ordered asynchronous processes in multi-agent systems. Physica D 204(1-2), 70–82 (2005), http://www.sciencedirect.com/science/article/pii/S0167278905001338

21. Das, S., Sarkar, A., Sikdar, B.K.: Synthesis of reversible asynchronous cellular automata for pattern generation with specific hamming distance. In: Sirakoulis, G.C., Bandini, S. (eds.) ACRI 2012. LNCS, vol. 7495, pp. 643–652. Springer, Heidelberg (2012), http://dx.doi.org/10.1007/978-3-642-33350-7_66

22. Eisele, M.: Long-range correlations in chaotic cellular automata. PLoS One 5(8), e11793 (2010), http://dx.doi.org/10.1371

23. Dennunzio, A., Formenti, E., Manzoni, L.: Computing issues of asynchronous CA. Fundamenta Informaticae 120(2), 165–180 (2012), http://dx.doi.org/10.3233/FI-2012-755

24. Dennunzio, A., Formenti, E., Manzoni, L., Mauri, G.: m-asynchronous cellular automata. In: Sirakoulis, G.C., Bandini, S. (eds.) ACRI 2012, vol. 7495, pp. 653–662. Springer, Heidelberg (2012), http://dx.doi.org/10.1007/978-3-642-33350-7_67

25. Droste, M., Gastin, P.: Asynchronous cellular automata for pomsets without auto-concurrency. In: Sassone, V., Montanari, U. (eds.) CONCUR 1996. LNCS, vol. 1119, pp. 627–638. Springer, Heidelberg (1996), http://dx.doi.org/10.1007/3-540-61604-7_80

26. Droste, M., Gastin, P., Kuske, D.: Asynchronous cellular automata for pomsets. Theoretical Computer Science 247(1-2), 1–38 (2000), http://dx.doi.org/10.1016/S0304-3975(00)00166-3

27. Fatès, N.: Asynchronism induces second order phase transitions in elementary cellular automata. Journal of Cellular Automata 4(1), 21–38 (2009), http://hal.inria.fr/inria-00138051

28. Fatès, N.: Critical phenomena in cellular automata: perturbing the update, the transitions, the topology. Acta Physica Polonica B - Proceedings Supplement 3(2), 315–325 (2010), http://www.actaphys.uj.edu.pl/sup3/abs/s3p0315.htm

29. Fatès, N.: Does *life* resist asynchrony? In: Adamatzky, A. (ed.) Game of Life Cellular Automata, pp. 257–274. Springer, London (2010), http://dx.doi.org/10.1007/978-1-84996-217-9_14

30. Fatès, N.: A note on the density classification problem in two dimensions. Exploratory papers presented at AUTOMATA 2012, La Marana, Corse, France (2012), http://hal.inria.fr/hal-00727558

31. Fatès, N.: A note on the classification of the most simple asynchronous cellular automata. In: Kari, J., Kutrib, M., Malcher, A. (eds.) AUTOMATA 2013. LNCS, vol. 8155, pp. 31–45. Springer, Heidelberg (2013)

32. Fatès, N., Gerin, L.: Examples of fast and slow convergence of 2D asynchronous cellular systems. Journal of Cellular Automata 4(4), 323–337 (2009)

33. Fatès, N., Morvan, M.: An experimental study of robustness to asynchronism for elementary cellular automata. Complex Systems 16, 1–27 (2005), http://www.complex-systems.com/abstracts/v16_i01_a01.html

34. Fatès, N., Morvan, M., Schabanel, N., Thierry, E.: Fully asynchronous behavior of double-quiescent elementary cellular automata. Theoretical Computer Science 362, 1–16 (2006), http://dx.doi.org/10.1016/j.tcs.2006.05.036

35. Fatès, N., Regnault, D., Schabanel, N., Thierry, É.: Asynchronous behavior of double-quiescent elementary cellular automata. In: Correa, J.R., Hevia, A., Kiwi, M. (eds.) LATIN 2006. LNCS, vol. 3887, pp. 455–466. Springer, Heidelberg (2006), http://dx.doi.org/10.1007/11682462_43

36. Ferber, J., Müller, J.-P.: Influences and reaction: a model of situated multiagent systems. In: Proceedings of the 2nd International Conference on Multi-agent Systems, pp. 72–79 (1996)

37. Fukś, H., Skelton, A.: Orbits of the bernoulli measure in single-transition asynchronous cellular automata. In: Fatès, N., Goles, E., Maass, A., Rapaport, I. (eds.) Proceedings of Automata 2011. Discrete Mathematics and Theoretical Computer Science Proceedings, DMTCS, pp. 95–112 (2011), http://www.dmtcs.org/dmtcs-ojs/index.php/proceedings/article/view/dmAP0107

38. Gács, P.: Deterministic computations whose history is independent of the order of asynchronous updating. CoRR cs.DC/0101026 (2001), http://arxiv.org/abs/cs.DC/0101026

39. Gharavi, R., Anantharam, V.: Effect of noise on long-term memory in cellular automata with asynchronous delays between the processors. Complex Systems 6(3), 287–300 (1992), http://www.complex-systems.com/abstracts/v06_i03_a05.html

40. Grilo, C., Correia, L.: Effects of asynchronism on evolutionary games. Journal of Theoretical Biology 269(1), 109–122 (2011), http://dx.doi.org/10.1016/j.jtbi.2010.10.022

41. Hoffmann, J., Fatès, N., Palacios, H.: Brothers in arms? on AI planning and cellular automata. In: Coelho, H., Studer, R., Wooldridge, M. (eds.) Proceedings of ECAI 2010. Frontiers in Artificial Intelligence and Applications, vol. 215, pp. 223–228. IOS Press (2010), http://www.booksonline.iospress.nl/Content/View.aspx?piid=17702

42. Hoseini, M., Tan, Z., You, C., Pavicic, M.: Design of a reconfigurable pulsed quad-cell for cellular-automata-based conformal computing. International Journal of Reconfigurable Computing 7907, Article ID 352428 (2010),
http://dx.doi.org/10.1155/2010/352428

43. Huberman, B.A., Glance, N.: Evolutionary games and computer simulations. Proceedings of the National Academy of Sciences, USA 90, 7716–7718 (1993)

44. Kanada, Y.: The effects of randomness in asynchronous 1d cellular automata (poster). Artificial Life IV (1994),
http://www.kanadas.com/CA/AsyncCA/AsyncCAext.pdf

45. Kuske, D.: Emptiness is decidable for asynchronous cellular machines. In: Palamidessi, C. (ed.) CONCUR 2000. LNCS, vol. 1877, pp. 536–551. Springer, Heidelberg (2000), http://dx.doi.org/10.1007/3-540-44618-4_38

46. Kuske, D.: Weighted asynchronous cellular automata. Theoretical Computer Science 374(1-3), 127–148 (2007), http://dx.doi.org/10.1016/j.tcs.2006.11.031

47. Lee, J.: A simple model of asynchronous cellular automata exploiting fluctuation. Journal of Cellular Automata 6(4-5), 341–352 (2011),
http://www.oldcitypublishing.com/JCA/JCAabstracts/
JCA6.4-5abstracts/JCAv6n4-5p341-352Lee.html

48. Lee, J., Adachi, S., Peper, F.: Reliable self-replicating machines in asynchronous cellular automata. Artificial Life 13(4), 397–413 (2007),
http://dx.doi.org/10.1162/artl.2007.13.4.397

49. Lee, J., Adachi, S., Peper, F., Mashiko, S.: Delay-insensitive computation in asynchronous cellular automata. Journal of Computer and System Sciences 70(2), 201–220 (2005), http://dx.doi.org/10.1016/j.jcss.2004.10.009

50. Lee, J., Adachi, S., Peper, F., Morita, K.: Asynchronous game of life. Physica D 194(3-4), 369–384 (2004), http://dx.doi.org/10.1016/j.physd.2004.03.007

51. Lee, J., Zhu, Q.S.: A direct proof of turing universality of delay-insensitive circuits. International Journal of Unconventional Computing 8(2), 107–118 (2012),
http://www.oldcitypublishing.com/IJUC/IJUCabstracts/
IJUC8.2abstracts/IJUCv8n2p107-118Lee.html

52. Lumer, E.D.L., Nicolis, G.: Synchronous versus asynchronous dynamics in spatially distributed systems. Physica D: Nonlinear Phenomena 71(4), 440–452 (1994),
http://www.sciencedirect.com/science/article/pii/0167278994900108

53. Macauley, M., McCammond, J., Mortveit, H.: Dynamics groups of asynchronous cellular automata. Journal of Algebraic Combinatorics 33(1), 11–35 (2011),
http://dx.doi.org/10.1007/s10801-010-0231-y

54. Macauley, M., McCammond, J., Mortveit, H.S.: Order independence in asynchronous cellular automata. Journal of Cellular Automata 3(1), 37–56 (2008),
http://www.oldcitypublishing.com/JCA/JCAabstracts/JCA3.1abstracts/
JCAv3n1p37-56Macauley.html

55. Macauley, M., Mortveit, H.S.: Coxeter groups and asynchronous cellular automata. In: Bandini, S., Manzoni, S., Umeo, H., Vizzari, G. (eds.) ACRI 2010. LNCS, vol. 6350, pp. 409–418. Springer, Heidelberg (2010),
http://dx.doi.org/10.1007/978-3-642-15979-4_43

56. Mamei, M., Roli, A., Zambonelli, F.: Emergence and control of macro-spatial structures in perturbed cellular automata, and implications for pervasive computing systems. IEEE Transactions on Systems, Man, and Cybernetics, Part A 35(3), 337–348 (2005), http://dx.doi.org/10.1109/TSMCA.2005.846379

57. Manzoni, L.: Asynchronous cellular automata and dynamical properties. Natural Computing 11(2), 269–276 (2012),
http://dx.doi.org/10.1007/s11047-012-9308-y

58. Messinger, S.M., Mott, K.A., Peak, D.: Task-performing dynamics in irregular, biomimetic networks: Research articles. Complexity 12(6), 14–21 (2007), http://dx.doi.org/10.1002/cplx.v12:6

59. Minoofam, S.A.H., Bastanfard, A.: Square kufic pattern formation by asynchronous cellular automata. In: Bandini, S., Manzoni, S., Umeo, H., Vizzari, G. (eds.) ACRI 2010. LNCS, vol. 6350, pp. 79–82. Springer, Heidelberg (2010)

60. Muscholl, A.: On the complementation of bchi asynchronous cellular automata. In: Shamir, E., Abiteboul, S. (eds.) ICALP 1994. LNCS, vol. 820, pp. 142–153. Springer, Heidelberg (1994), http://dx.doi.org/10.1007/3-540-58201-0_64

61. Nakamura, K.: Asynchronous cellular automata and their computational ability. Systems, Computers, Controls 5(5), 58–66 (1974)

62. Nehaniv, C.L.: Evolution in asynchronous cellular automata. In: Proceedings of the Eighth International Conference on Artificial Life, pp. 65–73. MIT Press (2003)

63. Nehaniv, C.L.: Asynchronous automata networks can emulate any synchronous automata network. International Journal of Algebra and Computation 14(5-6), 719–739 (2004), http://dx.doi.org/10.1142/S0218196704002043

64. Newth, D., Cornforth, D.: Asynchronous spatial evolutionary games. Biosystems 95(2), 120–129 (2009), http://dx.doi.org/10.1016/j.biosystems.2008.09.003

65. Noual, M.: Synchronism vs asynchronism in boolean networks. CoRR abs/1104.4039 (2011), http://arxiv.org/abs/1104.4039

66. Overeinder, B.J., Sloot, P.M.A.: Application of time warp to parallel simulations with asynchronous cellular automata. In: Proceedings of the 1993 European Simulation Symposium, pp. 397–402 (1993)

67. Peper, F., Adachi, S., Lee, J.: Variations on the game of life. In: Adamatzky, A. (ed.) Game of Life Cellular Automata, pp. 235–255. Springer, London (2010), http://dx.doi.org/10.1007/978-1-84996-217-9_13

68. Pighizzini, G.: Asynchronous automata versus asynchronous cellular automata. Theoretical Computer Science 132(2), 179–207 (1994), http://dx.doi.org/10.1016/0304-39759490232-1

69. Priese, L.: A note on asynchronous cellular automata. Journal of Computer and System Sciences 17(2), 237–252 (1978), http://www.sciencedirect.com/science/article/pii/0022000078900077

70. Radicchi, F., Vilone, D., Meyer-Ortmanns, H.: Phase transition between synchronous and asynchronous updating algorithms. Journal of Statistical Physics 129(3), 593–603 (2007), http://dx.doi.org/10.1007/s10955-007-9416-8

71. Rajewsky, N., Santen, L., Schadschneider, A., Schreckenberg, M.: The asymmetric exclusion process: Comparison of update procedures. Journal of Statistical Physics 92(1-2), 151–194 (1998), http://dx.doi.org/10.1023/A%3A1023047703307

72. Regnault, D.: Proof of a phase transition in probabilistic cellular automata. In: Béal, M.-P., Carton, O. (eds.) DLT 2013. LNCS, vol. 7907, pp. 433–444. Springer, Heidelberg (2013), http://dx.doi.org/10.1007/978-3-642-38771-5

73. Regnault, D., Schabanel, N., Thierry, E.: Progresses in the analysis of stochastic 2D cellular automata: A study of asynchronous 2D minority. Theoretical Computer Science 410(47-49), 4844–4855 (2009), http://dx.doi.org/10.1016/j.tcs.2009.06.024

74. Rolf, J., Bohr, T., Jensen, M.H.: Directed percolation universality in asynchronous evolution of spatiotemporal intermittency. Physical Review E. 57(3), R2503–R2506 (1998)

75. Rouquier, J.B., Morvan, M.: Coalescing cellular automata: Synchronization by common random source for asynchronous updating. Journal of Cellular Automata 4(1), 55–78 (2009), http://www.oldcitypublishing.com/JCA/JCAabstracts/JCA4.1abstracts/JCAv4n1p55-77Rouquier.html

76. Rouquier, J.B., Regnault, D., Thierry, É.: Stochastic minority on graphs. Theoretical Computer Science 412(30), 3947–3963 (2011), http://dx.doi.org/10.1016/j.tcs.2011.02.028

77. Ruxton, G., Saravia, L.: The need for biological realism in the updating of cellular automata models. Ecological Modelling 107(2), 105–112 (1998)

78. Saif, M.A., Gade, P.M.: The prisoner's dilemma with semi-synchronous updates: evidence for a first-order phase transition. Journal of Statistical Mechanics: Theory and Experiment 2009(7), P07023 (2009), http://dx.doi.org/10.1088/1742-5468/2009/07/P07023

79. Sarkar, A., Mukherjee, A., Das, S.: Reversibility in asynchronous cellular automata. Complex Systems 21(1), 71 (2012), http://www.complex-systems.com/abstracts/v21_i01_a05.html

80. Schneider, O., Worsch, T.: A 3-state asynchronous CA for the simulation of delay-insensitive circuits. In: Sirakoulis, G.C., Bandini, S. (eds.) ACRI 2012. LNCS, vol. 7495, pp. 565–574. Springer, Heidelberg (2012), http://dx.doi.org/10.1007/978-3-642-33350-7_58

81. Schönfisch, B., de Roos, A.: Synchronous and asynchronous updating in cellular automata. BioSystems 51, 123–143 (1999)

82. Sharifulina, A., Elokhin, V.: Simulation of heterogeneous catalytic reaction by asynchronous cellular automata on multicomputer. In: Malyshkin, V. (ed.) PaCT 2011. LNCS, vol. 6873, pp. 204–209. Springer, Heidelberg (2011)

83. Silva, F., Correia, L.: A study of stochastic noise and asynchronism in elementary cellular automata. In: Sirakoulis, G.C., Bandini, S. (eds.) ACRI 2012. LNCS, vol. 7495, pp. 679–688. Springer, Heidelberg (2012), http://dx.doi.org/10.1007/978-3-642-33350-7_70

84. Spicher, A., Fatès, N., Simonin, O.: Translating discrete multi-agents systems into cellular automata: Application to diffusion-limited aggregation. In: Filipe, J., Fred, A., Sharp, B. (eds.) ICAART 2009. CCIS, vol. 67, pp. 270–282. Springer, Heidelberg (2010)

85. Stark, W.R., Hughes, W.H.: Asynchronous, irregular automata nets: the path not taken. BioSystems 55, 107–117 (2000)

86. Suzudo, T.: Searching for pattern-forming asynchronous cellular automata – an evolutionary approach. In: Sloot, P.M.A., Chopard, B., Hoekstra, A.G. (eds.) ACRI 2004. LNCS, vol. 3305, pp. 151–160. Springer, Heidelberg (2004)

87. Suzudo, T.: Spatial pattern formation in asynchronous cellular automata with mass conservation. Physica A: Statistical Mechanics and its Applications 343, 185–200 (2004), http://dx.doi.org/10.1016/j.physa.2004.06.067

88. Takada, Y., Isokawa, T., Peper, F., Matsui, N.: Construction universality in purely asynchronous cellular automata. Journal of Computer and System Sciences 72(8), 1368–1385 (2006), http://dx.doi.org/10.1016/j.jcss.2006.04.006

89. Taouali, W., Viéville, T., Rougier, N.P., Alexandre, F.: No clock to rule them all. Journal of Physiology-Paris 105(1-3), 83–90 (2011), http://www.sciencedirect.com/science/article/pii/S092842571100026X

90. Toffoli, T.: Integration of the phase-difference relations in asynchronous sequential networks. In: Ausiello, G., Böhm, C. (eds.) ICALP 1978. LNCS, vol. 62, pp. 457–463. Springer, Heidelberg (1978), http://dx.doi.org/10.1007/3-540-08860-1_34

91. Tomassini, M., Venzi, M.: Artificially evolved asynchronous cellular automata for the density task. In: Bandini, S., Chopard, B., Tomassini, M. (eds.) ACRI 2002. LNCS, vol. 2493, pp. 44–55. Springer, Heidelberg (2002), http://dx.doi.org/10.1007/3-540-45830-1_5

92. Tošić, P.T.: On modeling large-scale multi-agent systems with parallel, sequential and genuinely asynchronous cellular automata. Acta Physica Polonica B - Proceedings Supplement 4(2), 217–235 (2011), http://doi.org/10.5506/APhysPolBSupp.4.217

93. Vanneschi, L., Mauri, G.: A study on learning robustness using asynchronous 1D cellular automata rules. Natural Computing 11(2), 289–302 (2012), http://dx.doi.org/10.1007/s11047-012-9311-3

94. Vielhaber, M.: Computation of functions on n bits by asynchronous clocking of cellular automata. Natural Computing (to appear, available for download "online first", 2013), http://dx.doi.org/10.1007/s11047-013-9376-7

95. von Neumann, J.: Theory of self-reproducing automata. University of Illinois press Urbana (1966); Burks, A. (ed.)

96. Wacker, S., Worsch, T.: Phase space invertible asynchronous cellular automata. In: Formenti, E. (ed.) Proceedings of AUTOMATA & JAC. EPTCS, vol. 90, pp. 236–254 (2012), http://dx.doi.org/10.4204/EPTCS.90.19

97. Worsch, T.: (Intrinsically?) universal asynchronous CA. In: Sirakoulis, G.C., Bandini, S. (eds.) ACRI 2012. LNCS, vol. 7495, pp. 689–698. Springer, Heidelberg (2012), http://dx.doi.org/10.1007/978-3-642-33350-7_70

A Note on the Classification of the Most Simple Asynchronous Cellular Automata

Nazim Fatès

Inria Nancy Grand-Est, LORIA UMR 7503,
54 600, Villers-lès-Nancy, France
nazim.fates@loria.fr

Abstract. This text presents some notes on the classification of simple rules in one and two dimensions. We focus on the 256 Elementary Cellular Automata and the 64 totalistic rules with von Neumann neighbourhood. The updating scheme is fully asynchronous updating, that is, only one cell is updated randomly and uniformly at each time step.

While a partial classification of such rules has been proposed some years ago, very few progress has been made since then. In order to spot the obstacles to a complete classification, we here mainly adopt an experimental approach based on the observations of the space-time diagrams. We also give some sketch of proofs when possible and underline the interesting open problems.

1 Introduction

This note looks at the problem as to whether asynchronous cellular automata (CA) are simpler or more difficult to study that their synchronous counterparts. This question may seem naive at first sight: since there are some asynchronous CA that are universal in many senses [8,12], the complexity of their dynamics is maximal. However, the question might be more interesting if we restrict its scope to some finite sets of rules such as the 256 Elementary Cellular Automata (ECA) or, in two dimensions, to the 64 totalistic rules with nearest neighbours interaction.

ECAs have a wide diversity of behaviours and we refer to the work of Schüle and Stoop for a recent development on their classification [11]. As far as asynchronous ECAs are concerned, we proposed classification of a subset of these rules based on the measure of the convergence time to a fixed point [4]. We employed fully asynchronous updating, that is, only one cell is updated at random at each time step. This updating scheme greatly simplifies the study of the dynamics of the rules as no simultaneity is allowed in the transitions. In the case of α-asynchronous dynamics, where cells are updated independently with a given probability, the work or Regnault et al. [5] and Fukś and Skelton [6] showed that the analysis turns out to be much more intricate. The two-dimensional case was tackled for the 64 totalistic rules with von Neumann neighbourhood but then again, understanding the dynamics was much more difficult and we could only propose a few rigorous calculations of the convergence properties [3].

J. Kari, M. Kutrib, and A. Malcher (Eds.): AUTOMATA 2013, LNCS 8155, pp. 31–45, 2013.

How can we give a more complete view on these simple asynchronous CA? We propose here to observe experimentally the behaviour of the rules that have not been completely understood yet. When possible, we will sketch some proofs of their convergence properties. Our aim is to determine whether the complexity displayed by the simple rules relies only on the synchronous updating. If so, then we can expect that by putting randomness in the updating, many mechanisms that make the system complex will be broken and the system will be easier to study. However, it may also well be that randomness overwhelms the behaviour in such a manner that it makes the system much more difficult to study...

2   Definitions

For the sake of simplicity, we begin by defining one-dimensional cellular automata. These definitions will be adapted to the two-dimensional case in Sec. 4. Let $\Lambda = (\mathbb{Z}/n\mathbb{Z})$ represent a set of n cells arranged in a ring. A cellular automaton is a dynamical system constituted of *cells* that are arranged on Λ; each cell can hold a *state* which is binary (denoted by 0 and 1), and a *configuration* is the state of the system at a given time ; the configuration space is $\mathcal{E}_n = \{0, 1\}^\Lambda$, it is finite and we have $|\mathcal{E}_n| = 2^n$.

We denote by $|x|_P$ the number of occurrences of a pattern P in x. The *density* $\rho(x)$ of a configuration $x \in \mathcal{E}_n$ is the ratio of 1s in this configuration: $\rho(x) = |x|_1/n$. We denote by $\mathbf{0} = 0^\Lambda$ and $\mathbf{1} = 1^\Lambda$ the two special uniform configurations. A cellular automaton is defined by using a neighbourhood $\mathcal{N} = \{n_1, \ldots, n_\nu\}$. It is a set of size ν, where an element $n_i \in \Lambda$ represents the displacement that links a cell to its i-th neighbour. The behaviour of a CA is given by a local transition function $f : Q^\nu \to Q$ which specifies how a cell updates its states according to the state of the cells in its neighbourhood. An *Elementary Cellular Automaton* (ECA) is defined with the neighbourhood $\mathcal{N}_3 = \{-1, 0, +1\}$ and a *local transition rule*, a function $f : \{0, 1\}^3 \to \{0, 1\}$. For a given ring size n, the *global transition rule* associated to f with a synchronous updating is the function $f : \mathcal{E}_n \to \mathcal{E}_n$ that maps a configuration x^t to a configuration x^{t+1} such that: $\forall i \in \Lambda,\ x_i^{t+1} = f(x_{i-1}^t, x_i^t, x_{i+1}^t)$.

We are here interested in examining the behaviour of CA under *fully asynchronous updating*, that is, when only one cell is updated at each time step. Let $(U_t)_{t \in \mathbb{N}}$ be a sequence of random variables that define at each time step which cell is updated. A fully asynchronous ECA is the stochastic process $(x^t)_{t \in \mathbb{N}}$ defined recursively with $x^0 = x$ and:

$$x_i^{t+1} = \begin{cases} f(x_{i-1}^t, x_i^t, x_{i+1}^t) & \text{if } i = U_t \\ x_i^t & \text{otherwise.} \end{cases}$$

2.1   Classification of Rules and States

The state space of a synchronous CA can be represented as an oriented graph where the vertices are the configurations and where an edge links a configuration and its successor. Because of the deterministic nature of the system, this graph can be described as a collection of connected components where each connected component is itself a collection of trees rooted on one cycle (this type of graph is also called a pseudo-forest). The leaves of the tree are garden-of-Eden configurations, the configurations on the trees represent the transient configurations and the configurations on the cycle represent the periodic configurations.

In a truly asynchronous system, cycles no longer exist and the structure of the graph described above does not hold any more. The behaviour of the system can be described with a Markov chain, which allows one to divide the state space into two types of configurations: the recurrent and transient configurations. The recurrent configurations are the states that are visited an infinite number of times while the transient configurations are visited only for a restricted (random) amount of time. As it is usual in Markov chain theory, this division can be formally established by partitioning the state space into *communication classes*, that is, classes that are created by an equivalence relation which relates two configurations that are reachable one from the other. (By convention each configuration communicates with itself).

A special attention can be given to the *fixed points*, that is, to the communication classes of size 1. Indeed, the synchronous and asynchronous systems share the same fixed points. Fixed points physically represent the stabilisation of the system and in the case where the CA are used as a model of computation, they can be interpreted as the end of a calculus (a good example is given by the density classification problem, see e.g. [2,1]). In this work, we are interested in classifying the rules according to the existence and reachability of their fixed points and according to the maximum time needed to reach a fixed point.

Formally, for a given CA rule and a given system size n, let T_x represent the *rescaled convergence time to a fixed point*, when starting from $x \in Q^A$: it is the actual time t need to attain a fixed point divided by n. This is a random variable, whose realisation depends on the sequence of updates that has been chosen. We are interested in $E[T_x]$, the average time needed to converge to a fixed point and more specifically by the maximum of this quantity over all configurations of size n. For a ring size n, the *worst expected convergence time in average* (WECT) of the CA is defined by:

$$\text{WECT}(n) = \max_{\{x \in Q^A\}} E[T_x]$$

3   Elementary Cellular Automata

Our aim now is to re-examine the classification of the rules according to the scaling of WECT as a function of the system size n. Of course, such a classification will be relevant only if the form of the function can be directly related to the actual behaviour of the system. Our thesis is that the WECT is not a mere quantitative estimation but that, in fact, it can be considered as a "signature" of the behaviour of the CA under fully asynchronous updating.

Before we jump into the scrutiny of the rules, let us first present a notation to refer to the ECA. The most common way to refer to an ECA f is to use the Wolfram code, that is, a number between 0 and 255 calculated with the formula: $W(f) = 2^0 f(0,0,0) + 2^1 f(0,0,1) + \cdots + 2^7 f(1,1,1)$. In words, this code corresponds to the decimal equivalent of the bits of the transition table of the ECA, with the least significant bit $f(0,0,0)$ on the left (the table has thus to be "reversed").

As a complementary way to study these rules, we propose to refer to an ECA by its "transition code" (T-code in short). We associate each transition to a letter according to the code of this table:

A	B	C	D	E	F	G	H
000	001	100	101	010	011	110	111

We refer to an ECA as the list of letters that represent the active transitions, that is, the transitions which produce a change of state. For example, the majority rule is associated to the code DE since only the transitions $(1,0,1)$ and $(0,1,0)$ are active. The identity rule is denoted by the special code I.

Note that the ordering of the T-code differs from Wolfram's code: the first four letters A, B, C, D and the last four letters E, F, G, H, have 0 and 1 as a center cell, respectively[1]. This ordering has the following advantage. First, knowing the code, it is very easy to get the symmetric rule obtained by the permutation of left and right: the new T-code is simply obtained by exchanging the letters B and C, on the one hand, and F and G, on the other hand. To get the rule symmetric by exchanging the 0 and 1 states, the letters A and H, B and G, C and F, D and E should be exchanged.

The second advantage of the notation is to provide a kind of "profile" of the rule as it points out the effect of each transition individually. For instance, a rule which has many active transitions is likely to produce more activity (changes in the cells' state) than a rule with less active transitions. Moreover, as each transition is labelled separately, it is easy to group transitions with similar effects when only one cell is updated. In particular:

- A and H indicate if the state 0 or 1 are quiescent, respectively.
- B and F (resp. G and C) commend the movement of 01 (resp. 10) frontiers.
- D and E enable the merging of regions of consecutive 0s and 1s, respectively.

The role of these groups of transitions will be made clearer when analysing the rules in more detail. In this note, ECAs will be referred to by their classical Wolfram code and by their T-code. As the symmetries mentioned above allow us to reduce the state space to 88 equivalent classes, we will use for the study of each class one rule, and unless otherwise stated, we will take the rule that has the smallest Wolfram code and call this rule *the minimal representative rule*.

3.1   Double-Quiescent Rules

We start by presenting the main results that have already been established for the *double-quiescent* rules, for which $f(0,0,0) = 0$ and $f(1,1,1) = 1$. (Their T-code does not have an A or an H.) Interested readers should refer to Ref. [4] for a full development of the following theorem.

---

[1] This means that all happens as if the transitions (x, y, z) were sorted out with the order yxz instead of xyz.

Theorem 1. *Among the 24 minimal double-quiescent ECA, 20 converge with a finite WECT, and 4 have an infinite WECT. Their WECT falls into the following categories:*

$$0, \ln n, \Theta\{n\}, \Theta\{n^2\}, \Theta\{2^n\}, \infty$$

Table 1. Classification of 24 representative rules under fully asynchronous updating. Note that not all of the rules are minimal representatives. The arrows ←, →, ⤻ denote the possible movements of the frontiers to the left, to the right or to both directions, respectively. The + signs denote the possibility to merge consecutive regions of 0s or 1s with transitions E and D, respectively. See Ref. [4] for more details.

behaviour	ACE	(#)	rule	01	10	010	101	WECT
identity	204	(1)	I	·	·	·	·	0
coupon collector	200	(2)	E	·	·	+	·	$\Theta(\ln n)$
	232	(1)	DE	·	·	+	+	
monotone	206	(4)	B	←	·	·	·	$\Theta(n)$
	132	(2)	BC	←	→	·	·	
	234	(4)	BDE	←	·	+	+	
	250	(2)	BCDE	←	→	+	+	
	202	(4)	BE	←	·	+	·	
	192	(4)	EF	→	·	+	·	
	218	(2)	BCE	←	→	+	·	
	128	(2)	EFG	→	←	+	·	
biased random walk	242	(4)	BCDEF	⤻	→	+	+	
	130	(4)	BEFG	⤻	←	+	·	
random walk	226	(2)	BDEF	⤻	·	+	+	$\Theta(n^2)$
	170	(2)	BDEG	←	←	+	+	
	178	(1)	BCDEFG	⤻	⤻	+	+	
	194	(4)	BEF	⤻	·	+	·	
	138	(4)	BEG	←	←	+	·	
	146	(2)	BCEFG	⤻	⤻	+	·	
biased random walk	210	(4)	BCEF	⤻	→	+	·	$\Theta(2^n)$
no fixed-point convergence	198	(2)	BF	⤻	·	·	·	other type
	142	(2)	BG	←	←	·	·	
	214	(4)	BCF	⤻	→	·	·	
	150	(1)	BCFG	⤻	⤻	·	·	

3.2 Beyond DQECA: Towards the Classification of the 256 ECAs

We now examine empirically the convergence of the other ECAs by looking at their space-time diagrams and propose some classes of behaviour. Though these classes are first defined empirically, they are meant to be constructed analytically since the membership to each class can be decided by calculating the WECT (and sometimes additional properties such as the type of fixed points that are reached).

Very Fast Converging Rules. There is a set of rules which appear to converge rapidly to a fixed point. We conjecture that these rules converge in a time that is logarithmic with respect to the size of the configuration. We divide this set into two classes:

- RCH: rapid convergence to a homogeneous fixed point,
- RCN: rapid convergence to a non-homogeneous fixed point.

In the RCH class, we find the following 16 minimal rules:

0, 2, 8, 10,	EFGH, BEFGH, EGH, BEGH,
18, 24, 26, 32,	BCEFGH, CEGH, BCEGH, DEFGH,
34, 40, 42, 50,	BDEFGH, DEGH, BDEGH, BCDEFGH,
56, 58, 74, 106.	CDEGH, BCDEGH, BEH, BDEH.

On the left column, we give the Wolfram code and on the right column, we give the T-code. We keep this convention in the following.

We represent below space-time diagrams of four rules from this class:

0 - EFGH   26 - BCEGH   58 - BCDEGH   74 - BEH

These diagrams should be interpreted as follows. Time goes from bottom to top; square in blue and white represent cells with states 0 and 1, respectively. The time is rescaled by a factor $1/n$: the transition from one line to the other is obtained after n updates. (This explains some discontinuities in the groups of cells). The ring size is fixed to $n = 50$ and the random evolution is represented over 30 time steps. Recall that the space is a ring, which explains that some sets of coloured cells seem to "appear".

It should also be noted that the initial configuration is made of half of the cells contiguously set to 1 and 0. This choice was made in order to allow for a better visualisation of the transmission of information than with a random initial condition.

In the RCN class, we find the following 10 minimal rules:

4, 5, 12, 13,	FGH, AFGH, GH, AGH,
36, 44, 72, 76,	DFGH, DGH, EH, H,
77, 104	AH, DEH.

We represent below space-time diagrams of four rules from this class:

   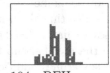

4 - FGH   5 - AFGH   72 - EH   104 - DEH

Linear Convergence. We now turn our attention to the rules which converge in linear time as a function of n. Surprisingly, we identified only two rules in this class:

78, 94	BH, BCH.

This contrasts with the fact that there are 10 DQECA with the same type of behaviour.

We represent below space-time diagrams of these two rules:

78 - BH   94 - BCH

Production of Stripes. There are a certain number of rules which produce stripes. However, by contrast with the two previously examined rules, these stripes form a background above which particles may travel and merge or annihilate. We call this class STR; it is constituted of the 10 following minimal rules:

6, 7, 14, 15,	BFGH, ABFGH, BGH, ABGH,
22, 23, 30, 37,	BCFGH, ABCFGH, BCGH, ADFGH,
38, 45	BDFGH, ADGH.

We represent below space-time diagrams of four rules from this class:

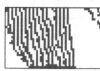   

6 - BFGH   37 - ADFGH   38 - BDFGH   45 - ADGH

The 7 first ECAs of this class produce 01-stripes; ECA 37 and 45 produce 001-stripes (which implies that the system can be observed to stabilise only if n is a multiple of 3). The case of ECA 38 is much less clear and deserves to be examined more carefully.

Non-converging Rules. The last class of rules, class NC, is constituted of the rules for which no obvious convergence is observed when looking at the (finite) simulations. This class can be subdivided into the three following classes:

- class PSL: Partial stabilisation with localised evolution,
- class NPF: rules that possess no fixed point,
- class NLE: noise-like evolution.

In the PSL class, we find 4 minimal rules:

28, 29, 73, 108.	CGH, ACGH, AEH, DH.

We represent below space-time diagrams of four rules from this class:

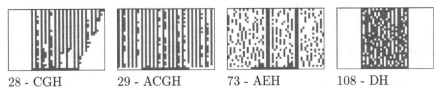

28 - CGH   29 - ACGH   73 - AEH   108 - DH

The class NPF is constituted of the rules for which it is possible to show formally that there exists no fixed point (see a proof below). There are 39 such rules, which correspond to the 13 following minimal representatives rules:

1, 3, 9, 11,	AEFGH, ABEFGH, AEGH, ABEGH,
19, 25, 27, 33,	ABCEFGH, ACEGH, ABCEGH, ADEFGH,
35, 41, 43, 51,	ABDEFGH, ADEGH, ABDEGH, ABCDEFGH,
57.	ACDEGH.

We represent below space-time diagrams of four rules from this class:

1 - AEFGH   27 - ABCEGH   43 - ABDEGH   57 - ACDEGH

Last, we put in the NLE class the remaining 9 minimal rules:

46, 54, 60, 62,	BDGH, BCDFGH, CDGH, BCDGH,
90, 105, 110, 122,	BCEH, ADEH, BDH, BCDEH,
126.	BCDH.

We represent below space-time diagrams of four rules from this class:

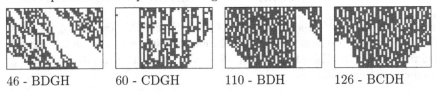

46 - BDGH   60 - CDGH   110 - BDH   126 - BCDH

From the sole observation of the space-time diagrams, it is not clear whether their WECT is infinite or whether it scales exponentially with the ring size n.

3.3 Sketch of Proofs

Logarithmic Convergence. To show the logarithmic convergence of the rules of class RCH and RCN, we can for instance exhibit a function $F : Q^n \to \mathbb{N}$ for which for each configuration x the probability to decrease (at least) by a constant quantity is proportional to $F(x)$. This is for instance easy to do with ECA o: by taking $\forall x \in \mathcal{E}_n, F(x) = |x|_1$, we recover the rules on the coupon-collecting process already shown for the rule E and the majority rule DE (see Ref. [4] for a proof). However, finding such a function for the other rules is not straightforward, even for ECA 2 (BEFGH), although this rule has only one single transition that updates to 1. Indeed, some space-time diagrams indicate that the problem of proving the logarithmic convergence of this rule needs new specific techniques to be tackled in all its generality.

Linear Convergence. Proving the linear convergence of the two rules of class LIN seems straightforward. It is interesting to compare the 10 DQECA that also have a linearly scaling WECT with those which contain an additional H transition in their T-code. We see that only B and BC do not change their class of behaviour: the presence of a non-quiescent state significantly alters the transmission of information except for these two rules. In their specific case, it is easy to understand why H is not affecting the behaviour: B and BC can be described as an expansion to the left or in both directions of state 1; the transition H then only puts 0s in the middle of zones of 1s without perturbing the propagation process.

Stripe Production. It can be observed experimentally that for the rules that produce 01-stripes, the convergence depends on the parity of the ring size: for an even value of n, the system converges to a fixed by the annihilation of particles that follow a random walk. For odd values of n, no convergence is possible as a single particle lives for ever and can not disappear by annihilation. For all these rules, our conjecture is thus that the WECT scales quadratically with n on the even values of n and is infinite for the other values. The same can of course be generalised to ECA 37 and 45 for sizes that are multiples of 3. As mentioned earlier, the case of ECA 38 appears as much more delicate and constitutes an interesting open problem.

About the Rules Showing No Convergence. For the rules of the PSL class, proving that their WECT is infinite looks rather easy. It is indeed possible to construct a non-converging configuration of arbitrary size by joining stable and non-stable parts together. For instance, for the rule DH (ECA 108), the configurations $0^{n-3}1\dot{0}1$ and $0^{n-3}1\dot{1}1$ are sent respectively to each other each time the unstable cell (shown with a dot) is updated. We leave the proof for the other rules as an exercise for the interested readers.

Now, let us examine the class NCP. Figure 1 is a modified de Bruijn diagram that gives the transitions that apply on each cell of a given configuration. Informally, it can be understood as a transducer where the configuration is parsed from left to right and where the last two digits are remembered. One switches from one step to the other according to the new state that is read (into brackets on the figure) and the transition that applies is the letter on the arrow. A configuration can thus be transformed as a sequence of letters where each letter specifies the transition that can apply (see e.g. Ref. [4] for examples).

As a consequence, a given configuration is a fixed point of a rule if its sequence of letters contains no letter that is in the T-code of the rule. It can thus be shown that a necessary and sufficient condition for a rule not to admit any fixed point is the impossibility to make a cycle on the de Bruijn diagram without producing a letter

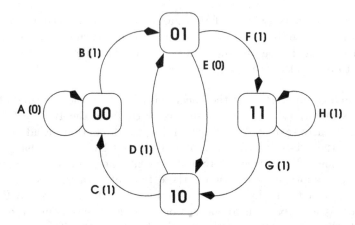

Fig. 1. De Bruijn diagram with letters of the T-code associated to the transitions

that is in the T-code of the rule. It is easy to show that a rule which has this property verifies all the following conditions: (a) it contains an A and an H; (b) it contains either a D or an E; (c) it contains either a B, a C, or an E; (d) it contains either a D, an F, or a G; (e) it contains a B, a C, an F, or a G. We searched automatically the rules that verify these five conditions and obtained the members of class NPF.

Last but not least, let us evoke the interesting case of the members of the NLE class. First, all these rules but ADEH have in common that **0** is their only fixed point. Indeed, if the T-code of a rule contains the letters B and D (or, symmetrically C and D), then **0** and **1** are the only potential fixed points (their existence is of course conditioned by A and H). This can be noticed by looking at the de Bruijn diagram (see Fig. 1) and noticing that all cycles of length greater than 1 are "broken".

As a consequence, it can be easily seen that if the T-code of a rule contains a B and D (or C and D), contains an H and does not contain an E, then this rule has an infinite WECT. Indeed, for any ring size, the last 1 can not disappear at this would imply that transition E is active. This sets the case of the following rules:

rules:	46, 54, 60, 62, 110, 126	BDGH, BCDFGH, CDGH, BCDGH, BDH, BCDH.

There remain three rules, that can be analysed individually. We begin by the rule BCEH (ECA 90) which corresponds to an XOR operation on the left and right neighbours. This rules admits **0** as a fixed point and $(110)^{n/3}$ as an additional fixed point when n is a multiple of 3. We conjecture that this rule is metastable, that is, it has a WECT that scales exponentially with the ring size. To establish this result is another interesting exercise.

Rule ADEH (ECA 105) has the specificity to possess only one fixed point $(1001)^{n/4}$ for the ring sizes that are multiples of 4. However, even for this particular value of n, it can be verified that the fixed point can not be attained as this would necessitate one of the transitions B, C, F or G to be active.

The last case that remains is rule BDEH (ECA 122). It can be noticed that the T-code of the rule differs from rule BCEH (ECA 90) only by the additional presence of D, which does not modify the reachability of the fixed point **0**. We therefore conjecture that this rule is also a metastable one.

4   Classification of the Two-Dimensional Totalistic Rules

In order to complete our view on the classification of the most simple rules, we now briefly look at the two-dimensional case, with a specific question in mind: are there behaviours that are somewhat "specific" of this dimension or do they reduce to the cases previously seen ?

We now use a square grid with periodic boundary conditions $\Lambda = (\mathbb{Z}/L\mathbb{Z})^2$. For the sake of homogeneity, we denote by $n = L^2$ the total number of cells of the grid and still express the WECT as a function of n. We will consider only the von Neumann neighbourhood: $\mathcal{N}_5 = \{(0,0),(1,0),(0,1),(0,-1),(-1,0)\}$.

The local functions we study are defined from $\{0,1\}^5$ to $\{0,1\}$ and we focus on the functions that do not depend on the particular values of each cell but only on the number of 1s in the neighbourhood. These rules, known as the *totalistic rules*, can be written as: $\phi(q_1,\ldots,q_5) = f(q_1+\cdots+q_5)$, where $f : \{0,\ldots,5\} \to \{0,1\}$.

There are 64 such totalistic rules. We associate to each function f the code Ti where $i = f(0)\cdot 2^0 + f(1)\cdot 2^1 + \cdots + f(5)\cdot 2^5$. These can also be represented by a transition table; the table of T10 is:

s	0	1	2	3	4	5
$f(s)$	0	1	0	1	0	0

By construction, all the rules are invariant under the spatial symmetries (rotations by 90 degrees and reflections). However, a rule may not be invariant by the exchanging 0 and 1. There are $2^3 = 8$ rules which are invariant by 0/1 exchange and there are 26 minimal representative rules (that is, the rules with the smallest code number when the 0/1 exchange is applied).

We propose here to briefly re-examine the classification we proposed with Gerin where were mainly interested by the difference between polynomial and non-polynomial types of convergence [3]. We now endeavour to give a more precise description of the various behaviours.

Coupon Collector. (WECT: logarithmic): T0, T8, T16, T20.
The convergence of T0 is clear; we conjecture that the three other rules also converge in logarithmic time. Below is an example of the evolution of T20:

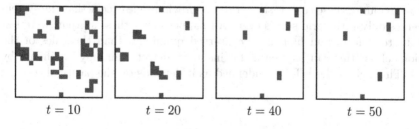

$t = 10$ \qquad $t = 20$ \qquad $t = 40$ \qquad $t = 50$

Fast Monotonous Convergence. (WECT: linear): T32, T36, T40, T48.
The system converges rapidly towards a fixed point with the optional presence of "islands" or "seas". Below is an example of the evolution of T36:

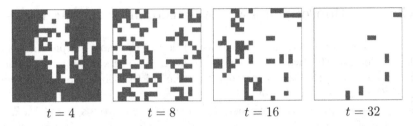

$t = 4$ $\qquad$ $t = 8$ $\qquad$ $t = 16$ $\qquad$ $t = 32$

It is interesting to note that T60, the symmetric of T48, corresponds to the rule of the Bootstrap percolation. Remark that only special initial conditions can allow us to see why these rules have a linear and not a logarithmic convergence. For instance, we believe that for T36 and T40, the configuration that has the greatest WECT is the configuration where all cells are in state 1 but one, which is in state 0.

Checkerboard-Like Convergence. (WECT: ?): T2, T3, T4, T14, T34.
The system converges towards a checkerboard-like pattern. We refer to the work of Regnault et al. for a description of this type of convergence [9,10]. (This author has focused his work on the minority rule but the rules of this class appear to follow the same type of dynamics.) Below is an example of the evolution of T34:

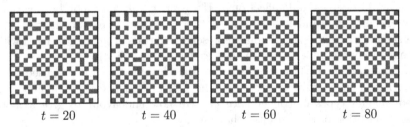

$t = 20$ $\qquad$ $t = 40$ $\qquad$ $t = 60$ $\qquad$ $t = 80$

We do not know what are the scaling laws of the WECT for these type of dynamics and leave the question as another open problem.

Checkerboard Convergence. (WECT: undefined): T6, T7, T38.
The behaviour of these rules is similar to the previous one except that the system converges only if the grid size is even. All happens as if these systems were less tolerant to defects and had more conserved quantities than the rules of the previous class (this can happen if, for instance, defects can only annihilate by pairs). This makes the WECT undefined as it depends on the parity of n.

Metastable Behaviour. (WECT: exponential): T10, T11, T12, T18, T44.
The system seems not to converge but there nevertheless exists a path that leads
the system to a fixed point. Below is an example of the evolution of T10:

$t = 100$ $t = 200$ $t = 500$ $t = 1000$

As already noted by Gerin [3], it is a challenge to discriminate experimentally
the metastable rules from the non-converging ones. Indeed, it is not possible
to "see" this difference experimentally (only for small-size grids, but these sizes
can also be non-representative of the larger sizes). Here, contrary to the one-
dimensional case (see the case of rule BCEF above), we would like to show that
the distance to a fixed point does not decrease with time (in average) but we do
not know how to explicitly "measure" this distance.

This problem was tackled by Hoffmann [7] et al. for the specific case of rule
T10. A solver that used the planning techniques was used to determine the
sequence of updates that would lead to a fixed point. As a positive spin-off,
the planner not only was used to find actual solutions, but it also provided an
automatic means for proving that one fixed point was reachable with a number
of updates that varied linearly with the number of cells. An upper bound on
the convergence time was provided but an lower bound is still missing. It is also
an open problem to generalise these techniques (or new techniques) to other
metastable rules.

Partially Stabilising. (WECT: infinite): T24, T25, T52.
The system partially stabilises on some parts while some other parts remain
unstable. Below is an example of the evolution of T24:

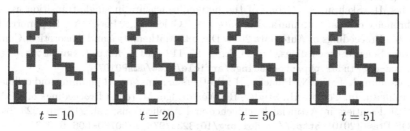

$t = 10$ $t = 20$ $t = 50$ $t = 51$

Erratic Non-converging. (WECT: infinite): T1, T5, T9 T13, T17, T21, T22
T25, T26, T28, T30, T42 .
The system evolves with noise-like patterns without finding a fixed point. It is
an open problem to show the non-convergence of these rules. A simple proof was
produced for T42, which is the parity rule, by showing that applying a transition
on a cell can not make it stable [3] (it can however stabilise its neighbours).

5   Discussion

This text presented some empirical analysis on the classification of fully asynchronous rules. Though there are cases where the randomness of the updating did simplify the dynamics, we observed that in general, the very problem of predicting the average convergence time to a fixed point was difficult, even when the rules were selected for their simplicity. Among the most crucial problems to complete the classification, it appears that proving logarithmic convergence of some one-dimensional rules and proving the metastability of some two-dimensional rules are good questions for the study of asynchrony in cellular automata.

Acknowledgements. The author expresses his gratitude to his collaborators with whom he established the results here presented. We particularly thank L. Gerin, M. Morvan, N. Schabanel, E. Thierry and D. Regnault. All comments, corrections, and ideas about this text are welcome.

References

1. Bušić, A., Fatès, N., Mairesse, J., Marcovici, I.: Density classification on infinite lattices and trees. Electronic Journal of Probability 18(51), 1–22 (2013), http://ejp.ejpecp.org/article/view/2325
2. Fatès, N.: Stochastic cellular automata solutions to the density classification problem - when randomness helps computing. Theory of Computing Systems 53(2), 223–242 (2013), http://dx.doi.org/10.1007/s00224-012-9386-3
3. Fatès, N., Gerin, L.: Examples of fast and slow convergence of 2D asynchronous cellular systems. Journal of Cellular Automata 4(4), 323–337 (2009)
4. Fatès, N., Morvan, M., Schabanel, N., Thierry, E.: Fully asynchronous behavior of double-quiescent elementary cellular automata. Theoretical Computer Science 362, 1–16 (2006)
5. Fatès, N., Regnault, D., Schabanel, N., Thierry, É.: Asynchronous behavior of double-quiescent elementary cellular automata. In: Correa, J.R., Hevia, A., Kiwi, M. (eds.) LATIN 2006. LNCS, vol. 3887, pp. 455–466. Springer, Heidelberg (2006)
6. Fukś, H., Skelton, A.: Orbits of the bernoulli measure in single-transition asynchronous cellular automata. In: Fatès, N., Goles, E., Maass, A., Rapaport, I. (eds.) Proceedings of Automata 2011. Discrete Mathematics and Theoretical Computer Science Proceedings, DMTCS, pp. 95–112 (2011), http://www.dmtcs.org/dmtcs-ojs/index.php/proceedings/article/view/dmAP0107
7. Hoffmann, J., Fatès, N., Palacios, H.: Brothers in arms? on AI planning and cellular automata. In: Coelho, H., Studer, R., Wooldridge, M. (eds.) Proceedings of ECAI 2010. Frontiers in Artificial Intelligence and Applications, vol. 215, pp. 223–228. IOS Press (2010), http://dx.doi.org/10.3233/978-1-60750-606-5-223
8. Peper, F., Adachi, S., Lee, J.: Variations on the game of life. In: Adamatzky, A. (ed.) Game of Life Cellular Automata, pp. 235–255. Springer, London (2010), http://dx.doi.org/10.1007/978-1-84996-217-9_13
9. Regnault, D., Schabanel, N., Thierry, E.: Progresses in the analysis of stochastic 2D cellular automata: A study of asynchronous 2D minority. Theoretical Computer Science 410(47-49), 4844–4855 (2009), http://dx.doi.org/10.1016/j.tcs.2009.06.024

10. Rouquier, J.B., Regnault, D., Thierry, E.: Stochastic minority on graphs. Theoretical Computer Science 412(30), 3947–3963 (2011),
    http://dx.doi.org/10.1016/j.tcs.2011.02.028
11. Schüle, M., Stoop, R.: A full computation-relevant topological dynamics classification of elementary cellular automata. Chaos 22(4), 043143 (2012),
    http://dx.doi.org/10.1063/1.4771662
12. Worsch, T.: (Intrinsically?) universal asynchronous CA. In: Sirakoulis, G.C., Bandini, S. (eds.) ACRI 2012. LNCS, vol. 7495, pp. 689–698. Springer, Heidelberg (2012), http://dx.doi.org/10.1007/978-3-642-33350-7_70

A Survey on
m-Asynchronous Cellular Automata*

Enrico Formenti

Nice Sophia Antipolis University, CNRS, I3S, UMR 7271,
06900 Sophia Antipolis, France
enrico.formenti@unice.fr

Abstract. The paper after briefly surveying main asynchronous models in cellular automata will report recent developments in the study of m-ACA, a new general framework for studying asynchrony in cellular spaces.

1 Introduction

Last twenty years witnessed the rapid growth of the domain of complex systems both from the theoretical and the application point of view. In parallel, a number of formal models were developed in order to reproduce their behavior and, possibly, deduce general properties from the formal models using a number of knowledge domains going from theoretical computer science to mathematics.

Cellular automata play a central role in this context because of their three main characteristics: locality, uniformity, synchronicity. (which is present in most complex systems at the point that is often taken as a definition of complex system): the emergence of a complex collective behavior starting from local interactions between simple individuals.

A cellular automaton consists in an infinite set of identical finite automata arranged on a regular lattice ($\mathbb{Z}$ in this article). Each finite automaton takes its state from a finite set S, called the set of *states* or the *alphabet*. The state is updated according to a *local rule* λ which take into account the state of the automaton and the one of a fixed finite neighborhood of neighboring automata. All automata in the lattice are updated in parallel.

This simple definition of the model contrasts the huge variety of long-term dynamical behaviors which has attracted the attention of many researchers (see [25, 13, 17, 12, 1] for recent results and a comprehensive bibliography). At the same time, this great variety of behaviors qualifies CA as very useful models in applications [26, 11, 10, 19, 3, 6, 32, 18].

Applications also motivated the introduction of a number of variants of CA model. Each new model is meant to highlight peculiar properties. For example, this paper focus on asynchrony. This last property turns out to be interesting in

---

* This work has been partially supported by the French National Research Agency project EMC (ANR-09-BLAN-0164).

J. Kari, M. Kutrib, and A. Malcher (Eds.): AUTOMATA 2013, LNCS 8155, pp. 46–66, 2013.

a number of different context ranging from modeling chemical reactions in living cells, to asynchronous computation and communication in distributed systems, and so on. As non-uniformity [16], asynchrony can also be useful to introduce inside CA more realistic features as noise [31].

The first part of the paper briefly survey the most known manners of dealing with asynchrony in CA. We do absolutely not pretend to be exhaustive or complete. We just review those models that motivate the studies reported in the rest of the paper. This second part of the paper introduces a new model for asynchrony which aims at generalizing existing ones (at some extent) and at the same time to offer enough theoretical "hooks" to be able to significantly analyze the long-term behavior. The basic idea is to augment the classical CA model with a measure μ over the integers. At each time step, a set of integers τ (finite or infinite) is extracted according to μ. The elements of τ are the indexes of the sites that are allowed to be updated, the cells with index in $\mathbb{Z} \setminus \tau$ leave their state unchanged. We call this new model m-ACA. Clearly, some work has to be done at the formal level to adapt the existing definitions to take into account the fact that in the new situation one works with family of functions and not with a single function (*the global function*) like in the classical setting. This have also to be combined with the fact of drawing sites to be updated using the measure μ.

After briefly surveying models related to m-ACA that can be found in literature, the paper reviews main results and ideas about m-ACA exploring both the dynamics and some set theoretic properties. The final section contains the seeds for a new research program which we believe will illustrate the "usefulness" of this new model in the study of the asynchrony in cellular automata.

2   The General Framework

Notation. For all $i, j \in \mathbb{Z}$ with $i \leq j$ (resp., $i < j$) let $[i, j] = \{k \in \mathbb{N} \mid i \leq k \leq j\}$ (resp., $[i, j) = \{k \in \mathbb{N} \mid i \leq k < j\}$). The set of positive integers (resp., reals) is denoted by $\mathbb{N}_+$ (resp., $\mathbb{R}_+$). Given a set X, $\mathcal{P}(X)$ denotes the collection of subsets of all X.

Let S be a finite alphabet. A *configuration* is a function from $\mathbb{Z}$ to S. The *configuration set* $S^{\mathbb{Z}}$ is usually equipped with the metric d defined as follows:

$$\forall x, y \in S^{\mathbb{Z}} \; d(x, y) = 2^{-n} \, , \text{ where } n = \min\{i \in \mathbb{N} \mid x_i \neq y_i \text{ or } x_{-i} \neq y_{-i}\}$$

The set $S^{\mathbb{Z}}$ is a Cantor space i.e., a compact, totally disconnected and perfect topological space. For any pair $i, j \in \mathbb{Z}$, with $i \leq j$, and any configuration $x \in S^{\mathbb{Z}}$ we denote by $x_{[i,j]}$ the word $x_i \cdots x_j \in S^{j-i+1}$. Similarly, for every $u \in S^{\ell}$ and for every $i, j \in [0, \ell)$, $u_{[i,j]} = u_i \dots u_j$ is the portion of a word inside $[i, j]$. In both the previous notations, $[i, j]$ can be replaced by $[i, j)$, with the obvious meaning. A configuration x is said to be a-finite for some $a \in S$ if the number of positions i with $x_i \neq a$ is finite.

Formally, a (one-dimensional) CA is a structure (S, λ, r) where S is the *alphabet* or *set of states*, $r \in \mathbb{N}$ is the *radius*, and $\lambda : S^{2r+1} \to S$ is the *local rule* of the automaton. The local rule λ induces a *global rule* $F : S^{\mathbb{Z}} \to S^{\mathbb{Z}}$ which describes the new global state of the CA after one time step

$$\forall x \in S^{\mathbb{Z}}, \ \forall i \in \mathbb{Z}, \qquad F(x)_i = \lambda(x_{i-r}, \ldots, x_i, \ldots, x_{i+r}) \ .$$

The *space-time diagram* of initial configuration c can be represented by a bi-infinite figure, where for the sake of simplicity we set $c^t(j) := F^t(c)_j$:

$$
\begin{array}{l|l|l}
t = 0 & \ldots c_{-2} \ c_{-1} \ c_0 \ c_1 \ c_2 \ldots & = c \\[1ex]
t = 1 & \ldots c^1_{-2} \ c^1_{-1} \ c^1_0 \ c^1_1 \ c^1_2 \ldots & = F(c) \\[1ex]
\vdots & \vdots \ \vdots \ \vdots \ \vdots \ \vdots \ \vdots \ \vdots & \vdots \\[1ex]
t & \ldots c^t_{-2} \ c^t_{-1} \ c^t_0 \ c^t_1 \ c^t_2 \ldots & = F^t(c) \\[1ex]
\vdots & \vdots \ \vdots \ \vdots \ \vdots \ \vdots \ \vdots \ \vdots & \vdots
\end{array}
$$

Space-time diagrams are a nice visual tool that might sometimes provide intuitions on the dynamical behavior or emergent phenomena. In Section 4.4 we will see that this is exactly the case.

An *activation function* v i.e., a function from $\mathbb{N}$ to $\mathcal{P}(\mathbb{Z})$ is our main tool to control synchronicity. Indeed, at any time step $t \in \mathbb{N}$, $v(t)$ tells which sites are active and must be updated; all other cells are left unchanged. Therefore, one can redefine the global function at time $t \in \mathbb{N}$ using v as follows. For time step $t = 0$,

$$\forall x \in S^{\mathbb{Z}}, \ \forall i \in \mathbb{Z}, \ F_v(x)_{0,i} = x_i \ .$$

For time step $t > 0$, define $\forall x \in S^{\mathbb{Z}}, \ \forall i \in \mathbb{Z}$

$$F_v(x)_{t+1,i} = \begin{cases} \lambda(F_v(x)_{t,i-r}, \ldots, F_v(x)_{t,i}, \ldots, F_v(x)_{t,i+r}) & \text{if } i \in v(t+1) \ , \\ F_v(x)_{t,i} & \text{otherwise} \ . \end{cases}$$

Remark that choosing v such that $\forall t \in \mathbb{N}, v(t) = \mathbb{Z}$, it means that all cells are updated at each time step i.e., we recover the classical CA setting. Summing up, one can give the following formal definition.

Definition 1 (ACA). *An Asynchronous Cellular Automaton (ACA) is structure (S, λ, r, v) where (S, λ, r) is a CA and v is an activation function.*

The main novelty with ACA vs. CA is that in ACA one does no more have a single global function but there is a family of global functions. This implies that all notions concerning dynamical behavior have to be adapted to work with family of functions.

Let $\mathcal{T}$ be a *monoid of continuous functions* from $S^{\mathbb{Z}}$ to $S^{\mathbb{Z}}$ where Id denotes the *identity* map on $S^{\mathbb{Z}}$. The family $\mathcal{T}$ is said to be *sensitive to initial conditions* (or, simply, *sensitive*) if there exists $\varepsilon > 0$ such that for any $x \in S^{\mathbb{Z}}$ and any $\delta > 0$, there is an element $y \in S^{\mathbb{Z}}$ with $d(x,y) < \delta$ such that $d(T(x), T(y)) \geq \varepsilon$ for some $T \in \mathcal{T}$. Furthermore, the family $\mathcal{T}$ is said to be *positively expansive* (or, briefly, *expansive*) if there exists a constant $\varepsilon > 0$ such that for every pair of distinct elements $x, y \in S^{\mathbb{Z}}$, we have $d(T(x), T(y)) \geq \varepsilon$ for some $T \in \mathcal{T}$.

Sensitivity and expansivity are elements of instability for a system whose dynamics are described by the family $\mathcal{T}$. The following notions instead refer to elements of stability for $\mathcal{T}$.

A configuration $x \in S^{\mathbb{Z}}$ is said to be an *equicontinuity point* for $\mathcal{T}$ if $\forall \varepsilon > 0$ $\exists \delta > 0$ such that $\forall y \in S^{\mathbb{Z}}$, $d(x,y) < \delta$ implies that $\forall T \in \mathcal{T}$, $d(T(x), T(y)) < \varepsilon$. The family $\mathcal{T}$ is *equicontinuous* if every configuration is an equicontinuity point for $\mathcal{T}$ or, equivalently, $\forall \varepsilon > 0 \ \exists \delta > 0$ such that $\forall x, y \in S^{\mathbb{Z}}$, $d(x,y) < \delta$ implies that $\forall T \in \mathcal{T}$, $d(T(x), T(y)) < \varepsilon$. The family $\mathcal{T}$ is said to be *almost equicontinuous* if the set E of all equicontinuity points for $\mathcal{T}$ is residual (i.e., E contains a countable intersection of open dense subsets).

The family of functions $\mathcal{T}_\nu$ induced by an ACA with activation function ν defined as follows

$$\mathcal{T}_\nu = \bigcup_{t \in \mathbb{N}} \{F_\nu(\cdot)_t\}$$

An ACA is sensitive (resp. expansive) (resp. equicontinuous) (resp., almost equicontinuous) iff its induced family of functions is sensitive (resp. expansive) (resp. equicontinuous) (resp., almost equicontinuous).

Modifying the activation function one can also introduce in a natural way the notion of non-determinism, simply saying that υ is defined from $\mathbb{N}$ to $\mathcal{P}(\mathcal{P}(\mathbb{Z}))$. However, even if this subject will not be developed in this paper, it suggests the idea that different choices of ν may bring to distinct models of asynchronism. The next sections, briefly review the most known ones that can be found in literature.

3   Asynchrony in Cellular Automata Literature

This section briefly surveys models and results from recent. Literature is really huge and it cannot be exhaustively reported in these few pages. We have chosen to survey only those models that inspired us directly the pathway to m-ACA model.

3.1   Fully Asynchronous CA

One of the possible approaches to asynchrony is to assume that *two updates never happen at the same time*. This means that only one cell updates at every time step. The resulting dynamics is determined not only by the local rule of the automaton, but also from an updating function whose image contains only singletons.

Definition 2. *A fully-ACA is a quadruple* $C_v = (S, \lambda, r, v)$ *where S is a finite set called the* alphabet, $r \in \mathbb{N}$ *is the* radius, $\lambda : S^{2r+1} \to S$ *is the* local rule, *and v is the* activation function. *For fully-ACA the function v respect the following property:*

$$\forall t \in \mathbb{N} \qquad v(t) = \{i\}$$

That is, exactly one cell is updated at every time step.

It is interesting to consider the behaviour of a fully-ACA when the sequence is not fixed. In fact, we can consider a family of fully-ACA defined in the following way:

$$C = \{C_v \mid \forall t \in \mathbb{N} \, |v(t)| = 1\}$$

A family of fully-ACA is characterized by the triple (S, λ, r) of the alphabet, local rule, and radius in common between all the fully-ACA of the family. In this way we can differentiate between properties that holds only when a particular updating function is selected from the ones that can hold independently from the particular choice of cells to be updated.

A first property that was studied is the relation between injectivity and surjectivity. A family C of fully-ACA is α-injective (resp. α-surjective) when every fully-ACA $C_v \in C$ is injective (resp. surjective). Contrarily to classical CA, those properties are equivalent for fully-ACA.

Proposition 1 ([28]). *Let $C = (S, \lambda, r)$ be a family of fully-ACA. Then the following statements are equivalent:*

1. *C is α-injective;*
2. *C is α-surjective;*
3. *λ is center-permutative.*

The equivalence of two "global" properties with a "local" property is a recurring theme for fully-ACA. In fact permutativity appears to be a sufficient condition for obtaining many interesting dynamical behaviours.

Dynamical Properties. Classical properties that are interesting to study in this new setting are sensitivity, expansivity and transitivity. It is easy to see that for any class C of fully-ACA there exists at least one activation function v whose corresponding fully-ACA C_v is not sensitive (resp. expansive) (resp. transitive). Hence, we say that a family of fully-ACA $C = (S, \lambda, r)$ is α-sensitive (resp. α-expansive) (resp. α-transitive) it there exists an activation function v for which the fully-ACA $C_v = (S, \lambda, r, v)$ is sensitive (resp. expansive) (resp. transitive).

A first link was found between the presence of a leftmost or rightmost local rule and sensitivity.

Proposition 2 ([28]). *Let $C = (S, \lambda, r)$ be a family of fully-ACA with $r > 0$. If λ is either leftmost or rightmost permutative then C is α-sensitive.*

It is important to point out that, like for classical CA [7], leftmost and rightmost permutativity are only sufficient but not necessary conditions to obtain α-sensitivity. When both leftmost and rightmost permutativity are present the dynamical behavior changes and expansivity is obtained.

Proposition 3 ([28]). *Let $C = (S, \lambda, r)$ be a family of fully-ACA with $r > 0$. If λ is both leftmost and rightmost permutative then C is α-expansive.*

It is interesting to note that there exist rightmost permutative local rules that give α-sensitivity but not α-expansivity.

Example 1. Let $C = (\{0, 1\}, \lambda, 1)$ be a family of fully-ACA with λ the shift rule (i.e., $\forall a, b, c \in \{0, 1\}$, $\lambda(a, b, c) = c$. This rule is rightmost permutative and, by Proposition 2, C is α-sensitive. However, given two configurations $x, y \in S^{\mathbb{Z}}$ with $d(x, y) = \delta$ and with all the differences between x and y in negative position, independently of the updating function chosen the distance between the orbits of the two configurations cannot grow larger than δ.

Transitivity, like sensitivity, only requires permutativity either in the leftmost or the rightmost position.

Proposition 4 ([28]). *Let $C = (S, \lambda, r)$ be a family of fully-ACA with $r > 0$. If λ is either leftmost or rightmost permutative then C is α-transitive.*

Remark 1. For sensitivity and transitivity there is an easy necessary condition that can be used to decide quickly if a fully-ACA $C_v = (S, \lambda, r, v)$ is not sensitive and transitive. To obtain both sensitivity and transitivity the updating function must be such that $\bigcup_{i \in \mathbb{N}} v(i)$ is infinite (i.e., it is a subset of $\mathbb{Z}$ that is unbounded either in the positive or in the negative values).

To obtain expansivity the necessary condition is more stringent: $\bigcup_{i \in \mathbb{N}} v(i)$ must be unbounded in both the negative and the positive values.

A first idea to reduce the dependence of the dynamics of the particular sequence chosen was to find if the property defined by an activation function was *stable*. A property was defined to be stable for an activation function v if the property also holds for all activation function v' such that $v(t) = v'(t)$ on all but a finite number of elements of $\mathbb{N}$.

In [28], it has been proved that there exists a sequence for which sensitivity is a stable property. Similar results holds for expansivity and transitivity.

Turing Completeness. Another question that was investigated in the fully-ACA setting was to establish whenever the model allows computations to be performed and the power of such a computation both in term of Turing-completeness [29] and in term of slowdown of the simulation of a Turing Machine.

It is possible to use the lattice $S^{\mathbb{Z}}$ as the tape of a Turing machine in which, in addition to the symbol written in a cell of the tape, the state of the machine and some control information are encoded.

An activation function v respect is called *universal* when:

$$\forall i \in \mathbb{N} \qquad |\{t \in \mathbb{N} \mid v(t) = i\}| = \infty$$

That is, when every cell is updated infinitely many time. When v satisfies such a property, it is possible to simulate a Turing Machine. However, depending on the particular activation function, the simulation can be arbitrarily slow. In [14], it has been proved that the simulation of a Turing Machine working in time $T(n)$ can be simulated in time $O(T(n)^2)$, hence, differently from other models like register machines, the simulation is not exponentially slower but, in some sense, it is "fast". For further computation aspects of asynchronous CA we address the reader to [27, 33].

3.2   Stochastic Fully Asynchronous CA

Even if it is interesting to study the dynamics of fully-ACA when the updating function is fixed, when modeling real-life processes there is almost always a stochastic component involved. Therefore, the model of fully-ACA has been extended by choosing the cell to be updated by means of a stochastic process. An *Elementary Cellular Automaton* (ECA) is a (one-dimensional) CA with radius 1 and set of states $S = \{0, 1\}$. An ECA of local rule λ is *doubly quiescent* if $\lambda(0, 0, 0) = 0$ and $\lambda(1, 1, 1) = 1$. In [20], Fates *et al.* studied doubly quiescent ECA over finite rings of size n (with periodic boundary conditions). The authors devised the following update policy. At each time step $t \in \mathbb{N}$ an integer $i \in \{0, \ldots, n - 1\}$ is drawn with uniform probability and they set $v(t) = i$. A complete classification of the expected convergence time (when a convergence to a configuration was possible) towards a fixed point (i.e., a configuration consisting of either all 0 or of all 1). The classification consists in the following seven classes.

Class	Behavior	Conv. time
I	Identity	0
II	Coupon collector	$\Theta(n \ln n)$
III	Monotonic	$\Theta(n^2)$
IV	Biased random walk	$\Theta(n^2)$
V	Random walk	$\Theta(n^3)$
VI	Biased random walk	$\Theta(n2^n)$
VII	Divergent	Divergent

3.3 α-Asynchronous CA

A slight relaxation of the asynchrony condition of fully-ACA lead to the notion of α-asynchronous CA (α-ACA). Every cell has a (not necessarily fair) coin that is tossed at every time step to decide if the cell has to update or not. The type of coin is fixed for every cell. That is, a certain value $\alpha \in (0, 1)$ is chosen and every cell updates with probability α (and remain unchanged with probability $1 - \alpha$).

Like in the case of stochastic ACA, the study of α-ACA has been carried on the restricted class of doubly quiescent ECA with focus on convergence time towards a fixed point.

Theorem 1 ([21]). *The behaviour of* 52 *of the* 64 *different doubly quiescent ECA under α-asynchronous dynamics is the following:*

- 48 *ECA converge to a random fixed point from any initial configuration with a time dependent from α that is one of the following:* 0, $\Theta\left(\frac{\log n}{\log(1-\alpha)}\right)$, $\Theta\left(\frac{n}{\alpha} + \frac{1}{\alpha(1-\alpha)}\right)$, $O\left(\frac{n}{\alpha(1-\alpha)}\right)$, $O\left(\frac{n}{\alpha^2(1-\alpha)}\right)$, $\Theta\left(\frac{n^2}{\alpha(1-\alpha)}\right)$;
- *Two of them diverges;*
- *Two of them converges with a small probability if the length of the automaton is even and diverges otherwise.*

The classification of the behavior of the last 12 doubly quiescent ECA remains an open problem. We found this work interesting and deep. What follows in this article is an attempt to give a more general setting and provide new tools in order to solve some of these open questions.

Among the open questions raised in [21], one concerns the analysis of the time needed for a finite configuration to converge to a stable configuration (i.e., a fixed point) and more in particular, if there exists an α-asynchronous CA with a *phase transition* between a polynomial and an exponential convergence time. This question has been solved very recently in [30].

4 m-ACA

More general forms of asynchrony should involve more complex updating sequences in which possibly infinite sets of cells are updated at each time step and the there are correlations between updated sites. If the formal modeling of such general systems is easy, one cannot say the same thing about the analysis of the long-term behavior. Therefore, one should tradeoff between full generality, maximal non-determinism and capability of analysis. In this section, we propose to constrain non-determinism using probability measures over the set of integers (i.e. over the set of cells that should be updated in parallel at each time step). Therefore, the new model is nothing but a classical CA with the addition of a probability measure μ which is used to extract the set of cells to update. More formally,

Definition 3 (m-ACA). *An m-ACA $\mathcal{C}$ is a quadruple (S, r, λ, μ) where S is a finite alphabet, $r > 0$ is the* radius, *$\lambda : S^{2r+1} \to S$ is the* local rule *and μ is a probability measure on the Borel σ-algebra on $\mathcal{P}(\mathbb{Z})$.*

Given the measure μ, we say that the *activation function ν is generated by μ* if for all $t \in \mathbb{N}$, the set $\nu(t) \in \mathcal{P}(\mathbb{Z})$ is extracted using μ. Therefore, F_ν is the global function of the m-ACA.

Denote by $\mathcal{S}$ the set of all activation functions. In the model proposed in this paper, μ is used to extract the subset of $\mathbb{Z}$ indicating which cells are allowed to be updated. At each time step, a new extraction is performed and we made the hypothesis that extractions are independent. Therefore, it is natural to consider the product measure μ_s of the measure μ to measure sets of activation functions i.e., subsets of $\mathcal{S}$ (μ_s always exists and is unique, see [22, Thm. B, pag. 157]).

Consider the power set of integers $\mathcal{P}(\mathbb{Z})$ ordered by set inclusion. Then, a *filter* on $\mathcal{U}$ on $\mathcal{P}(\mathbb{Z})$ is a subset of $\mathcal{P}(\mathbb{Z})$ such that $\mathbb{Z} \in \mathcal{U}$, $A \cap B \in \mathcal{U}$ for any $A, B \in \mathcal{U}$ and $\emptyset \notin \mathcal{U}$; moreover it has the upward closure property i.e., if $A \in \mathcal{U}$ and $A \subseteq B$, then $B \in \mathcal{U}$. A set $\mathcal{U} \in \mathcal{P}(\mathbb{Z})$ is an *ultrafilter* if it is a filter and for any $A \subseteq \mathcal{P}(\mathbb{Z})$ it follows that either $A \in \mathcal{U}$ or $(\mathcal{P}(\mathbb{Z}) \setminus A) \in \mathcal{U}$. For $i \in \mathbb{Z}$, denote $\mathcal{U}_i$ the *principal ultrafilter* of element i i.e., the collection of all subset of $\mathcal{P}(\mathbb{Z})$ containing the integer i.

We stress that each cell $i \in \mathbb{Z}$ is updated with a probability given by $\mu(\mathcal{U}_i)$.

4.1   Fair and Quasi-Fair Measures

As we have already said, we are interested in studying m-ACA where the probability measure associated has some interesting properties. First of all, all cell should have the a non-zero probability of being updated. This is a necessary requirement for allowing the information exchange within region of the cellular space and hence allow the computing (in the Turing sense) capabilities [14]. For similar reasons, no cell should be updated with probability 1. Moreover, the event "update all cells" should have zero probability since, more or less, this corresponds to turn back to the classical CA model. Indeed, in order to totally avoid mimicking the classical model, we require even more, all events concerning an infinite number of cells should have zero probability. More formally,

Definition 4. *A probability measure μ over a σ-algebra of $\mathcal{P}(\mathbb{Z})$ is fair if it satisfies the following properties:*

1. *$\forall i \in \mathbb{Z}$, $0 < \mu(U_i) < 1$,*
2. *$\forall I \in \mathcal{P}(\mathbb{Z})$ $(|I| < \infty) \Rightarrow \mu\left(\bigcap_{i \in I} U_i\right) = \prod_{i \in I} \mu(\mathcal{U}_i)$,*
3. *$\forall I \in \mathcal{P}(\mathbb{Z})$ $(|I| = +\infty) \Rightarrow \mu\left(\bigcap_{i \in I} U_i\right) = 0$,*

where U_i is the ultrafilter $\mathcal{U}_i$ or its complement.

The second condition in the definition of fair measure simply tells that cells update independently. Remark that this condition is not sufficient to avoid the extremal cases discussed in the introduction to this section. The following example shows that the necessity of the third requirement on fair measures to avoid the possibility of having infinite sets of integers with positive measure.

Example 2. Consider the measure $\mu : \mathcal{P}(\mathbb{Z}) \to [0, 1]$ defined as follows:

$$\forall i \in \mathbb{Z}, \ \mu(\mathcal{U}_i) = \frac{i}{c(i)}$$

where $c(i) = i + 1$ if $i \equiv 3 \mod 4$, $i - 1$ otherwise. Consider the set $I \subseteq \mathbb{N}$ of odd prime integers. Then,

$$\mu\left(\bigcap_{i \in I} \mathcal{U}_i\right) = \prod_{i \in I} \mu\left(\mathcal{U}_i\right) = \prod_{i \in I} \frac{i}{c(i)} = \frac{\pi}{4}.$$

Remark that for any set $S \in \mathcal{P}(\mathbb{Z})$, if the cardinality of S is finite then

$$0 < \mu\left(\bigcap_{i \in I \setminus S} \mathcal{U}_i\right) < 1 .$$

The following shows how to deduce a fair measure from a Bernoulli measure over $\{0, 1\}$.

Example 3. Consider the Bernoulli measure β over $\{0, 1\}$ such that $\beta(1) = a$ and $\beta(0) = 1 - a$. It is not difficult to verify that the measure μ_β defined as $\forall i \in \mathbb{Z}$, $\mu_\beta(\mathcal{U}_i) = a$ is fair. We call μ_β the *Bernoulli fair measure* induced by β.

Clearly, any m-ACA induced by a Bernoulli fair measure is an α-asynchronous CA and vice versa. It is also clear that the class of m-ACA is strictly bigger than the one of α-asynchronous CA since not all fair measures are Bernoulli fair measures.

Fair measures have some interesting properties which reveal very useful when studying m-ACA dynamics. First of all, the measure of an ultrafilters or of complements of ultrafilters is uniformly bounded. More formally, in [15, Lemma 1 and Remark 5], it is proved the following.

Proposition 5. *For any fair measure μ there exist two constants ϵ, ξ such that*

$$\forall I \in \mathcal{P}(\mathbb{Z}), \, 0 < \epsilon < \mu\left(\bigcap_{i \in I} U_i\right) < \xi < 1$$

where U_i is the ultrafilter $\mathcal{U}_i$ or its complement and $|I| < \infty$.

Fair measures are a pretty large class but it is still not clear how large it is the class of measures that respects the design principle that we have discussed at the beginning of the section. A first step in this direction consists in considering measures that behave much like a fair measure in the sense that they have the same set of null measure. Before giving the formal definition we need some preliminary definition.

Given a sigma-algebra Σ over $\mathbb{Z}$, $\mathcal{M}_\Sigma$ denotes the set of all measures over Σ.

Definition 5. *A function $f : \mathcal{M}_\Sigma \to \mathcal{M}_\Sigma$ is zero-preserving if*

$$\forall \mu \in \mathcal{M}_\Sigma, \, \forall A \in \Sigma \qquad \mu(A) = 0 \iff (f(\mu))(A) = 0 .$$

Denote by $\mathfrak{Z}$ the set of all zero-preserving functions from $\mathcal{M}_\Sigma$ to itself.

In other words, a zero-preserving function takes a measure μ over Σ into another measure μ' over Σ such they have the same sets of null measure (and of course the same sets of full measure). The idea is that if μ is fair then μ' is not far from being fair since it will satisfy at least conditions 1 and 3 of fair measures. Indeed, we can give the following

Definition 6. A quasi-fair measure *is the image of a fair measure under a zero-preserving function. Let* $\mathfrak{A}_{\mathrm{QFAIR}}$ *be the set of all quasi-fair measures.*

Given a set of measures $M \subseteq \mathcal{M}_\Sigma$, the *zeta-closure* $\mathfrak{Z}(M)$ of M is the set of measures which are image of some measure in M via a zero-preserving function, more formally

$$\mathfrak{Z}(M) = \bigcup_{f \in \mathfrak{Z}} \bigcup_{\mu \in M} \{f(\mu)\} \ .$$

Since the composition of two zero-preserving functions is a zero-preserving function, the class of quasi-fair measures is closed under composition by zero-preserving functions.

Proposition 6. $\mathfrak{Z}(\mathfrak{A}_{\mathrm{QFAIR}}) = \mathfrak{A}_{\mathrm{QFAIR}}$.

The above proposition tells us that the class of $\mathfrak{A}_{\mathrm{QFAIR}}$ measures is the largest class of measures that one can obtain by using zero-preserving functions but it does say anything if there are other possibilities for extending the class of measures that respect the defining principles discussed so far. However, $\mathfrak{A}_{\mathrm{QFAIR}}$ is large enough to allow to take into account complex dependencies between cells update since the condition 2 of fair measures is no more necessarily satisfied. The following example shows that there exists a quasi-fair measure which is not fair and hence $\mathfrak{A}_{\mathrm{QFAIR}}$ is a real extension of $\mathfrak{A}_{\mathrm{FAIR}}$.

Example 4. Choose $\epsilon \in (0,1)$ and define μ as follows:

$$\forall I \in \mathcal{P}(\mathbb{Z}), \ \mu\left(\bigcap_{i \in I} U_i\right) = \begin{cases} \frac{\epsilon^n}{n} & \text{if } n = |I| < \infty \text{ and } I \neq \emptyset \\ 0 & \text{otherwise} \end{cases}$$

where U_i is the ultrafilter $\mathcal{U}_i$ or its complement. Clearly, μ is not fair since it does not satisfy condition 2 of fair measures. Consider the Bernoulli fair measure μ_ϵ and define a function f as follows

$$\forall \xi \in \mathcal{M}_\Sigma, \ f(\xi) = \begin{cases} \mu & \text{if } \xi = \mu_\epsilon \\ \xi & \text{otherwise} \end{cases}$$

Since f is zero-preserving μ is a quasi-fair measure.

4.2 Set Theoretic Properties

Set theoretic properties like surjectivity and injectivity are very important when studying the dynamics since they are often necessary condition for the presence of a given dynamical behavior. For example, injectivity is a necessary and sufficient condition for reversibility [23], while surjectivity is often necessary for the presence of chaotic behavior [8, 1, 13] and strictly related to other dynamical properties [9, 2]. Moreover, both surjectivity and injectivity are one of the most well-known of dimension sensitive properties. Indeed, they are decidable in dimension one [4] and undecidable for dimension two or grater [24].

Definition 7. *An m-ACA $C = (S, \lambda, r, \mu)$ is surjective (resp. injective) iff for all activation functions ν, $F_\nu(\cdot)_1$ is surjective (resp. injective). C is μ-almost surely surjective (resp., injective) iff*

$$\mu\left(\{\nu(1) \mid F_\nu(\cdot)_1 \text{ is surjective (resp. injective)}\}\right) = 1 \ .$$

Permutativity is an easy-to-verify combinatorial property which is strictly connected with surjectivity and injectivity.

Definition 8. *A CA local rule $\lambda : \{0,1\}^{2r+1} \to \{0,1\}$ is center-permutative if and only if for all $(x_1, \ldots, x_r), (y_1, \ldots, y_r) \in \{0,1\}^r$ it holds*

$$\lambda(x_1, \ldots, x_r, 0, y_1, \ldots, y_n) \neq \lambda(x_1, \ldots, x_r, 1, y_1, \ldots, y_n) \ .$$

An m-ACA is center-permutative if its local rule is center-permutative.

The following results links all the three notions introduced above.

Theorem 2 ([15]). *For any measure $\mu \in \mathfrak{A}_{\text{QFAIR}}$ and for any m-ACA $C = (S, \lambda, r, \mu)$, the following statements are equivalent:*

1. *C is μ-almost surely surjective;*
2. *C is μ-almost surely injective;*
3. *C is center-permutative.*

Example 5. The shift map σ is a bijective CA. For any measure $\mu \in \mathfrak{A}_{\text{QFAIR}}$, the m-ACA version $(\{0,1\}, 1, \sigma, \mu)$ is not surjective. Indeed, consider an activation function ν such that $\nu(1) = \{i\}$ for some $i \in \mathbb{Z}$ and a configuration $y \in \{0,1\}^{\mathbb{Z}}$ such that $y_i = 0$ and $y_{i+1} = 1$. Then, any possible pre-image x should have $x_{i+1} = 1$ since the site $i+1$ is not updated but this implies $y_i = 1$ contradicting the former hypothesis. By Theorem 2, the shift map is not even μ-almost surely surjective since it is not center-permutative.

Example 6. Consider the xor CA $C = (\{0,1\}, 1, \lambda)$ with local rule defined as follows

$$\forall x, y, z \in \{0,1\}, \ \lambda(x, y, z) = y \oplus z$$

where $\oplus$ is the usual xor operation. It is well-known that C is surjective but not injective. Given a measure $\mu \in \mathfrak{A}_{\text{QFAIR}}$, its m-ACA version $C = (\{0,1\}, 1, \lambda, \mu)$ is μ-almost surely surjective since λ is center-permutative. Indeed, this m-ACA is surjective. Given any activation function ν and any configuration y, let us build a pre-image x such that $F_\nu(x)_1 = y$. We build the part with positive index, the negative one is very similar. At stage $i = 0$, define $x_0 = y_0$ if $\nu(1)_0 = 0$, otherwise let $x_0 = a$ and $x_1 = (1 - a) \cdot y_0 + a \cdot (1 - y_0)$ for $a \in \{0,1\}$. At stage n, we have two cases

1. x_n has been defined at the previous stage. If $v(1)_n = 0$ then leave x_n unchanged. If $v(1)_n = 1$ then let $x_{n+1} = (1 - x_n) \cdot y_n + x_n \cdot (1 - y_n)$.
2. x_n has not been defined at the previous stage. Define $x_n = y_n$ if $v(1)_n = 0$, otherwise let $x_n = a$ and $x_{n+1} = (1 - a) \cdot y_n + a \cdot (1 - y_n)$ for $a \in \{0, 1\}$.

By compactness, the process described above completely constructs the pre-image x.

From the previous simple examples we deduce that the situation about surjectivity and injectivity is quite different from classical CA. However, from the decidability point of view nothing changes like it is stated by the following.

Proposition 7 ([15]). *For any measure $\mu \in \mathfrak{A}_{QFAIR}$, μ-almost surely surjectivity is decidable for one-dimensional CA and undecidable in greater dimensions.*

4.3 About the Dynamical Behavior

This section surveys the (still few) knonw dynamical properties of m-ACA. Some of the notions concerning families of global functions have been introduced in the previous sections, here also the measure of the set of activation functions giving rise to a certain behavior is taken into account. Results and examples in this section are taken directly from [15].

Definition 9. *Consider an m-ACA $\mathcal{C} = (S, \lambda, r, \mu)$, a real number $p \in [0, 1]$, and an activation function $v \in \mathcal{P}(\mathbb{Z})^{\mathbb{N}}$ generated by μ. The m-ACA $\mathcal{C}$ is said to be either p–equicontinuous or p–almost equicontinuous or p–sensitive or p–expansive if $\mu_s(\Upsilon) = p$, where Υ is the set of all sequence v with respect to which $\mathcal{C}$ has that behavior.*

The remainder of the this section focuses on the situations when the above dynamical properties happen *almost surely*, i.e., when $p = 1$.

Example 7. Let λ_σ be the local rule of the classical CA shift map σ. The m-ACA $\mathcal{C} = (\{0, 1\}, \lambda_\sigma, 1, \mu)$ is almost surely sensitive. Indeed, consider any sequence v with the following property: for all $n \in \mathbb{N}$ there exists a time t such that $n - i \in v_{t+i}$ for each $i \in [0, n]$, i.e., each cell of position $n, n - 1, \ldots, 0$ is updated respectively at time $t, t + 1, \ldots, t + n$. Now, for any such a sequence v, any configuration x, and any integer $n \in \mathbb{N}$, consider the configuration y such that $y_{[-n,n]} = x_{[-n,n]}$ and $y_i \neq x_i$ for every $i > n$. So, the $(n+t)$–th element T of the family $\mathcal{T}_v$ is such that $T(y)_0 \neq T(x)_0$. Thus, $\mathcal{T}_v$ is sensitive or, in other words, $\mathcal{C}$ is sensitive w.r.t. v. Furthermore, by the second Borel-Cantelli Lemma, one finds that the set of all the updating sequences v with the above property has measure equal to one. Therefore, $\mathcal{C}$ is almost surely sensitive.

Definition 10. *Consider an m-ACA $\mathcal{C} = (S, \lambda, r, \mu)$ and let v be an activation function generated by μ. A word $w \in S^k$ is s-blocking w.r.t. v for some integer $s \in [1, k]$ if there exists an offset $j \in [0, k - s]$ such that*

$$\forall i \in \mathbb{Z}, \ \forall x, y \in [w]_i, \ \forall T \in \mathcal{T}_v, \quad T(x)_{[i+j,i+j+s]} = T(y)_{[i+j,i+j+s]} \tag{1}$$

Let $p \in \mathbb{R}$ with $0 \leq p \leq 1$. A word $w \in S^k$ is said to be (p,s)-blocking for some integer $s \in [1,k]$ if $\mu_s(\Upsilon) = p$, where Υ is the set of activation functions w.r.t. which w is s-blocking.

Example 8. Let $\mathcal{C} = (\{0,1\}, \lambda, 1, \mu)$ be an m-ACA where λ is the majority rule, i.e., $\lambda(a,b,c) = \lfloor (a+b+c)/2 \rfloor$. The word $w = 00$ is 2-blocking w.r.t. any sequence $v \in \mathcal{P}(\mathbb{Z})^{\mathbb{N}}$. In fact, we have that for all $a \in \{0,1\}$, $\lambda(a,0,0) = \lambda(0,0,a) = 0$. That is, w remains unchanged w.r.t. all possible activation functions and then it is a $(1,2)$-blocking word.

In order to state that a word w is blocking w.r.t. a given activation function v, Condition (1) from Definition 10 prescribes that the equality holds independently of where w is placed inside configurations. The fact that the equality holds for some positions does not imply that it is also true for all other positions as it is illustrated by the following example.

Example 9. Let $\mathcal{C}$ be the m-ACA of Example 8. Consider the activation function $v = (\mathbb{Z} \setminus \{0,1\}, \mathbb{Z} \setminus \{0,1\}, \ldots)$. The word $w = 01$ satisfies (1) only for $i = 0$.

Given an m-ACA and a word $w \in \{0,1\}^*$, there can be activation functions w.r.t. which w is blocking and others w.r.t. which w is not.

Example 10. Let $\mathcal{C} = (S, \lambda, r, \mu)$ be any m-ACA which is v-sensitive for some $v \in \mathcal{P}(\mathbb{Z})^{\mathbb{N}}$. Clearly $\mathcal{C}$ admits no blocking word w.r.t. v. However, any word is blocking w.r.t. the activation function $(\emptyset, \emptyset, \ldots)$.

Given an m-ACA $\mathcal{C} = (S, \lambda, r, \mu)$ and an activation function $v \in \mathcal{P}(\mathbb{Z})^{\mathbb{N}}$, denote by E_v the set of all equicontinuity points for the family $\mathcal{T}_v$. Recall that in the classical CA setting, almost equicontinuity is characterized by the presence of a r-blocking word. Concerning the m-ACA context, this can be rephrased as follows: there exists a (p,r)-blocking word $\Leftrightarrow$ the m-ACA is p-almost equicontinuous. Proposition 8 shows a strong result for the left-to-right implication, namely, there exists a residual set of points which are equicontinuity points w.r.t. all activation functions in a set of μ_s-measure p. The opposite implication is not yet completely understood.

Proposition 8. *Consider an m-ACA $\mathcal{C} = (S, \lambda, r, \mu)$ with $\mu \in \mathcal{M}_\Sigma$. If $\mathcal{C}$ admits a (p,r)-blocking word for some $p \in [0,1]$, then there exists a subset $\Upsilon \subseteq \mathcal{P}(\mathbb{Z})^{\mathbb{N}}$ with $\mu_s(\Upsilon) = p$ such that the set $\bigcap_{v \in \Upsilon} E_v$ is residual.*

Corollary 1. *Consider an m-ACA $\mathcal{C} = (S, \lambda, r, \mu)$ with $\mu \in \mathcal{M}_\Sigma$. If $\mathcal{C}$ admits a (p,r)-blocking word w for some $p \in [0,1]$, then $\mathcal{C}$ is p-almost equicontinuous.*

The following result is a first step towards a possible proof that p-almost equicontinuous m-ACA admit a (p,r)-blocking word.

Proposition 9. *Consider an m-ACA $\mathcal{C} = (S, \lambda, r, \mu)$ with $\mu \in \mathcal{M}_\Sigma$. Consider the set Υ of all sequences $v \in \mathcal{P}(\mathbb{Z})^{\mathbb{N}}$ w.r.t. which $\mathcal{C}$ admits an r-blocking word. Then, the set $\bigcap_{v \in \Upsilon} E_v$ is residual.*

The following proposition is a further witness that the new setting gives a new genuine model which is quite different from classical CA. Indeed, in classical CA, expansive CA are surjective but not injective [5].

Proposition 10. *Consider an m-ACA $C = (S, \lambda, r, \mu)$ with $\mu \in \mathfrak{A}_{\mathrm{QFAIR}}$. If C is almost surely expansive then C is μ-almost surely injective.*

4.4   Experiments

In order to explore m-ACA dynamics further one can turn to experiments in the hope to have new intuitions. At present we are going to experiment with only one m-ACA, namely, the shift map σ and try to analyze both the effect of different measures μ and of initial measures with which the initial configuration is extracted. Three classes of experiments are reported in this section. Each class of experiments is illustrated by two figures, a space-time diagram and a quantitative diagram. In the space-time diagram time goes downward, the state 1 is represented by a black box, 0 by a white one. The quantitative diagram reports the value of 3 curves. The density of ones w.r.t. zeroes (colored in red) and the number of alternates (colored in blue) during the evolution of the m-ACA. An alternate is the boundary between a sequence of cells in state 1 and a sequence of cells in state 0, or viceversa. This can be quickly computed counting the number of patterns 01 or 10 in the current configuration. The third curve is the value of the measure μ (colored in green). Remark that this time the a value i on the x axis represents the ultrafilter $\mathcal{U}_i$ and the value on the y axis is the measure of $\mathcal{U}_i$. The value of μ are then repeated periodically with period 100 and rescaled to fit the same range with the other two curves.

From the first experiment we can see that the m-ACA behaves more or less like a shift CA on the right part of the space-time diagram and like the identity in the leftmost part of the space-time diagram. This agrees with the distribution of values of μ.

From the second experiment, we deduce that now the m-ACA behaves more like a shift. Sort initial segments of zeroes or ones tend to disappear rather quickly and a (slow) process of homogenization seems to start. This is confirmed by the curve of alternates. Remark that this curve seems to stabilize. Indeed, more experiments (not reported here for lack of space) confirmed that the curve continue decreasing during time although very slowly. In the third experiment, the initial measure with which the initial configuration is extracted has been changed so to produce a large majority of ones, μ is the same as in the first experiments. Again, we experience the rapid decrease of alternates in the first part of the evolution and it become slower and slower when time grows. Summing up all the three experiments showed that there is some kind of homogenization process that takes place. The curve of alternates seem to confirm it and to illustrate that the speed of homogenization depends more on μ than on the measure with which the initial configuration is extracted.

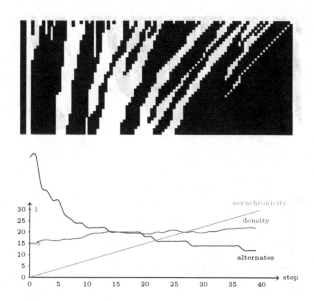

Experiment 1. An evolution of the shift m-ACA. The measure μ takes values in $[0.01, 0.99]$, grows linearly with i between 0 and 100 and then it repeats periodically. The initial configuration is extracted using a uniform measure over $\{0, 1\}$.

4.5 Exploring a New Research Direction

This section is going to explore an new research direction suggested from previous experiments. We shall concentrate on the evolutions of alternates. Assume that the current configuration contains the pattern $x_1 x_2 \ldots x_6 = 111000$ which contains one alternate and consider a generic local rule λ of a CA of radius 1 such that $\lambda(111) = 1$ and $\lambda(000) = 0$ (i.e., it is a doubly quiescent ECA). Let us try to understand what can be the possible images of 111000 under each possible updating policy. Assume that x_2 as to be updated then, according to λ, its image is 1. Remark that if x_2 is not updated, its image is also going to be 1. The same reasoning can be applied to x_5, this cell is going to conserve the state 0 independently of the updating policy. Consider now to update x_3, its new value depends on $\lambda(110)$. While it would have been 1 in case of no update. Similarly, the new value of x_4 is zero if there are no updates, $\lambda(100)$ otherwise. Therefore according the to the values of λ and to the update policy, the alternate can change of position, stay or even give birth to a new alternate. Figure 1, illustrates all the possible cases according to the update policy and the probability with which they might happen if one assumes that $\alpha = \mu(\mathcal{U}_{x_3})$ and $\beta = \mu(\mathcal{U}_{x_4})$

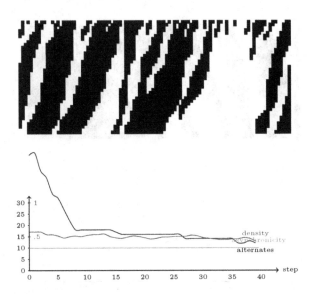

Experiment 2. Another evolution of the shift m-ACA. The measure μ takes constant value .33. The initial configuration is extracted using a uniform measure over $\{0, 1\}$.

Figure 2 specializes Figure 1 to the case of the shift map and shows how alternates have moved. Since all updates are independent it is easy to see that in this case

$$\mathbb{P} \text{ (the alternate moves to the left)} \; = \alpha$$
$$\mathbb{P} \text{ (the alternate does not move)} \; = 1 - \alpha$$
$$\mathbb{P} \text{ (the alternate moves to the right)} = 0$$

Therefore, in this case, the probability of moving for an alternate does not depend on β but only on α. A *segment* is the set of cells between two successive alternates. Assume that the successive alternate to the right w.r.t. to the one we have considered above is between sites y and $y + 1$. Moreover, assume that $\gamma = \mu (\mathcal{U}_y)$. Clearly, the length of the segment makes a biased random walk according to the updating probabilities of the alternates by which it is defined.

Figure 3 illustrates the state graph of the random-walk with the corresponding transitions probabilities which can be easily computed from α and γ. Remark that the state 0 is absorbing, indeed, the shift map cannot create new alternates and therefore when a segment disappears, it is forever. Disappearance of short segments is precisely what we have remarked in the experiments of the previous section. At this point one might try to observe the density of segments to determine if the homogenization process that seems to take place in experiments can be expressed formally.

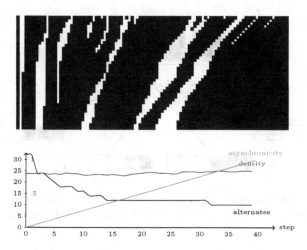

Experiment 3. Another evolution of the shift m-ACA. The measure μ is like in the first experiment. The initial configuration is extracted using a Bernoulli measure over $\{0, 1\}$ of ratio 0.8.

Denote $X_n(c)$ the random variable representing the number of alternates in the configuration c for cells with index between $-n$ and n divided by $2n + 1$. The density of alternates for a configuration c is given by

$$\delta(c) = \limsup_{n \to \infty} X_n(c)$$

Of course, what interests us is understanding the behavior of δ along orbits of the shift map, in other words we need to study the random process $\{X_n^n(c)\}_{t \geq 0}$ in which X_n^n represents the value of X_n after n iterations of the shift m-ACA started on the configuration c. Since there are no alternates creation, it is clear that

$$\mathbb{E}\left[X_{n+1}^{n+1} \mid X_n^n, X_{n-1}^{n-1}, \ldots, X_0^0\right] \leq X_n^n \qquad \cdot$$

and hence $\{X_n^n(c)\}_{t \geq 0}$ is a super-martingale. Remark that for all $n \in \mathbb{N}$, $\mathbb{E}[X_n^n] \leq 1$. Then, by the convergence theorem for super-martingales one concludes that $\lim_{n \to \infty} X_n^n(c) = k$ for some real $k > 0$ for μ-almost all updating functions ν extracted using μ. Let us prove that $k = 0$. Indeed, since the process converges to k, for any $\epsilon > 0$ there must be a large enough $n \in \mathbb{N}$ such that $|X_n^n - k| < \epsilon$. Consider now all the segments of size $\ell < n$ in between the cells of index $-n$ and n. We have seen that the length of these segments perform a random walk with 0 as an absorbing state. It means that after a time large enough they will have disappeared with non-zero probability. Since the shift map cannot create new segments we have that the density must have decreased to some $k' < k$.

The long analysis above proves that for μ-almost all activation functions generated by μ, for η-almost all initial configurations c, there is a long-term homogenization process which turns c into a "mono-chromatic" configuration i.e.,

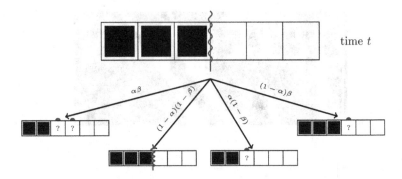

Fig. 1. Alternate dynamics according to a generic doubly quiescent ECA local rule λ. A question mark indicates that the new value depends on the local rule.

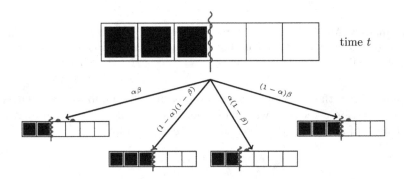

Fig. 2. Alternate dynamics according to the shift map. Remark that the alternate moves left or right according to the probabilities indicated on the arrows label.

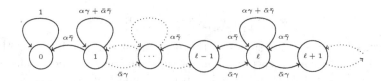

Fig. 3. The biased random walk characterizing segment length. Remark the absorbing state. The symbol $\bar{\xi}$ means $1 - \xi$.

a configuration with density of alternates equal to zero. We believe that similar formal tools and ideas can be applied successfully to all other doubly quiescent ECA extending the classification given in [21] to the the whole $\mathbb{Z}$.

Aknowledgments. The author warmly thanks the companions of the scientific adventure on m-ACA started these last years: Luca Manzoni (Nice Sophia Antipolis University, France), Giancarlo Mauri and Alberto Dennunzio (Università Milano-Bicocca). The author also would like to sincerely thanks Jarkko Kari (University of Turku, Finland) Martin Kutrib and Andreas Malcher (University of Giessen, Germany), chairs of AUTOMATA 2013, for giving the opportunity of this invited paper.

Bibliography

1. Acerbi, L., Dennunzio, A., Formenti, E.: Conservation of some dynamical properties for operations on cellular automata. Theoretical Computer Science 410(38-40), 3685–3693 (2009)
2. Acerbi, L., Dennunzio, A., Formenti, E.: Surjective multidimensional cellular automata are non-wandering: A combinatorial proof. Information Processing Letters 113(5-6), 156–159 (2013)
3. Alarcon, T., Byrne, H.M., Maini, P.K.: A cellular automaton model for tumour growth in inhomogeneous environment. Journal of Theoretical Biology 225, 257–274 (2003)
4. Amoroso, S., Patt, Y.N.: Decision procedures for surjectivity and injectivity of parallel maps for tesselation structures. Journal of Computer and System Sciences 6, 448–464 (1972)
5. Blanchard, F., Cervelle, J., Formenti, E.: Some results about the chaotic behavior of cellular automata. Theor. Comput. Sci. 349(3), 318–336 (2005)
6. Cattaneo, G., Dennunzio, A., Farina, F.: A full cellular automaton to simulate predator-prey systems. In: El Yacoubi, S., Chopard, B., Bandini, S. (eds.) ACRI 2006. LNCS, vol. 4173, pp. 446–451. Springer, Heidelberg (2006)
7. Cattaneo, G., Dennunzio, A., Margara, L.: Chaotic subshifts and related languages applications to one-dimensional cellular automata. Fundamenta Informaticae 52, 39–80 (2002)
8. Cattaneo, G., Formenti, E., Margara, L., Mauri, G.: On the dynamical behavior of chaotic cellular automata. Theoretical Computer Science 217(1), 31–51 (1999)
9. Cattaneo, G., Dennunzio, A., Margara, L.: Solution of some conjectures about topological properties of linear cellular automata. Theoretical Computer Science 325, 249–271 (2004)
10. Chaudhuri, P., Chowdhury, D., Nandi, S., Chattopadhyay, S.: Additive Cellular Automata Theory and Applications, vol. 1. IEEE Press, New York (1997)
11. Chopard, B.: Cellular automata and lattice boltzmann modeling of physical systems. In: Rozenberg, G., et al. (eds.) Handbook of Natural Computing, pp. 287–331. Springer (2012)
12. Dennunzio, A., Di Lena, P., Formenti, E., Margara, L.: On the directional dynamics of additive cellular automata. Theoretical Computer Science 410, 4823–4833 (2009)
13. Dennunzio, A., Di Lena, P., Formenti, E., Margara, L.: Periodic orbits and dynamical complexity in cellular automata. Fundamenta Informaticae 126, 183–199 (2013)
14. Dennunzio, A., Formenti, E., Manzoni, L.: Computing issues of asynchronous CA. Fundamenta Informaticae 120(2), 165–180 (2012)
15. Dennunzio, A., Formenti, E., Manzoni, L., Mauri, G.: m-asynchronous cellular automata: from fairness to quasi-fairness. Natural Computing (in press, 2013)

16. Dennunzio, A., Formenti, E., Provillard, J.: Non-uniform cellular automata: Classes, dynamics, and decidability. Information and Computation 215, 32–46 (2012)
17. Dennunzio, A., Formenti, E., Weiss, M.: Multidimensional cellular automata: closing property, quasi-expansivity, and (un)decidability issues. Theoretical Computer Science (to appear, 2013)
18. Dennunzio, A., Guillon, P., Masson, B.: Sand automata as cellular automata. Theoretical Computer Science 410, 3962–3974 (2009)
19. Farina, F., Dennunzio, A.: A predator-prey cellular automaton with parasitic interactions and environmental effects. Fundamenta Informaticae 83(4), 337–353 (2008)
20. Fatès, N., Morvan, M., Schabanel, N., Thierry, E.: Fully asynchronous behaviour of double-quiescent elementary cellular automata. Theoretical Computer Science 362, 1–16 (2006)
21. Fatès, N., Regnault, D., Schabanel, N., Thierry, É.: Asynchronous behavior of double-quiescent elementary cellular automata. In: Correa, J.R., Hevia, A., Kiwi, M. (eds.) LATIN 2006. LNCS, vol. 3887, pp. 455–466. Springer, Heidelberg (2006)
22. Halmos, P.R.: Measure theory. Graduate texts in Mathematics, vol. 38. Springer (1974)
23. Hedlund, G.A.: Endomorphisms and automorphisms of the shift dynamical system. Mathematical Systems Theory 3, 320–375 (1969)
24. Kari, J.: Reversibility and surjectivity problems of cellular automata. J. Comput. Syst. Sci. 48(1), 149–182 (1994)
25. Kari, J.: Theory of cellular automata: A survey. Theoretical Computer Science 334, 3–33 (2005)
26. Kier, L.B., Seybold, P.G., Cheng, C.-K.: Modeling Chemical Systems using Cellular Automata. Springer (2005)
27. Lee, J., Adachi, S., Peper, F., Mashiko, S.: Delay-insensitive computation in asynchronous cellular automata. J. Comput. Syst. Sci. 70, 201–220 (2005)
28. Manzoni, L.: Asynchronous cellular automata and dynamical properties. Natural Computing 11(2), 269–276 (2012)
29. Nakamura, K.: Asynchronous cellular automata and their computational ability. Systems, Computers, Control 5, 58–66 (1974)
30. Regnault, D.: Proof of a phase transition in probabilistic cellular automata. In: Béal, M.-P., Carton, O. (eds.) DLT 2013. LNCS, vol. 7907, pp. 433–444. Springer, Heidelberg (2013)
31. Schönfisch, B., de Roos, A.: Synchronous and asynchronous updating in cellular automata. BioSystems 51, 123–143 (1999)
32. Wolfram, S.: A new kind of science. Wolfram-Media (2002)
33. Worsch, T.: Towards intrinsically universal asynchronous CA. Natural Computing (in press, 2013)

Elementary Cellular Automata
with Memory of Delay Type

Ramon Alonso-Sanz

Universidad Politecnica de Madrid, ETSIA (Estadistica, GSC),
Ciudad Universitaria, 28040, Madrid, Spain
ramon.alonso@upm.es

Abstract. The effect of memory of delay type in the dynamics of elementary cellular automata is presented in this study.

Keywords: cellular automata, memory.

1   Introduction : Cellular Automata with Memory

Cellular Automata (CA) are discrete, spatially explicit extended dynamic systems. A CA system is composed of a grid of adjacent cells arranged as a regular lattice, which evolves in discrete time steps. Each cell is characterized by an internal state whose value belongs to a finite set. The updating of these states is done simultaneously according to a common local transition rule (ϕ) involving only the neighborhood ($\mathcal{N}$) of each cell [10].

Conventional CA are Markovian (ahistoric, memoryless) : The next state of a cell depends solely on its current neighborhood configuration. Thus, if $\sigma_i^{(T)}$ is taken to denote the state value of the generic cell i at time-step T, the cell values evolve by iteration of the mapping :

$$\sigma_i^{(T+1)} = \phi(\{\sigma_{j\in\mathcal{N}_i}^{(T)}\})$$

A seemingly natural way of implementing an explicit dependence in the dynamics of the past states is to take into account a summary (s) of them.

Either in the way (first summary, then rule):

$$s_j^{(T)} = s(\sigma_j^{(1)},\ldots,\sigma_j^{(T-1)},\sigma_j^{(T)}) \rightarrow \sigma_i^{(T+1)} = \phi(\{s_{j\in\mathcal{N}_i}^{(T)}\}) \qquad (1)$$

or in the way (first rule, then summary),

$$f_i^{(T)} = \phi(\{\sigma_{j\in\mathcal{N}_i}^{(T)}\}) \rightarrow \sigma_i^{(T+1)} = s(f_i^{(1)},\ldots f_i^{(T-1)},f_i^{(T)}) \qquad (2)$$

Both (1), referenced as *embedded* memory, and (2) referenced as *delay* memory, are extensions to the standard framework where the mapping ϕ remains unaltered, but every cell retains historic memory of its past states by means of the trait state s. So to say, cells canalize memory.

J. Kari, M. Kutrib, and A. Malcher (Eds.): AUTOMATA 2013, LNCS 8155, pp. 67–83, 2013.

We have studied the memory implementation given by (1) in previous works [1], so that this article is devoted to the delay-type memory implementation given by (2). Only elementary CA rules will be taken into account in this initial study.

Average Memory

Historic memory can be weighted by applying a geometric discounting process in which the state $f_i^{(T-\tau)}$, obtained τ time steps before the last round, is actualized to $\alpha^\tau f_i^{(T-\tau)}$, α being the *memory factor* lying in the $[0,1]$ interval. This well known mechanism fully takes into account the last round ($\alpha^0 = 1$), and tends to *forget* the older rounds.

Thus the dynamics with the delay memory mechanism is implemented at time-step T for every cell i as:

(i) First the map ϕ is applied:

$$f_i^{(T)} = \phi(\{\sigma_{j\in\mathcal{N}_i}^{(T)}\})$$

(ii) The unrounded weighted mean (m) of the f-states is then computed:

$$m_i^{(T)} = \frac{f_i^{(T)} + \sum_{t=1}^{T-1} \alpha^{T-t} f_i^{(t)}}{1 + \sum_{t=1}^{T-1} \alpha^{T-t}} \equiv \frac{\omega_i(T)}{\Omega(T)} = \frac{f_i^{(T)} + \alpha\omega_i(T-1)}{\Omega(T)} \tag{3}$$

(iii) Then, the new state is obtained by rounding the $m_i^{(T)}$ by comparing it to the landmark 0.5 if $\sigma \in \{0,1\}$, assigning the last state in case of an equality to this value, so that:

$$\sigma_i^{(T+1)} = \mathcal{H}(m_i^{(T)}) = \begin{cases} 1 & if \ m_i^{(T)} > 0.5 \\ f_i^{(T)} & if \ m_i^{(T)} = 0.5 \\ 0 & if \ m_i^{(T)} < 0.5 \end{cases} \tag{4}$$

The choice of the memory factor α simulates the long-term or remnant memory effect. The limit case $\alpha = 1$ corresponds to a memory with equally weighted records (*full* memory, equivalent to *majority* memory), whereas $\alpha \ll 1$ intensifies the contribution of the most recent states and diminishes the contribution of the more remote states (short-term working memory). In general, the choice $\alpha = 0$ leads to the ahistoric model. In the $\sigma \in \{0,1\}$ scenario, α-memory is only effective if $\alpha > 0.50$ due to the rounding mechanism described in step (iii). This memory implementation will be referred to as α-memory.

It is remarkable that this geometric memory mechanism is not *holistic* but *accumulative* in its demand for knowledge of past history: The whole $\{f_i^{(t)}\}$ series needs not be known to calculate the term $w_i^{(T)}$ of the memory *charge* $m_i^{(T)}$ in (3), while to (sequentially) calculate $w_i^{(T)}$ one can resort to the already calculated $w_i^{(T-1)}$ and compute: $w_i^{(T)} = f_i^{(T)} + \alpha w_i^{(T-1)}$. Consequently, only one number per cell needs to be stored. This positive property is accompanied by the drawback of any weighted average memory : It computes with real numbers, which is not in the realm of proper CA, that works only with integer arithmetics.

Computationally it is a saving if instead of calculating $m_i^{(T)}$ for every cell, we calculate the numerator $w_i^{(T)}$ all across the lattice and compare the $2w_i^{(T)}$ figures to the factor $\Omega(T)$.

2 Elementary CA

Elementary rules are one-dimensional CA with two possible values at each site ($\sigma \in \{0,1\}$), with rules operating on nearest neighbors ($r = 1$). These rules are characterized by a sequence of binary values (β) associated with each of the eight possible triplets $\left(\sigma_{i-1}^{(T)}, \sigma_i^{(T)}, \sigma_{i+1}^{(T)}\right)$:

$$
\begin{array}{cccccccc}
111 & 110 & 101 & 100 & 011 & 010 & 001 & 000 \\
\beta_1 & \beta_2 & \beta_3 & \beta_4 & \beta_5 & \beta_6 & \beta_7 & \beta_8
\end{array}
\tag{5}
$$

The *rule number* of elementary CA is $\mathcal{R} = \sum_{i=1}^{8} \beta_i 2^{8-i} \in [0, 255]$.

Legal rules are *reflection symmetric* (so that 100 and 001 as well as 110 and 011 yield identical values), and *quiescent* ($\beta_8 = 0$). These restrictions leave 32 possible *legal* rules of the form: $\beta_1\beta_2\beta_3\beta_4\beta_2\beta_6\beta_40$.

The computer code in Table 1 generates the α-memory patterns of the rule 254 up to $T = 8$, for both embedded and delay memories. Full $\alpha=1.0$ memory is considered in the code in Table 1, whose output is given also in Table 1. In this very particular scenario, the actual σ-patterns are coincident for embedded and delay memories. What is relevant is the toy-example given via rule 254 in Table 1 is the demonstration of the *inertial* effect that memory exerts, impeding the *speed of light* expansion of the spatio-temporal pattern of rule 254 (11111110).

Figures 1 and 2 show the spatio-temporal patterns of the sixteen elementary legal rules affected by memory when starting from a single live cell [1]. The spatio-temporal evolution is shown up to $T = 25$. In Fig. 1 the memory factor varies from 0.6 to 1.0 by 0.1 intervals. In Fig. 2 very low memory charge is considered, i.e., the memory factor α is very close to 0.50, the limit of its effectiveness.

As a rule, the transition from the ahistoric scenario to the fully historic $\alpha = 1.0$ is fairly gradual, so that the patterns become gradually shrink as more historic

---

[1] Starting from a single active site, history does not affect the dynamics of the remaining sixteen legal ECA rules, either by its immediate extinction, e.g., rule 32, or by the absence of spread of activity beyond the initial live cell, e.g., rule 4.

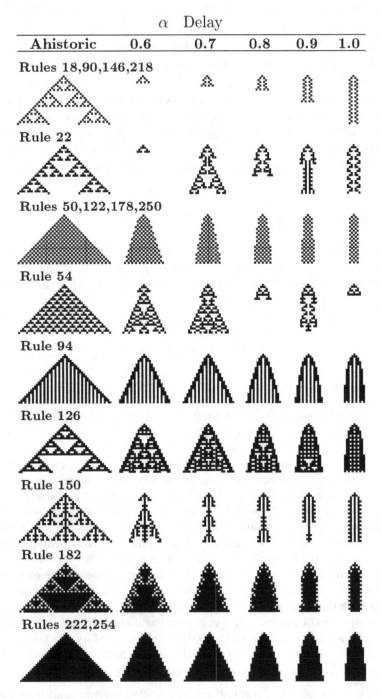

Fig. 1. Elementary legal rules active from a single cell

Table 1. A $MATLAB^{\circledR}$ program for rule 254 with memory

```
function cam
T=8;SR=254;alpha=1.0;N=11;
[srb]=binarynumber(SR);left=[N 1:N-1];right=[2:N 1];
for memo=1:2
    [SIGMA,OMEGA,omega]=init(T,N,alpha);
    switch memo
      case 1     % Embedded
       for t=1:T
        SIGMAH(t,:)=SIGMA;S=SIGMA;
        omega=(alpha*omega)+SIGMA;OMEGAX=OMEGA(t);
        for i=1:N
         if(2*omega(i)>OMEGAX)S(i)=1;end;  % Memory
         if(2*omega(i)<OMEGAX)S(i)=0;end
        end
        [SIGMA]=RULE(S,N,sbr,left,right);  % Rule
        HS(t,:)=S;
       end
      case 2     % Delay
       for t=1:T
        SIGMAH(t,:)=SIGMA;
        [S]=RULE(SIGMA,N,sbr,left,right);  % Rule
        SIGMA=S;HS(t,:)=S;
        omega=(alpha*omega)+SIGMA;OMEGAX=OMEGA(t);
        for i=1:N
         if(2*omega(i)>OMEGAX)SIGMA(i)=1;end% Memory
         if(2*omega(i)<OMEGAX)SIGMA(i)=0;end
        end
       end
    end
    subplot(2,4,2*(memo-1)+1);image(33*SIGMAH);axis image;axis('off'):
    if(memo==1)title('σ embedded');else;title('σ delay');end
    subplot(2,4,2*(memo-1)+2);imagesc(33*HS,[0,44]);axis image;axis('off');
    if(memo==1)title('s');else;title('f');end
end
print camemory.eps -depsc

function [SIGMA]=RULE(S,N,sbr,left,right);
    for i=1:N
        SIGMA(i)=srb(8-(4*S(left(i))+2*S(i)+S(right(i))));
    end
function [SIGMA,OMEGA,omega]=init(T,N,alpha);
    SIGMA(1:N)=0; SIGMA((N+1)/2:(N+1)/2)=1;
    OMEGA(1)=1.0;omega(1:N)=0;
    for t=2:T;OMEGA(t)=1+alpha*OMEGA(t-1);end
function [BN] =binarynumber(rule);
    BN(1:8)=0;irtx=rule;
    for ix=1:8
        rest=mod(irtx,2);ratio=(irtx-rest)/2;BN(8-ix+1)=rest;irtx=ratio;
    end
```

σ embedded   s   σ delay   f

memory is retained (higher α). Rules 50, 122, 178,250, 94, and 222,254 are
paradigmatic of this smooth evolution. Rules 126 and 182 also present a gradual
evolution, although their patterns with high levels of memory models hardly
resemble the ahistoric ones. But the non-smooth effect of memory is also present
in Figs. 1-2. The somehow erratic effect of memory is particularly surprising in
the case of the group of rules{18,90,146,218}, in which extinction is found in all
the non-full memory scenarios of Fig. 1, but not in the full memory ($\alpha = 1.0$)

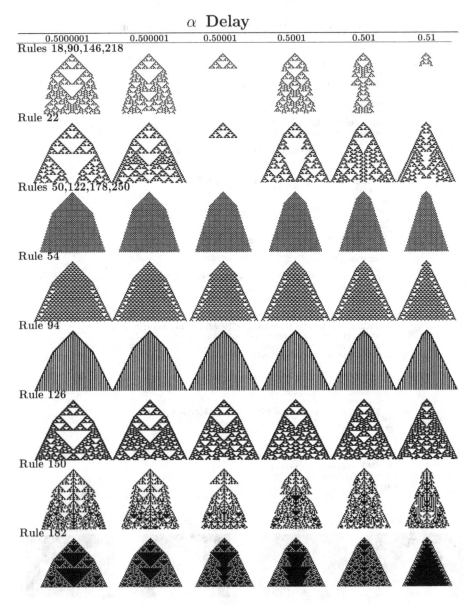

Fig. 2. Elementary legal rules active from a single cell with low memory

one, whereas in Fig. 2 extinction arises with α=0.50001 and α=0.51, but the remaining memory charges generate fairly interesting spatio-temporal patterns. Rule 22 also shows let us say unexpected extinctions: $\alpha = 0.6$ and $\alpha = 0.8$ in Fig. 1; again $\alpha = 0.50001$ in Fig. 2. Rule 54 extinguishes with $\alpha = 0.8$, and much surprisingly with full memory. As a rule, starting from a single site live cell, the strong inertial effect that full memory exerts tends to induce either periodic patters or very narrow patterns that expands at very low velocity. Thus, the case of rule 54 extinction with $\alpha = 1.0$ is rather atypical.

Figures 3 and 4 show the effect of memory on some ECA rules when starting at random: the values of sites are initially uncorrelated and chosen at random to be 0 (*white*) or 1 (*grey*) with probability 1/2. The pictures show also the differences in patterns (DP) resulting from reversing the center site value. The *damaged* region is enhanced with *black* pixels, corresponding to the site values that differed among the patterns generated with the two initial configurations. Patterns are shown up to $T = 81$, based on a line of size 135. Periodic boundary conditions are imposed on the edges in the simulations in Figs. 3-4. The memory factors implemented on them are indicated at the top of the figures.

Rule 18 (00010010) allows only dead cells with exactly one living neighbor to become alive. All living cells die. Although seemingly simple, rule 18 shows intriguing properties studied elsewhere. Memory has a dramatic effect on rule 18 in Fig.3. Even at the low value of $\alpha = 0.55$, the appearance of the spatio-temporal pattern completely changes, far from the distinctive inverted triangles world of the ahistoric pattern. Most of the structures generated with memory are short-living, but some of them persist in a periodic way. Some of the periodic structures are fairly complex, except in the fully historic model, in which case only simple periodic patterns of live cells survive.

As a rule, the effect of memory on the differences in patterns (DP) mimics that on the spatio-temporal patterns. In the case of rule 18 in Fig.3 for example, in the ahistoric model the perturbation grows close to the *speed of light* (with Lyapunov exponents $\lambda_L = \lambda_R \simeq 1$), but in the simulations with memory the DPs shrink to small periodic structures.

The chaotic linear legal rules 90 and 150 in Fig.3 show a much smoother evolution from the ahistoric to the full memory scenarios: no pattern evolves either to full extinction or to the preservation of only a few isolated persistent propagating structures (solitons). Rule 126 in Fig.4 evolves in a similar form. Particularly when comparing the ahistoric and fully historic patterns, which show a high degree of synchronization. The patterns with inverted triangles dominate the scene in the ahistoric spatio-temporal of rules 90, 150 and 126. Historic memory fuzzyfies this common appearance, particularly in the case of rule 150. The rules 90, 150 126 show a fairly gradual evolution from the ahistoric DP (for rules 90 and 150 exactly that generated starting with a single site active cell) to the DP with full memory, becoming increasingly depleted as historic memory increases, with no extinction for any α value. To avoid coined terms such as chaotic or random, the DP for these rules with not full memory could be described as *helter-skelter*.

The no-legal low-number rule 30 (Fig.4) evolves with memory very differently to the also low-number rule 18. The essentials of the ahistoric pattern remain regarding rule 30 with not full memory, albeit emerging interesting structures that in the embedded memory scenario where studied in [8]. Further study is due in the current delay memory implementation.

	α	
Ahistoric	0.55	0.60
0.65	0.70	1.00

Rule 18

Rule 90

Rule 150

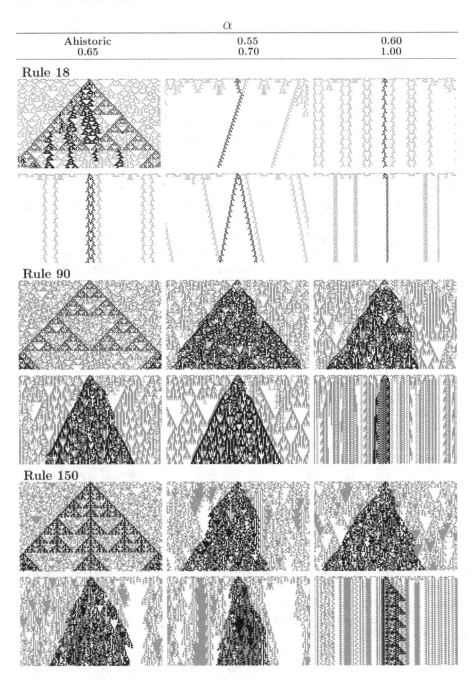

Fig. 3. Rules 18, 90 and 150 starting at random

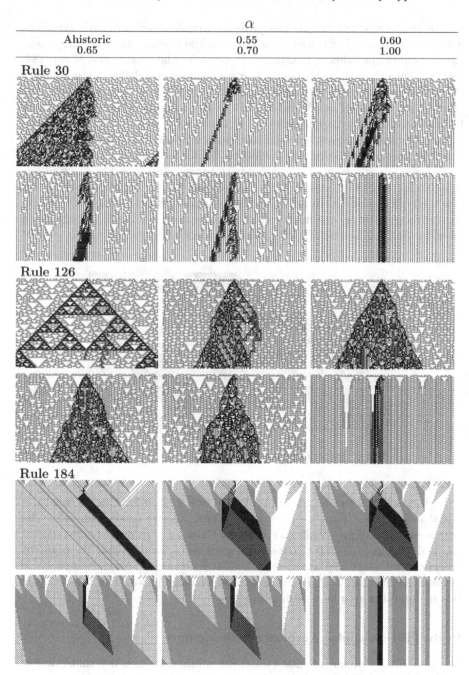

α

| Ahistoric | 0.55 | 0.60 |
| 0.65 | 0.70 | 1.00 |

Rule 30

Rule 126

Rule 184

Fig. 4. Rules 30, 126 and 184 starting at random

The *traffic* rule 184 (Fig.4) has proved particularly effective in solving the *density task*: to decide whether an arbitrary initial configuration contains a density of 1s above or below ρ_c, particularly $\rho_c = 0.5$. The effectiveness of rule 184, together with that of the also number conserving block cellular automata rules III and HPP, with embedded memory has been assessed in previous works ([3]-[4]. The assessment of its effectiveness with delay memory is planed for the near future. Nevertheless, the snapshots in Fig.4 may serve as a promising preamble. In fact the moderate (not too high, not too low) degrees of memory $\alpha = 0.65$ and 0.70 show that the pattern evolve to the all 1s configuration. This leads to a correct classification of the actual initial configuration in Fig. 4, which has $\rho_0 = 0.5259 > 0.5000$. Unexpectedly, the patterns for rule 184 with $\alpha = 0.55$ and $\alpha = 0.60$ are coincident. In any case, the dynamics with these memory charges also correctly classifies the initial configuration (please see Fig.5), though much later, by $T = 259$ instead of by $T < 90$ as happens with $\alpha = 0.55$ and $\alpha = 0.60$.

Fig. 5. Rule 184 with $\alpha = 0.60$ memory up to $T = 260$

Further study is due on the effect of delay-memory on ECA, far beyond this initial investigation (e.g., on rules 54 and 110, the two one-dimensional rules that seem to belong to Wolfram's complex Class IV.). In order to systematize the analysis, one can resort to the equivalence classes, formed under the negative, reflection and negative plus reflection transformations [13]. Memory is expected to affect all the rules of an equivalence class in a similar way. But the details of this hypothesis are to be scrutinized.

Probabilistic Cellular Automata with Memory

In probabilistic cellular automata the 0-1 β values defining a deterministic rule (5) become probabilities, thus real values in the $[0, 1]$ interval. As an example, the deterministic parity rule $[1, 0, 1, 0, 1, 0, 1, 0]$ may be *probabilized* to as $[0.9, 0, 0.9, 0, 0.9, 0, 0.9, 0]$. This is the case of Fig. 6, where the initial configuration is the same of Fig.3, so that due to the *proximity* of the probabilities (0.9) to the deterministic scenario (1.0), the general structure of the patterns in Fig.3 is recognizable in Fig.6, albeit *altered*, the paradigmatic example being the *imperfect* damage in the ahistoric scenario, and *stylized* as a result of the probabilization.

	α	
Ahistoric	0.55	0.60
0.65	0.70	1.00

Rule 150

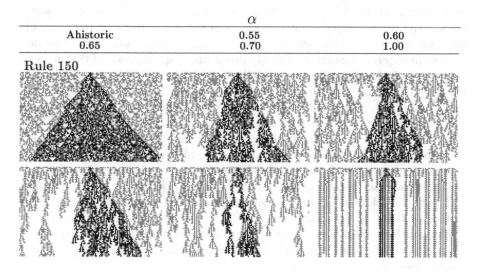

Fig. 6. The probabilistic rule $[0.9, 0, 0.9, 0, 0.9, 0, 9.9, 0]$ with memory

Introducing probabilities in the CA transition rules approaches the context to that of the Markov random fields (the basic tool in the study of *interacting particle systems*), and enables to study perturbations to deterministic automata, as well as transitional changes from one deterministic automata to another. The study of the statistical mechanics of probabilistic CA with memory appears as an interesting (though challenging) task.

3   Elementary Cellular Automata Rules as Memory

In the simulations so far, the length of the trailing memory is not limited. But it may be limited to the last τ time-steps. In the shortest scenario, $\tau=3$, in which case, elementary CA-rules (ψ) may be in turn implemented as memory rules (see in [2] the implementation of this approach with embedded memory) . Thus,

$$f_i^{(T)} = \phi(\{\sigma_{j \in \mathcal{N}_i}^{(T)}\}) \rightarrow \sigma_i^{(T+1)} = \psi(f_i^{(T-2)}, f_i^{(T)}, f_i^{(T-1)}) \qquad (6)$$

In the implementation adopted in (6) the time-step $T - 2$ plays the role of *left* cell, whereas time-step $T - 1$ plays the role of *right* cell. Other choices are, of course, feasible. Initially, $\sigma_i^{(2)} = f_i^{(1)}$, $\sigma_i^{(3)} = f_i^{(2)}$.

Figure 7 shows the effect on rule 150 of the CA-rules acting as memory when starting from a single active cell up to $T = 13$. The numbers of the ECA rules acting as memory appear on the top of every pattern. In a general scenario, rule 150 is affected by every memory rule except, of course, by the *identity* rule 204 (11001100). But in the scenario of Fig. 7 a subset of rules does not affect rule 150: $+68$, $+76$, $+100$, $+108$, $+196$, $+228$ and $+236$. Some ECA rules acting as memory lead rule 150 to extinction, e.g., $+8$ and $+128$, whereas others soon blacken the spatio-temporal pattern, e.g., $+23$ and $+215$. Patterns consisting of only two *branches*, are also traced in Fig. 7, e.g., $+4$ and $+132$. Some patterns with memory are reminiscent of the ahistoric one, e.g., $+6$ and $+148$, but as a normal effect, memory notably alters the spatio-temporal patterns, leading to patterns that are fairly unexpected regarding rule 150. The set of rules $+16$, $+24$, $+48$, $+56$, $+144$, $+152$, and $+184$ produce patterns with not any cell alive at some time-steps, which does not imply extinction after any of them. This kind of cataleptic episodes are only feasible when endowing cells with elementary rules as memory. As a rule, no general relevant concordance in Fig. 7 can be traced between the effect on rule 150 of *all* rules in the same equivalence class. Please, considerer as examples, the classes $\{60, 102, 153, 195\}$, $\{110, 124, 137, 193\}$. Anyway, reflected rules tend to produce similar memory effect, e.g., $\{8,64\}$, $\{13,69\}$, $\{29,71\}$, $\{30,86\}$, or $\{184,226\}$,.

Linear rules remain linear when cells are endowed with linear memory rules. Thus for example, the parity rule 150 endowed with $+150$ acting as memory would evolve as:

$$f_i^{(T)} = \sigma_{i-1}^{(T)} \oplus \sigma_i^{(T)} \oplus \sigma_{i+1}^{(T)} \rightarrow \sigma_i^{(T+1)} = f_i^{(T)} \oplus f_i^{(T-1)} \oplus f_i^{(T-2)}, \quad T \geq 3.$$

Incidentally, it is foreseeable that some rules endowed with ECA rules as delay memory, in particular those of type linear+linear, would produce interesting results regarding random number generation, as already proved in the embedded memory context [6].

The majority rule 232 acts selecting the most frequent (*mode*) of the last three f-state values: $\psi_{232}\big(f_i^{(T-2)}, f_i^{(T)}, f_i^{(T-1)}\big) = mode\big(f_i^{(T-2)}, f_i^{(T-1)}, f_i^{(T)}\big)$. The idea implemented by rule 232 regarding the three most recent values may be readily generalized to more than three time-steps. Thus, majority memory of the last τ f-states will operate as:

$$\sigma_i^{(T+1)} = mode\big(f_i^{(T-\tau+1)}, \ldots f_i^{(T-)}, f_i^{(T)}\big) \tag{7}$$

This kind of majority memory avoids the need of computing with real numbers, as α-memory does. So, it is in the realm of the CA discrete paradigm. But, unlike α-memory, which demands just one number per cell to be stored, majority memory of length τ demands precisely τ numbers per cell to be stored.

The lowest degree of memory conceivable is that of featuring cells by Boolean functions of their last two states: $\sigma_i^{(T+1)} = \psi\big(f_i^{(T)}, f_i^{(T-1)}\big)$. These mappings are characterized by a sequence of four binary values (β) associated with each of the four possible pairs $\big(f_i^{(T)}, f_i^{(T-1)}\big)$ (a two-bit analogue of the ECA codification):

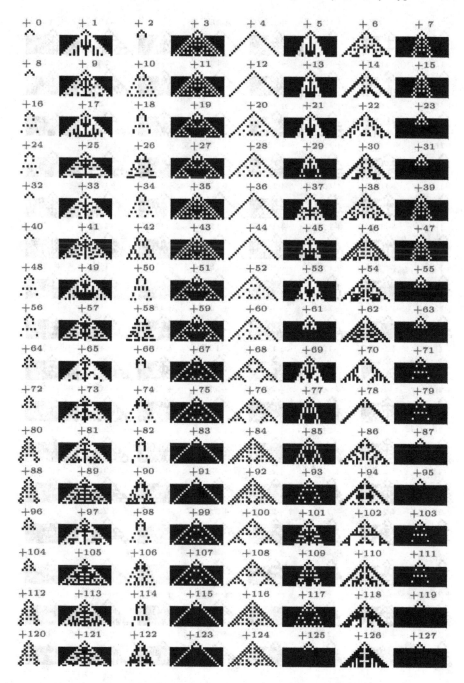

Fig. 7. Elementary rule 150 starting from a single active cell with CA-rules acting as memory

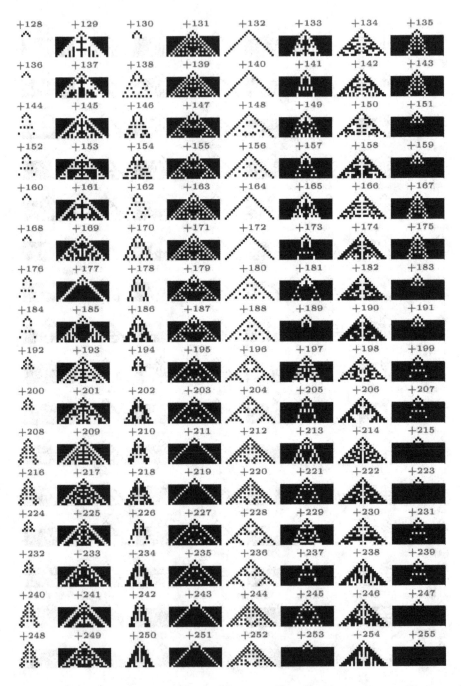

Fig. 7. (*Continued.*)

$$\begin{array}{c} 11\ 10\ 01\ 00 \\ \beta_1\ \beta_2\ \beta_3\ \beta_4 \end{array} \equiv \sum_{i=1}^{4} \beta_{\mathbf{s}} 2^{4-i} = \mathcal{R} \in [0, 15]$$

Thus, $\mathcal{R} = 12\,(1100)$ being the identity rule $\sigma_i^{(T+1)} = f_i^{(T)}$, $\mathcal{R} = 5\,(0101)$ reversing the last state: $\sigma_i^{(T+1)} = 1 \ominus f_i^{(T)}$, and $\mathcal{R} = 6\,(0110)$ being the parity rule: $\sigma_i^{(T+1)} = f_i^{(T-1)} \oplus f_i^{(T)}$. The parity ECA rule 150 in particular becomes with $\tau{=}2$ parity memory (i.e., R6):

$$f_i^{(T)} = \sigma_{i-1}^{(T)} \oplus \sigma_i^{(T)} \oplus \sigma_{i+1}^{(T)} \rightarrow \sigma_i^{(T+1)} = f_i^{(T)} \oplus f_i^{(T-1)}, \quad T > 2.$$

4   Conclusion and Future Work

The delay memory implementation mechanism studied here (1), together its closely related embedded one (2) studied in previous works [1], constitute a simple extension (of straightforward computer codification) of the basic paradigm allowing for an easy systematic study of the effect of memory in cellular automata (and other discrete dynamical systems). This may inspire some useful ideas in using cellular automata as a tool for modeling phenomena with memory. This task has been traditionally attacked by means of differential, or finite-difference, equations, with some (or all) continuous component. In contrast, full discrete models are ideally suited to digital computers. Thus, it seems plausible that further study on cellular automata with memory should prove profitable, and may be possible to paraphrase T.Toffoli [11] in presenting cellular automata with memory *as an alternative to (rather than an approximation of)* integro-differential equations in modeling phenomena with memory. Besides their potential applications, cellular automata with memory have an aesthetic and mathematical interest on their own, so that we believe that the subject is worth to studying.

Nearest and next-nearest ($r = 2$) one-dimensional CA, two-dimensional CA, and reversible [5] rules with delay type memory are planed to be studied in the near future. Asynchronous updating, probabilistic rules, multifractal properties [9], structurally dynamic cellular automata, and the effectiveness of CA rules with delay type memory in random number generation and in solving the density classification task will also come under scrutiny.

Acknowledgment. This work was supported by the Spanish MEC Project MTM2012-39101-C02-01.

Appendix

A Glimpse of Two-dimensional Cellular Automata with Memory

Let us mention here the effect of α-memory in a particular two-dimensional CA rule, that of the parity rule in the Moore neighbourhood $\mathcal{N}$ (summation modulo two):

$$f_{i,j}^{(T)} = \sum_{(k,l)\in\mathcal{N}_{i,j}} \sigma_{k,l}^{(T)}$$

Figure 8 shows the effect of memory up to $T = 18$ on the 2D parity rule starting from a single live cell. Non-low levels of memory tend to freeze the dynamics from the early time-steps, e.g. over 0.60 in Fig. 8. In the particular case of full memory small oscillators of short range in time are frequently generated, such as the period-two oscillator that appears as soon as $T = 3$ in Fig. 8. The group of evolution patterns shown in the [0.501,0.54] interval of α variation of Fig. 8, might not be expected to be generated by the parity rule, because they are too *sophisticated* for this simple chaotic rule. This is particularly so beyond the scope of Fig. 8, i.e., for $T > 18$, as Fig. 9 shows in the case of $\alpha = 0.501$, where memory induces patterns notably different to the ahistoric ones. These patterns tend to be framed in squares of size not more than $T \times T$, whereas in the ahistoric case, the patterns tend to be framed in $2T \times 2T$ square regions, so even a very small memory charge induces a very notable reduction in the affected cell area in the scenario of Fig. 8. Diffusion-Limited Aggregation like [12] simulation practitioners might be somehow inspired in the pattern formation dynamics shown in Fig. 9.

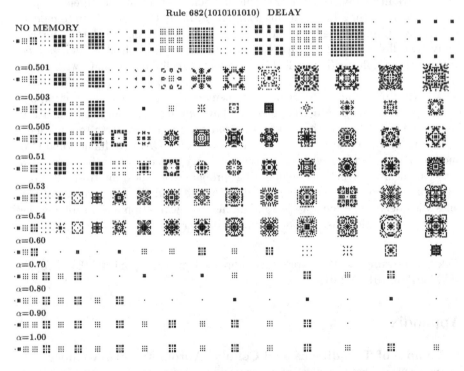

Fig. 8. The 2D parity rule with α-memory

α=0.501   **Rule 682(1010101010) DELAY**

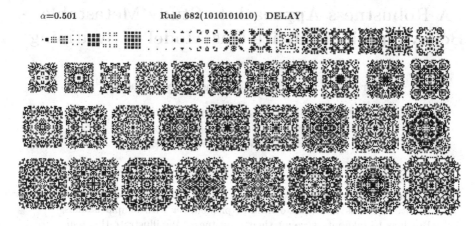

Fig. 9. The 2D parity rule with very low α-memory

References

1. Alonso-Sanz, R.: Discrete systems with memory. World Scientific Pub. (2011)
2. Alonso-Sanz, R., Martin, M.: Elementary cellular automata with elementary memory rules in cells: The case of linear rules. J. of Cellular Automata 1(1), 70–86 (2006)
3. Alonso-Sanz, R.: The HPP rule with memory and the density classification task. Int. J. of Modern Physics C 21(9), 1115–1128 (2010)
4. Alonso-Sanz, R., Bull, L.: A very effective density classifier two-dimensional cellular automaton with memory. J. Phys. A: Math. Theor. 42, 485101 (2009)
5. Alonso-Sanz, R.: Reversible cellular automata with memory: patterns starting with a single site seed. Physica D 175(1/2), 1–30 (2003)
6. Alonso-Sanz, R., Bull, L.: Random number generation by cellular automata with memory. Int. J. Modern Physics C 19(2), 351–367 (2008)
7. Alonso-Sanz, R., Bull, L.: Elementary cellular automata with minimal memory and random number generation. Complex Systems 18(2), 195–213 (2009)
8. Martinez, G.J., Adamatzky, A., Alonso-Sanz, R., Seck-Touh-Mora, J.C.: Complex dynamics emerging in Rule 30 with majority memory. Complex Systems 18(3), 345–365 (2009)
9. Sanchez, J.R., Alonso-Sanz, R.: Multifractal properties of R90 cellular automaton with memory. Int. J. Modern Physics C 15(10), 1461–1470 (2004)
10. Schiff, J.L.: Cellular automata: a discrete view of the world. Wiley (2008)
11. Toffoli, T.: Cellular automata as an alternative to (rather than an approximation of) differential equations in modeling physics. Physica D 10, 117–127 (1984)
12. http://en.wikipedia.org/wiki/Diffusion-limited_aggregation
13. Wuensche, A., Lesser, M.: The Global Dynamics of Cellular Automata. Addison-Wesley (1992)

A Robustness Approach to Study Metastable Behaviours in a Lattice-Gas Model of Swarming

Olivier Bouré[1,2], Nazim Fatès[2], and Vincent Chevrier[1]

[1] Université de Lorraine, LORIA UMR 7503,
Vandoeuvre-lès-Nancy, 54506, France
[2] Inria, Villers-lès-Nancy, F-54600, France

Abstract. Research in biology is increasingly interested in discrete dynamical systems to simulate natural phenomena with simple models. But how to take into account their robustness? We illustrate this issue by considering the behaviour of a lattice-gas model with an alignment-favouring interaction rule. This model, which has been shown to display a phase transition between an ordered and a disordered phase, follows ergodic dynamics. We present a method based on the study of stability and robustness, and show that the organised phase may result in several different behaviours. We then observe that behaviours are influenced asymptotically by the definition of the cellular lattice.

Keywords: Swarming behaviour, lattice-gas cellular automata, phase transitions, robustness, discretisation effects, resonance effects.

Introduction

Research on natural systems has thrived in the past years with the use of dynamical systems to simulate their behaviour. An interesting approach to the problem considers simple mathematical models, such as Turing's reaction-diffusion equations, may reproduce the mechanisms that Nature uses in many complex phenomena. When these models are hard to solve analytically, numerical simulations allow one to explore a wide variety of rules and to obtain statistical data by repeating experiments at a reduced cost. Simple discrete models, such as cellular automata, have been known to be a valuable tool to model complex natural phenomena, as their simplicity is often a good means to identify the role played by each component of the model and thus to make clear the necessary conditions for the emergence of a given behaviour [1].

However, the use of simple models inevitably alters the way entities interact with each other and could affect the system by introducing some unwanted behaviour [2]. Thus, when studying the behaviour of a model through simulation, it is necessary to distinguish which part of the behaviour emerges from the interaction rule, from the part induced by the simulation setting. This question amounts to determine the *robustness* of a model, that is, "the degree to which [its behaviour] is insensitive to effects that are not considered in the design" [3]. An intuitive method for detecting such effects consists in studying extensively

J. Kari, M. Kutrib, and A. Malcher (Eds.): AUTOMATA 2013, LNCS 8155, pp. 84–97, 2013.

the dynamics of the system under different simulation conditions and search for modifications of the behaviour (see *e.g.* [4,5]).

This paper considers the simulation of a complex phenomenon in the field of *collective motion*, that is, the coordinated movement of entities with local interaction. This family of models has been extensively studied in numerous natural systems [6,7], using various models from self-propelled particles [8] to cellular automata [9]. The goal was either to gain insight of into the mechanisms involved in the biological systems [10,11,12] or to provide a simulation tool for human crowds [13,14], as well as to design physically-inspired algorithms that perform on grids [15,16].

The *Vicsek model* was introduced in 1995 as a model of "self-propelled particles" moving at constant speed in a continuous space [17]. Assuming a stochastic direction-averaging rule, with a single parameter modulating the alignment behaviour from random to deterministic orientation, Vicsek *et al.* observed the *swarm instability*, that is, a phase transition that separates chaotic, random motion from complete alignment of the particles. Discrete versions of Vicsek's self-propelled particles were developed by Deutsch *et al.* on a square lattice [18,19] as well as Csahók and Vicsek on an hexagonal lattice [20]. Indeed, discrete dynamical systems such as lattice-gas cellular automata (LGCA) are well-suited tools for simulating complex systems with minimal computational cost because of their parallel, spatially-extended structure. In spite of the discretisation, these models show a conservation of the swarm instability transition [21], whereas the resulting dynamics shows the appearance of novel behaviours [22]. Our objective here is to assess the robustness of the behaviour, by studying the dependence of Deutsch's model [19] on the definition of the system's lattice.

The model's dynamics come with an additional difficulty: we will show that because the updating rule being stochastic and reversible makes the system *ergodic*. How can we then extract information about the dynamics in such an unstable environment? In fact, even though no configuration remains indefinitely stable, we will see that the system is subject to *metastability* [23], that is, it "can persist for a long period of time in a phase which is not the one favoured by the thermodynamic parameters" [24]. In other words, once randomly initialised, the system will quickly converge towards some specific type of configurations, or *pattern*, and hold it for long times until random fluctuations allow it to escape this pattern for another one. These patterns act as "basins of attraction" which can thus be used to study how the system organises in long times and for a large number of simulations. Our goal is to provide a first "map" of these basins and explain how they are linked to the robustness of the model.

After presenting a formal description of the model (Sec. 1), we determine the different patterns of the system by constraining the state space (Sec. 2), after which we quantify their stability by studying the influence of an increasing spatial size. We then reveal how the observation of the behaviour is influenced by resonance effects for any finite lattice (Sec. 3). Finally, we study how the lattice may introduce biases in the observations of the system's behaviour (Sec. 4), and finish by briefly discussing the implications of our approach (Sec. 5).

1   Deutsch Lattice-Gas Model of Swarming

1.1   Lattice-Gas Cellular Automata

A lattice-gas cellular automaton (LGCA) is a discrete dynamical system defined by a triplet $\{\mathcal{L}, \mathcal{N}, f_I\}$ where :

- $\mathcal{L} \subset \mathbb{Z}^2$ is the array that forms the cellular space.
- $\mathcal{N}$ is a finite set of vectors called the *neighbourhood*. It associates to a cell the set of its neighbouring cells. The sets $\mathcal{N}$ and $\mathcal{L}$ are such that for all $c \in \mathcal{L}$ and for all $n \in \mathcal{N}$, the *neighbour* $c + n$ is in $\mathcal{L}$.
- f_I is the *local interaction rule*.

In LGCA, neighbouring cells are connected via *channels* through which *particles* can travel from one cell to another. For the sake of simplicity, we will consider here that each channel is associated to a neighbour. Consequently, the number of channels is given by $\nu = \mathrm{card}(\mathcal{N})$.

We thus note the *configuration* x as the state of the automaton, which is defined as a function $x : \mathcal{L} \to \mathcal{Q} \subset \mathbb{N}^\nu$ which maps each cell to a set of states for the channels. Each channel contains a given number of particles represented by an element of $\mathbb{N}$. The state of a cell $c \in \mathcal{L}$ is denoted by $x_c = (x_1(c), ..., x_\nu(c)) \in \mathcal{Q}$, where $x_i(c) \in \mathbb{N}$ is the state of the i-th channel that connects cell c and its neighbour $c + n_i$, with $\mathcal{N} = \{n_1, \ldots, n_\nu\}$.

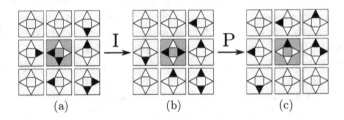

Fig. 1. The cycle of a LGCA cell (a) at initial state, (b) after interaction step I, (c) after propagation step P. By convention, black and white triangles represent occupied and empty channels respectively.

The dynamics of a LGCA arises from the successive applications of two transitions applied to all cells synchronously (see example on Fig. 1):

- The *interaction step* I reorganises the particles within each cell. The local transition $f_I : \mathcal{Q}^{\nu+1} \to \mathcal{Q}$ is denoted by:

$$x_c^I = f_I(x_c, x_{c+n_1}, \ldots, x_{c+n_\nu}), \text{ with } \mathcal{N} = \{n_1, \ldots, n_\nu\}. \qquad (1)$$

- The *propagation step* P relocates all particles simultaneously in the same channel of the corresponding neighbour in $\mathcal{N}$. The result of the local transition $f_P : \mathcal{Q}^{\nu+1} \to \mathcal{Q}$ is given by:

$$x_c^P = f_P(x_c^I, x_{c+n_1}^I, \ldots, x_{c+n_\nu}^I)$$
$$= (x_1^I(c - n_1), \ldots, x_\nu^I(c - n_\nu)) \qquad (2)$$

The evolution of the system from a time t to the following time $t + 1$ is determined by: $x^{t+1} = P \circ I(x^t)$. In this paper, initial configurations x^0 are generated from a uniform distribution of *density* ρ, where ρ is the probability for *each channel*, independently, to contain a particle.

1.2 Swarming in Lattice-Gas Cellular Automata

The swarm model we study is taken from the work of Deutsch *et al.* compiled in a dedicated book (see Ref. [19], chapter 8.2). It describes a probabilistic *swarming interaction* rule in which a cell reorganises its particles according to a probability distribution that maximises local alignment.

This transition is particle-conserving and uses its neighbourhood state as a director field to align the cell particles. In this paper, the neighbourhood is composed of the vectors of the 4 nearest cells: $\mathcal{N} = \{(1,0), (0,1), (-1,0), (0,-1)\}$. Moreover, an *exclusion principle* is imposed: a channel contains at most one particle. As a consequence, a configuration is a vector $x \in \mathcal{Q}^{\mathcal{L}}$ where the state for a cell c is a vector $x_c \in \mathcal{Q} = \{0,1\}^4$.

To maximise the alignment of particles within cells, the computation of the individual rule uses two parameters:

- The *local flux* $J_c(x) = \sum_{i=1}^{\nu} x_i(c) \cdot n_i$ the resulting particle direction in a cell c, with the neighbourhood $\mathcal{N} = (n_i)$.
- The *director field* $D_c(x) = \sum_{i=1}^{\nu} J_{c+n_i}(x)$ denotes the total flux of the neighbourhood of a cell c.

Now, let $k(x, c) = \sum_{i=1}^{\nu} x_i(c)$ be the the number of particles in a cell c, and $\Omega(k) \subset \mathcal{Q}$ the set of the possible states of a cell that contains k particles. For a cell $c \in \mathcal{L}$, the transition probability for the interaction step to update from a state x_c to a new state $x_c^I \in \Omega(k(x,c))$ in the presence of the director field $D_c(x)$ is given by:

$$P(x_c \to x_c^I) = \frac{1}{Z} \exp\left[\sigma . J_c(x^I) \cdot D_c(x)\right] \qquad (3)$$

where:

- The normalisation factor Z is such that $\sum_{x_c^I \in \Omega(k(x,c))} P(x_c \to x_c^I) = 1$.
- The *alignment sensitivity* σ is the control parameter controlling the intensity of the swarming effects.

With only the parameter σ to control the behaviour continuously from random direction to deterministic alignment[1], the model is fairly simple and thus easy to explore. An example of a local application of the rule is shown on Fig. 2.

---

[1] When $\sigma = 0$, all outcomes x^I that conserve the number of particles have an equal probability to be selected, making the interaction step completely random. Inversely, when $\sigma \to \infty$, the system becomes pseudo-deterministic, that is, the selection almost always picks one of the configurations that maximises the local alignment.

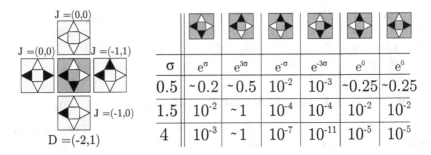

σ	e^{σ}	$e^{3\sigma}$	$e^{-\sigma}$	$e^{-3\sigma}$	e^{0}	e^{0}
0.5	~0.2	~0.5	10^{-2}	10^{-3}	~0.25	~0.25
1.5	10^{-2}	~1	10^{-4}	10^{-4}	10^{-2}	10^{-2}
4	10^{-3}	~1	10^{-7}	10^{-11}	10^{-5}	10^{-5}

Fig. 2. Example of the application of the swarm interaction rule for the central cell. Left: typical states for a cell and its neighbours, with neighbouring fluxes and the director field $\boldsymbol{D}_c(\boldsymbol{x})$ of the center cell. Right: elements of $\Omega(2)$ along with a table of the computed weights (Eq. 3) for different values of σ before normalisation to probability 1.

1.3   Recurrence and Ergodicity of Behaviours

An important property of the update rule is that, for a given transition $\boldsymbol{x}^t \to \boldsymbol{x}^{t+1} \to \boldsymbol{x}^{t+2}$, the probability that $\boldsymbol{x}^{t+2} = \boldsymbol{x}^t$ (up to an interaction) is strictly positive[2]. This implies that the Markov chain representing the evolution of the system is *recurrent*, that is, there is always a non-zero probability to go back to previously visited configurations. In other words, for a given initial configuration, any reachable configuration will be visited an infinite number of times over infinite simulation times: the behaviour thus consists strictly speaking of a random walk over the entire space of reachable configurations. Studying the system's dynamics shows that if the behaviour often converges towards a stable attraction point (Fig. 3-a), it is much more volatile for particular parameter values (Fig. 3-b). How then to study the behaviour in such unstable conditions?

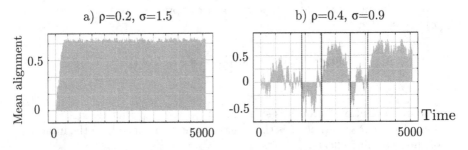

Fig. 3. Evolution of the mean alignment $\overline{\gamma}$ for different values of the density ρ and the sensitivity σ. Note how the behaviour "shifts" between several organised patterns.

The observations in Fig. 3 suggests that there exist distinct lower-energy attractors, which will appear more often from random configurations (attractivity)

---

[2] This can easily be proved by noting that the interaction that reverses all channels within cells is associated to a positive probability.

or remain present for longer simulation times (stability). Our approach consists in considering these sets of ordered and stable configurations, referred to as *patterns*, and use them to characterise the behaviour of the system by focusing on the regions of the parametrical space where the considered pattern is most stable and attractive. The next section is thus devoted to a thorough search for these patterns.

2   Observation and Identification of Patterns

In the literature, analytical approaches have been used to describe the organisation phenomenon occurring in this model [9]. However, a systematic experimental approach to explore the organisation process has to our knowledge not yet been carried out.

2.1   Monitoring the Behaviour

The first method is simply to inspect by eye the configurations ; three types of visualisations are used:

- The *density visualisation* (Fig. 4 -Left) displays how many particles are in a cell. Empty cells are white, cells with 1, 2 and 3 particles are light, medium or dark grey, respectively, and fully occupied cells with 4 particles are black.
- The *flux visualisation*(Fig. 4 -Middle) is a new representation that we introduce in order to facilitate the reading of the resulting particles direction within cells by associating a colour for each cell flux. A zero-flux cell is represented in white, while other types of flux show a different colour for each corresponding cardinal point: N (green), N-E (lime), E (yellow), S-E (orange), S (red), S-W (magenta), W (blue), N-W (cyan).
- The *channel visualisation* (Fig. 4 -Right) displays the state of channels by denoting the presence of a particle in a channel by a black triangle.

We also use a quantitative method with two *order parameters*:

- The *mean velocity* $\overline{\phi}$, introduced by Bussemaker *et al.*, averages horizontal and vertical momentum, in order to quantify a consensus in the direction of particles. For a configuration $\boldsymbol{x}$, it is defined by:

$$\overline{\phi}(\boldsymbol{x}) = \frac{1}{\mathrm{card}(\mathcal{L})} \left\| \sum_{c \in \mathcal{L}} J_c(\boldsymbol{x}) \right\|_\infty \quad \text{where } \|\boldsymbol{v}\|_\infty = |v_x| + |v_y|. \tag{4}$$

- To this parameter, we add the *mean alignment* $\overline{\gamma}$ to express whether particles of a cell are in average aligned with the flux of the neighbours of this cell:

$$\overline{\gamma}(\boldsymbol{x}) = \frac{1}{k(\boldsymbol{x})} \sum_{c \in \mathcal{L}} \frac{1}{\mathrm{card}(\mathcal{N})} J_c(\boldsymbol{x}) \cdot D_c(\boldsymbol{x}) \tag{5}$$

where $k(\boldsymbol{x}) = \sum_{c \in \mathcal{L}} k(\boldsymbol{x}, c)$ is the total number of particles. Its value varies in $[-1, 1]$: $\overline{\gamma} = 1$ indicates that all particles are aligned, and for $\overline{\gamma} = -1$, all particles are antialigned[3].

These two parameters are complementary as they capture two distinct aspects of the spatial organisation of particles: the mean alignment $\overline{\gamma}$ monitors whether particles are on average aligned or antialigned with the neighbouring fluxes, while $\overline{\phi}$ captures a global consensus in directions.

Experimental Protocol. Throughout the paper, the following protocol will be used to assess the resulting behaviour for each given setting (σ, ρ):

1. fix the lattice dimensions L and the parameters ρ and σ,
2. start from an initial configuration, randomly generated by a Bernoulli distribution where each channel has a probability ρ to contain a particle, and $1 - \rho$ to be empty,
3. iterate the system for a fixed *transition time* T_{tr},
4. average the value of the parameters for a *sampling time* T_{sa},
5. use visualisations and order parameters to classify the configuration,
6. repeat from step 2 several times.

2.2   Observation and Identification of Patterns

We already know from the literature that the model displays a phase transition separating a chaotic disorganised phase from an organised phase for critical values of the parameters (σ, ρ) [21]. Our classification completes this observation by distinguishing several patterns, shown in Fig. 4:

Random Pattern (R). This category includes all configurations that do not display any observable ordered phenomenon. It is characterized by a zero-mean velocity and a zero-mean alignment and corresponds to the parametrical region of low sensitivity σ and low particle density ρ.

Diagonal Stripe Pattern (DS). For higher values of (ρ, σ), the behaviour organises into a diagonal stripe, composed of cells containing two particles that points to the same two orthogonal directions, and travels diagonally through the lattice. It is quantitatively characterised by high values for both mean velocity $\overline{\phi}$ and mean alignment $\overline{\gamma}$.

Checkerboard Pattern (CB). For high values of the density ($\rho \in [0.3, 0.5]$)[4], the system surprisingly organises into regions where each cell contains two particles that are antialigned with the neighbours' fluxes. This observation is confirmed by a zero-velocity $\overline{\phi}$ and a *negative* mean alignment $\overline{\gamma}$.

---

[3] We borrow this term from spins systems in particle physics. Antialignment refers to the relationship between two particles whose directions are on the same axis, but in opposition.

[4] It can be shown that the system is symmetrical around $\rho = 0.5$, by exchanging 0s (no particle) and 1s (particle) in the channels.

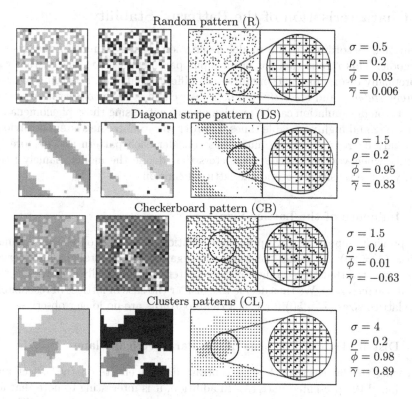

Fig. 4. (colour online) Major patterns, with associated visualisations and typical values for parameters. Configurations are obtained from random initial configuration, for $L = 25$, $t = 1000$.

Clusters Pattern (CL). When the sensitivity increases drastically ($\sigma > 2$), the system no longer organises into a diagonal stripe, but into a small number of clusters of collinear particles. These clusters travel through the lattice and occasionally meet by overlapping, but remain seemingly stable in the long run. It is characterised by a high mean alignment $\overline{\gamma}$ while the mean velocity $\overline{\phi}$ can take any value in $[0, 1]$.

These first observations show us that the transition from order to disorder does not consist only by the formation of a stripe. Most interestingly, although some patterns echo back to previous observations [19,22], the checkerboard constitutes a novel observation for this model. In order to determine if these observations are robust, we now propose to assess the stability of the patterns for various simulation settings.

3   Characterisation of the Patterns' Stability

Recall that according to the model description, the dynamics of the system is ergodic. This means that for given input parameters (ρ, σ), the system will theoretically disorganise and organise into different patterns, according to their inherent *stability* and *attractivity*. The measure and even the observation of stability through simulation can be problematic, as witnessing those phenomena involves long and highly-variable times. In order to estimate the system behaviour and study its robustness, we must thus consider each pattern and explore its stability when varying all the parameters that define the model, namely : the density ρ, the sensitivity σ and the lattice definition.

3.1   Influence of the Lattice Size

In a previous report [25], we presented additional patterns observed for small lattices $(L = 20)$. Although these types of organisation are stable, our observations suggested that the stability of these patterns dramatically decreases as the lattice size increases. We thus decide to consider the case of lattices of reasonably large lattice sizes $(L > 50)$ for which these patterns are no longer observed.

3.2   Distribution of Patterns in the Parametrical Plane

Increasing the lattice scale has by contrast limited effects on the aspect and evolution of the presented patterns. In addition, it is interesting to note that for most couples (ρ, σ), only one type of pattern appears preponderantly at different places and spread on the entire lattice. When conflicting forms of the pattern appear, they co-exist for some time but generally merge to a unique lattice-scale pattern:

- In the case of the diagonal stripe, several stripes of conflicting directions may appear simultaneously, until only one direction remains.
- The checkerboard pattern first appears scattered in several "regions" of local checkerboards of different directions (*e.g.* NW/SE versus NE/SW), until a unified checkerboard covers the entire lattice.

The corresponding parametrical regions for each major patterns are displayed on Fig. 5. Note that if it is difficult to observe experimentally more than one type of pattern anywhere *inside* these regions, inbetween settings (dashed lines) easily display pattern shifts and the occasional coexistence of several patterns of different types.

Our observations suggest that the presented patterns remain stable for large lattices, for long enough simulations times. It is however still not clear how is characterised the transition between a pattern to another, and whether the stability of the behaviour can be generalised for *any* lattice $\mathcal{L}$.

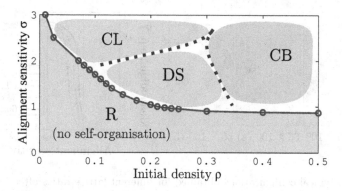

Fig. 5. Spatial distribution of the disordered and ordered phases in the density-sensitivity parametric plane. We divided the ordered phase into approximated regions of appearance for each observed patterns. The circles represent experimental observations of the phase transition.

3.3   Influence of the Lattice Size Ratio

The diagonal stripe is defined as a cluster of particles looping over the periodic boundaries of a *square* lattice. One may then wonder what happens when the lattice has unequal dimensions. We thus now consider as parameters $\rho = 0.2, \sigma = 1.5$, which match the diagonal stripe region, and a rectangular lattice $\mathcal{L} = (\mathbb{Z}/L_x\mathbb{Z}) \times (\mathbb{Z}/L_y\mathbb{Z})$, where L_x and L_y are respectively the width and height of the lattice. Several cases can be distinguished for the ratio L_x/L_y (see Fig. 6-Left):

– Integer or quasi-integer "regular" ratios (*e.g.* 100×50, 100×30) show a diagonal stripe pattern that loops one or several times over the periodic boundaries.
– For other "irregular" ratios (*e.g.* 60×100), the configuration displays an unfinished, distorted diagonal stripe, as it can no longer loop "regularly" over the periodic boundaries. However, over very long simulation times, the system might finally find a stable pattern (see 66×100 (b)).

From these observations, we conclude that the regularity of the lattice influences the behaviour of the system, by disturbing the regularity of the diagonal stripe pattern. We can quantify this phenomenon by considering the following process: starting from a fixed density $\rho = 0.2$ and given lattice dimensions (L_x, L_y), we measure the mean alignment $\overline{\gamma}$ after a few thousands steps for different values of the sensitivity σ. We thus obtain a plot of alignment $\overline{\gamma}$ versus sensitivity σ, displayed in Fig. 6-Right.

It is interesting to note that although the transition between the disordered and the ordered phases is always observed, the sharpness of the transition as well as the critical point σ_c slightly change from regular to irregular ratios. These observations support the hypothesis of a strong connection between the formation of the diagonal stripe pattern and the regularity of the lattice. Our interpretation of this phenomenon is that the diagonal stripe pattern emerges

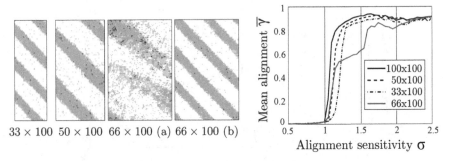

33×100 50×100 66×100 (a) 66×100 (b)

Fig. 6. Left: typical configurations obtained for different lattice ratios after 1000 time steps ; note that the case 66×100 is shown at two different times: at $t = 1000$ (a) and at $t = 10^6$ (b). Right: a quantification of the corresponding transitions, as plot of the mean alignment $\overline{\gamma}$ versus the alignment sensitivity σ, for different lattice ratios with transient and sampling times ($T_{\mathrm{tr}} = 10^5, T_{\mathrm{sa}} = 100$).

from the periodic interactions of diagonal clusters which is achieved more easily in regular lattices than in irregular ones. Therefore, it can be considered as a "resonance" effect caused by the finite lattice with periodic boundaries.

More generally, this means that a finite implementation of the model induces a bias in the behaviour of the system. Now this final statement questions our understanding of the dynamics: how much of the resonance effects tamper with the resulting behaviour? To tackle this issue, we propose to consider the case of an infinite lattice $\mathcal{L} = \mathbb{Z}^2$ and to compare the observed behaviour with the finite case.

4   Overcoming the Resonance Effects

Changing the implementation of the model from a finite to an infinite lattice suggests drastic changes in hypotheses. If the number of possible configurations is infinite, the probability to escape a given pattern through fluctuations becomes zero, and the behaviour can no longer be considered as metastable. Instead, we will observe the emergence of phases, that is, local behaviours that occur statistically everywhere on the lattice and remain stable.

In order to study the behaviour without long-term resonance effects, we propose to choose coherent values for the space and time dimensions of the simulations. This means that to estimate the behaviour in a given order of T, we need to use an equivalent size $L \approx T$ for the lattice. Similarly, to study the asymptotic behaviour, both dimensions must increase simultaneously when passing to the limit. As an example, we computed samples of lattice sizes $L = 1500$ and $L = 100$ respectively for ($T_{\mathrm{tr}} = 1400, T_{\mathrm{sa}} = 100$). As observed in Fig. 7, the difference in the resulting behaviours is significant, as captured by the evolution of order parameters versus the sensitivity σ:

– The transition between the disorganised and organised phases greatly differs between experiments: for the case $L = 100$, the transition is sharp and almost

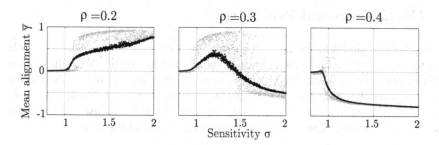

Fig. 7. The organisation phenomena for different values of σ at fixed ρ. Dots represent independent sampling for $(T_{\mathrm{tr}} = 1400, T_{\mathrm{sa}} = 100)$ and for different lattice settings – black accounts for $L = 1500$, and grey for $L = 100$.

immediate whereas for the case $L = 1500$, the transition is progressive. This observation seems to confirm the resonance effects identified in the last section.

- The plot for densities $\rho = 0.2$ and 0.4 confirms the existence of at least an "aligned" and an "antialigned" phase. The case $\rho = 0.3$ appears to show an intermediate case, but the precise transition is not visible.
- The differentiation between the diagonal stripe and the clusters pattern is *a priori* not apparent.

Our simulations are now too limited to assess asymptotic behaviours, as their cost both in terms of time and memory reached computational limits. However, they are sufficient to display tendencies in the organisation of particles and reveal divergent behaviours. In particular, we conjecture from the observation of order parameters that the asymptotic behaviour of the system divides up in at least three phases: disorganised, aligned and antialigned. Moreover, a preliminary visual experiment using a $L = 500$ lattice and $t = 500$ suggests a visible differentiation of behaviour between the diagonal stripe and the clusters pattern (see Fig. 8). Determining whether there exists a distinct phase for the diagonal stripe pattern is an interesting problem left for future work.

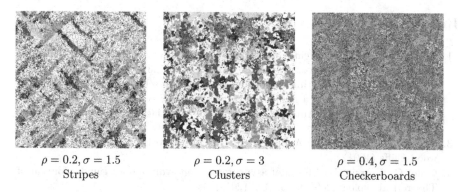

| $\rho = 0.2, \sigma = 1.5$ | $\rho = 0.2, \sigma = 3$ | $\rho = 0.4, \sigma = 1.5$ |
| Stripes | Clusters | Checkerboards |

Fig. 8. (colour online) Flux visualisation of large-scale configurations for non-biased simulations, with equal space and time dimensions ($t = 500, L = 500$)

5   Conclusions and Perspectives

In spite of the model following a stochastic updating rule controlled by the sole parameter σ, and behaviours being derived from random initial configuration determined only by their density ρ, a surprisingly high number of distinctive patterns could be identified. By simulating the model for conditions that were not planned in its original design, we discovered that the organised phase could result in unexpected behaviours that exhibit the limits of the model.

Identification of Novel Patterns. For instance, the stability of the checkerboard is an important result of this study: although particles try to maximise their own alignment, the global alignment remains negative. Even, our exploration of its robustness via variations of the lattice supported the idea that the system adopts an anti-aligned phase. It is however undeniable that the checkerboard is intrinsically linked to the synchronous updating scheme of the model, as showed in a previous work [26], which questions its "realism" with regards to a biological context.

Revealing Resonance Bias. Our experiments echo back to an unresolved issue on the nature of the transitions in this model of swarming. The swarm instability, the transition between the disordered and the ordered phases, has been previously documented in numerous studies of lattice-gas models as "weakly first-order" by Csahók *et al.* [20] and second-order by Bussemaker *et al.* [21].

Our simulations suggest that the diagonal stripe pattern is heavily subject to resonance effects, induced by simulations of finite lattice with periodic boundaries, over long times. In other terms, it means that the limits of time t and space L are non-commutative, that is, fixing L and studying the behaviour for $t \to \infty$ is not equivalent to fixing t and studying the behaviour for $L \to \infty$. According to our observation, this implies that the phase transition may appear first-order in the case of a finite lattice, but would actually be of higher-order in an open infinite space.

References

1. Ermentrout, G.B., Edelstein-Keshet, L.: Cellular automata approaches to biological modeling. Journal of Theoretical Biology 160(1), 97–133 (1993)
2. Chevrier, V., Fatès, N.: How important are updating schemes in multi-agent systems? an illustration on a multi-turmite model. In: Proceedings of the 9th International Conference on Autonomous Agents and Multiagent Systems, pp. 533–540 (2010)
3. Slotine, J., Li, W., et al.: Applied nonlinear control, vol. 66. Prentice hall, Englewood Cliffs (1991)
4. Grilo, C., Correia, L.: Effects of asynchronism on evolutionary games. Journal of Theoretical Biology 269(1), 109–122 (2011)
5. Bouré, O., Fatès, N., Chevrier, V.: Probing robustness of cellular automata through variations of asynchronous updating. Natural Computing 11(4), 553–564 (2012)

6. Vicsek, T., Zafeiris, A.: Collective motion. Physics Reports 517(3-4), 71–140 (2012)
7. Deutsch, A., Theraulaz, G., Vicsek, T.: Collective motion in biological systems. Interface Focus 2, 689–692 (2012)
8. Peruani, F., Ginelli, F., Bär, M., Chaté, H.: Polar vs. apolar alignment in systems of polar self-propelled particles. Journal of Physics: Conference Series 297(1), 012014 (2011)
9. Deutsch, A.: Orientation-induced pattern formation: Swarm dynamics in a lattice-gas automaton model. International Journal of Bifurcation and Chaos 6(9), 1735–1752 (1996)
10. Whitelam, S., Feng, E.H., Hagan, M.F., Geissler, P.L.: The role of collective motion in examples of coarsening and self-assembly. Soft Matter 5, 1251–1262 (2009)
11. Chopard, B., Ouared, R., Deutsch, A., Hatzikirou, H., Wolf-Gladrow, D.: Lattice-gas cellular automaton models for biology: From fluids to cells. Acta Biotheoretica 58, 329–340 (2010)
12. Hatzikirou, H., Brusch, L., Schaller, C., Simon, M., Deutsch, A.: Prediction of traveling front behavior in a lattice-gas cellular automaton model for tumor invasion. Computers Mathematics with Applications 59(7), 2326–2339 (2010)
13. Helbing, D., Isobe, M., Nagatani, T., Takimoto, K.: Lattice gas simulation of experimentally studied evacuation dynamics. Physical Review E 67, 067101 (2003)
14. Lerner, A., Chrysanthou, Y., Lischinski, D.: Crowds by example. Computer Graphics Forum 26(3), 655–664 (2007)
15. Kennedy, J., Eberhart, R.C.: A discrete binary version of the particle swarm algorithm. Systems, Man, and Cybernetics 5, 4104–4108 (1997)
16. Leung, H., Kothari, R., Minai, A.A.: Phase transition in a swarm algorithm for self-organized construction. Physical Review E 68(4), 046111 (2003)
17. Vicsek, T., Czirók, A., Ben-Jacob, E., Cohen, I., Sochet, O.: Novel type of phase transition in a system of self-driven particles. Physical Review Letters 75, 1226 (1995)
18. Deutsch, A.: Orientation-induced pattern formation: swarm dynamics in a lattice-gas automaton model. International Journal of Bifurcation and Chaos 6, 1735–1752 (1996)
19. Deutsch, A., Dormann, S.: Cellular Automaton Modeling of Biological Pattern Formation. Birkhauser Boston (2005)
20. Csahók, Z., Vicsek, T.: Lattice-gas model for collective biological motion. Physical Review E 52, 5297–5303 (1998)
21. Bussemaker, H.J., Deutsch, A., Geigant, E.: Mean-field analysis of a dynamical phase transition in a cellular automaton model for collective motion. Physical Review Letters 78(26), 5018–5021 (1997)
22. Peruani, F., Klauss, T., Deutsch, A., Voss-Boehme, A.: Traffic jams, gliders, and bands in the quest for collective motion of self-propelled particles. Physical Review Letters 106, 128101 (2011)
23. Manzo, F., Olivieri, E., Nardi, F., Scoppola, E.: On the essential features of metastability: Tunnelling time and critical configurations. Journal of Statistical Physics 115, 591–642 (2004)
24. Cirillo, E., Nardi, F., Spitoni, C.: Metastability for reversible probabilistic cellular automata with self-interaction. Journal of Statistical Physics 132, 431–471 (2008)
25. Bouré, O., Fatès, N., Chevrier, V.: A robustness approach to study metastable behaviours in a lattice-gas model of swarming, Tech. rep., LORIA – Inria Nancy Grand-Est – Université de Lorraine (2013)
26. Bouré, O., Fatès, N., Chevrier, V.: First steps on asynchronous lattice-gas models with an application to a swarming rule. Natural Computing (to appear)

Leakage Squeezing Using Cellular Automata

Sandip Karmakar and Dipanwita Roy Chowdhury

Indian Institute of Technology, Kharagpur, WB, India

Abstract. Leakage squeezing is a novel approach towards resisting side channel attacks against cryptographic implementations. It is seen that certain codes are ideal for leakage squeezing applications. However, in this paper we argue that few other cryptographic properties are essential for better squeezing. In this respect we analyze few Cellular Automata (CA) configurations towards suitability in leakage squeezing. It is argued that nonlinear cellular automata with respective cryptographic and code properties are ideal for applications in this scenario.

Keywords: Leakage Squeezing, Cellular Automata, Nonlinear Cellular Automata, Hybrid Nonlinear Cellular Automata.

1 Introduction

Cellular Automata are self-evolving systems of cells each of which updates itself per cycle following a rule embedded into it. Cellular Automata (CA) is known for its ability to generate pseudorandom sequences needed for various applications like VLSI testing and coding theory, [10]. Several researchers have attempted to apply the pseudorandomness of CA to cryptography. In this paper we describe a usage of CA in connection with both coding theory and cryptography.

Side channel attacks present great threat to cryptographic implementations. It is seen in literature that most of the standard cryptographic algorithms in block cipher, stream cipher, hash functions or other categories can be effectively analyzed using information about side channel leakage in practical time. Hence, it became necessary to protect sensitive information in cryptographic algorithms from side channel leakages. In this direction, a novel approach was introduced in [6], which does not store any sensitive algorithmic information in hardware registers for hardware implementations. The sensitive information is computed on the execution-time and again "masked" before storing. A detailed description of the scheme is given in the following section. This scheme is called leakage squeezing.

A formal analysis of the leakage squeezing schemes show that linear codes fit in correctly in the design. In this respect CA are directly applicable to such designs as a vast literature is available on design of linear codes using CA ([9]). However, in this paper, we argue that certain other cryptographic properties are mandatory for use in leakage squeezing scheme. We then analyze certain nonlinear hybrid CA configurations for matching in requirements of these applications. It is seen that we can get suitable CA for applications in leakage squeezing among the analyzed CA.

J. Kari, M. Kutrib, and A. Malcher (Eds.): AUTOMATA 2013, LNCS 8155, pp. 98–109, 2013.

This paper is organized as follows. Following introduction, we describe basic definitions related to CA and cryptographic properties in section 2. We describe the method of leakage squeezing in this section also. The technique and analysis of requirements of CA in leakage squeezing is described in section 3. Finally section 4 concludes the paper.

2 Preliminaries

Before describing the usage of Cellular Automata (CA) in leakage squeezing, in this section, we briefly discuss basics of CA, basic definitions of cryptographic properties and the concept of leakage squeezing. Detailed discussion of CA can be found in [9], while a detailed introduction of leakage squeezing and its analysis on first and second order can be found in [6] and [1] respectively.

2.1 Cellular Automata

In this subsection, we present the basic terminology of CA.

Definition 1. *Cellular Automata: A cellular automaton is a finite array of cells. Each cell is a finite state machine $C = (Q, f_c)$ where Q is a finite set of states and f a mapping $f_c : Q^n \to Q$. The mapping f_c, called local transition function. n is the number of cells the local transition function depends on. On each iteration of the CA each cell of the CA updates itself with respective f_c. Dimension of the cell array is called the dimension of the CA. Adjacent cells of a cell are called the neighbourhood of the CA.*

The number of neighbouring cells f_c depends on, may be same or different on different directions of the automaton. f_c may be same or different for cells across the automaton. The array of cells may be multi-dimensional. Hence, a huge number of CA configurations are possible. In this paper, we model rules as Boolean functions, so that, $Q = \{0, 1\}$. Each cell of the system is initialized with a Boolean value. Collectively, over the automaton it is referred to as the *seed*. In this paper, we have considered 1-dimensional CA only.

A 1-dimensional CA, each of whose rule depends on left and right neighbour and the cell itself is called a 3-neighbourhood CA. Similarly, if each cell depends on 2 left and 2 right neighbours and itself only, it is called 5- neighbourhood CA. A CA whose cells depend on 1 left and 2 right neighbouring cells is called a 4-neighbourhood right skew CA. A left skewed 4- neighbourhood CA can be defined similarly.

Definition 2. *Rule:The local transition function for a 3-neighbourhood CA cell can be expressed as follows:*
$q_i(t + 1) = f_c[q_i(t), q_{i+1}(t), q_{i-1}(t)]$
where f_c denotes the local transition function realized with a combinational logic, and is known as a rule of CA cell [9]. The decimal value of the truth table of the local transition function is defined as the rule number of the CA.

For example, for 1-dimensional 3-neighbourhood CA, Rule 30: $f_i = q_{i-1}(t) \oplus (q_{i+1}(t) + q_i(t))$, where $+$ is the Boolean or operator and $\oplus$ is the Boolean xor operator. This rule is extensively studied for application to cryptography [3].
Rule 60: $f_i = q_{i-1}(t) \oplus q_i(t)$.
Rule 90: $f_i = q_{i-1}(t) \oplus q_{i+1}(t)$.

Definition 3. *Uniform and Hybrid Cellular Automaton: A CA whose local transition function is same for all the cells is called uniform cellular automaton else it is called a hybrid cellular automaton.*

Definition 4. *Linear and Nonlinear Cellular Automaton: A CA whose local transition function in algebraic normal form (ANF) does not involve the (Boolean and) operator in any of the cell is called the linear cellular automaton. Otherwise, it is called a nonlinear CA. For example, rule, $f_i = q_{i-1}(t) \oplus q_{i+1}(t)$ employed in each cell is a linear cellular automaton, while rule, $f_i = q_{i-1}(t).q_{i+1}(t)$ employed in each cell is a nonlinear cellular automaton, where, $q_{i-1}(t)$ and $q_{i+1}(t)$ denotes left and right neighbours of the i-th cell at t-th instance of time.*

Any CA can be utilized to generate pseudorandom sequences of different degree of security by first selecting a seed and then updating each cell according to the transition functions. State values from the middle cell of the cell array may be taken output to represent generation of pseudorandom sequences.

2.2   Cryptographic Terms and Primitives

We now provide definitions involving cryptographic primitives. We will concentrate only on *boolean functions*.

Affine Function: A boolean function which involves its input variables in linear combinations (i.e., combinations involving $\oplus$) only, is called an *affine function*. For example, $f(x_1, x_2) = x_1 \oplus x_2$ is an *affine function*, while the function, $f(x_1, x_2) = x_1 \oplus x_2 \oplus x_1.x_2$ is not an *affine function*, where . is the boolean "and" operation.

Hamming Weight: Number of boolean 1's in a boolean function's truth table is called the hamming weight of the function. For example, hamming weight of $f(x_1, x_2) = x_1 \oplus x_2$ is, 2 and hamming weight of $f(x_1, x_2) = x_1.x_2$ is 1.

Balanced Boolean Function: If the hamming weight of a boolean function of n variables is 2^{n-1}, it is called a balanced boolean function. Thus, $f(x_1, x_2) = x_1 \oplus x_2$ is balanced, while $f(x_1, x_2) = x_1.x_2$ is not balanced.

Hamming Distance: Hamming weight of $f_1 \oplus f_2$ is called the hamming distance between f_1 and f_2. Thus, hamming distance between $f_1(x_1, x_2) = x_1 \oplus x_2$ and $f_2(x_1, x_2) = x_1.x_2$ is 1.

Nonlinearity: The minimum of the hamming distances between a function, f and all affine functions involving its input variables is nonlinearity of the function. Hence, nonlinearity of $f(x_1, x_2) = x_1.x_2$ is 1.

Resiliency: A boolean function of n variables is called to have a resiliency t, if for all possible subsets of variables of size less than or equal to t, on fixing values of those variables in each of the set, the resultant boolean function still remains balanced. For example, resiliency of $f(x_1, x_2) = x_1 \oplus x_2$ is 1, but resiliency of $f(x_1, x_2) = x_1.x_2$ is 0.

Algebraic Degree: The highest degree of a boolean function is called the *algebraic degree* of the boolean function. Thus, *algebraic degree* of $f(x_1, x_2) = x_1 \oplus x_2 \oplus x_1.x_2$ is 2.

2.3 d-Monomial Test

d-Monomial test is a statistical test for pseudorandomness proposed independently in [2] and [4]. It investigates boolean function representation of each output bit in terms of input bits. If boolean function is pseudorandom sequence generator, the it will have a d-degree monomials $\frac{1}{2}\binom{n}{d}$ many. A deviation will indicate non-randomness. For example, consider the function $f(x_1, x_2) = x_1 \oplus x_2$, it has 2 1-degree monomials and 0 2 degree monomial. It turns out that it has 2, 2-degree monomials less, hence it is very much non-pseudorandom. On the other hand $f(x_1, x_2) = x_1 \oplus x_1.x_2 \oplus \neg x_1.\neg x_2$ passes the test and is a good pseudorandom generator.

In spite of its simplicity, this test gained huge appriciation in cryptographic community. It proved to be a good tool in analyzing the degree of pseudorandomness of cryptographic systems. To the best of our knowledge, d-monomial test has not been applied to CA configurations previously. We explore different CA configurations under this test.

2.4 Leakage Squeezing

Leakage squeezing was introduced in [6] towards the aim of protecting cryptographic designs from unintentional leakages. The idea is not to store sensitive cryptographic data in registers, thus disabling direct access of sensitive data using side channel leakages. Instead of storing a single sensitive cryptographic information, two or more protected shares are stored. The sensitive data is masked using one or more masks, while bijections of masks are also stored. The design with single mask is studied in [6] and that with two masks for second-order leakage squeezing is studied in [1]. Certainly, consulting the papers ([6] and [1]) it becomes evident that higher order leakage squeezing can also be attempted, however, the hardware overhead and throughput need to be justified. Here, we briefly discuss the concept of leakage squeezing. We also produce the conditions on bijections derived in [6] and [1].

Leakage Squeezing of Order One [6]. Let, X be a shared variable. Instead of storing X in a register, we store two variables in registers. The design includes a masking generator. The masking generator generates an ideal pseudo-random mask M at every cycle of operation. The design also includes a bijection F : $\{0, 1\}^n \rightarrow \{0, 1\}^n$, where n is the bit-length of X and M. The actual shares stored in the design are, $S_1 = X \oplus M$ and $S_2 = F(M)$. Thus the sensitive variable X may be obtained as,

$$X = S_1 \oplus F^{-1}(S_2)$$
$$= X \oplus M \oplus M.$$

The invariant of each iteration of the cryptographic algorithm is, $X = S_1 \oplus F^{-1}(S_2)$. Thus during the following cycle a new mask is generated, M' (this process is called mask-refresh), the bijection F is applied and the new sensitive value X' is protected. It may be mentioned that F is known in public. Thus the strength of the scheme depends on pseudo-random mask M. The scheme is depicted in figure 1.

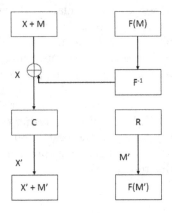

Fig. 1. Leakage Squeezing of Order One

Leakage squeezing of order one is studied in [6]. It is assumed that the architecture leaks in Hamming Weight model. It was derived in this paper that the condition for d^{th} order leakage squeezing is achieved when F is a $(2n, n, d+1)$ code.

Leakage Squeezing of Order Two [1]. Leakage squeezing of order two is studied in [1]. The scheme is as follows:

- Let, X be the sensitive variable.
- Let, F_1 and F_2 be two bijections from n bit strings to n bit strings.
- Let, M_1 and M_2 be two pseudo-random masks.

Then, use three shares in three registers, $S_1 = X \oplus M_1 \oplus M_2$, $S_2 = F_1(M_1)$ and $S_3 = F_2(M_2)$. The sensitive value X may thus be obtained from,

$$X = S_1 \oplus F_1^{-1}(S_2) \oplus F_2^{-1}(S_3)$$
$$= X \oplus M_1 \oplus M_2 \oplus M_1 \oplus M_2$$

Here, again it should be noted that F_1 and F_2 are known in public, thus, strength of the design depends on masking generators generating masks M_1 and M_2. Also, the invariant being $X = S_1 \oplus F_1^{-1}(S_2) \oplus F_2^{-1}(S_3)$, mask refreshes to generate M_1' and M_2' to store shares S_1', S_2' and S_3' to protect sensitive value X' in the following cycle and so on. The scheme is depicted in figure 2.

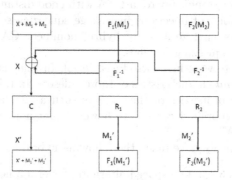

Fig. 2. Leakage Squeezing of Order Two

The paper, [1] has analyzed the requirements of bijections F_1 and F_2. The authors have again assumed leakage in Hamming Weight model. A number of conditions on F_1 and F_2 have been derived. For this paper, it suffices to state that if F_1 and F_2 are linear, d^{th} order leakage squeezing is achieved where d is the minimal distance of the code, $(x, F_1^{-1}(x), F_2^{-1}(x)); x \in GF_2^n$ (of rate $1/3$ and with three disjoint information sets) minus 1.

3   Leakage Squeezing Using Cellular Automata

It is seen that linear codes are ideal as bijective functions used in leakage squeezing schemes. Cellular Automata is studied extensively in coding theory [9]. There are algorithms for generating $(2n, n, d)$ codes using linear CA rules. Rules 90, 150, 102 are used extensively in generating $(2n, n, d)$ codes. These codes can provide leakage squeezing of order $d - 1$. Similarly, in case of order two leakage squeezing also as we have seen these codes are easily applicable as F_1 and F_2. However, being used in a cryptographic implementation linear codes present certain weaknesses.

Consider a linear bijection F. It follows that for some $n \times n$ matrix T, when M is of length n, $F(M) = T.M$. Note that T is publicly known and $F(M)$ is stored in a register. So, if leakage L is obtained from register containing $F(M)$, the information obtained about M is, $T^{-1}.L$, which in turn induces leakage information about sensitive variable X as, $T^{-1}.L \oplus S_1$. Therefore, it is evident that linear bijections or linear codes are not suitable for design of leakage squeezing schemes.

Analyzing the weaknesses of linear bijections as described above it follows that the bijections should not be easily invertible. In other words, nonlinearity is required for the bijections. In addition argumentively in a similar pattern it will follow that the bijections used in leakage squeezing need to be cryptographically robust. If $F(M)$ is unbalanced or less resilient the leakage through $F(M)$ is higher and therefore getting information about the sensitive value X.

In summary, cryptographically robust CA with good distance properties need to be studied for choice of bijections in leakage squeezing schemes. In the following subsection we analyze a set of hybrid nonlinear CA for candidacy as bijections of leakage squeezing schemes.

The rules used here were first introduced in [5]. In that paper, authors analyze the $d - monomial$ characteristics of those rulesets. In this paper, we study other cryptographic properties of the rulesets such as nonlinearity, resiliency, balancedness and algebraic degree. Note however that none of the rulesets are maximum length CA.

For the experiment we have taken the following hybrid CA rulesets:

1. *Ruleset 1*: Rules 30 and 60 spaced alternately over a 3-neighbourhood CA.
2. *Ruleset 2*: Rules 30, 60 and 90 spaced alternately over a 3-neighbourhood CA.
3. *Ruleset 3*: Rules 30, 60, 90 and 120 spaced alternatively over a 3-neighbourhood CA.
4. *Ruleset 4*: Rules 30, 60, 90, 120 and 150 spaced alternatively over a 3-neighbourhood CA.
5. *Ruleset 5*: Rules 30, 60, 90, 120, 150, 180, 210, 240 spaced alternatively over a 3-neighbourhood CA.
6. *Ruleset 6*: Rules 30, 60, 90, 120, 150, 180, 210, 240, 15, 45 spaced alternatively over a 3-neighbourhood CA.

The Boolean expressions of the used rules are tabulated in table 1.

3.1   Functional Model of CA for Testing Crypto-properties

For the experiment, we have taken an $(n + 1)$-cell *null-boundary* CA(*figure 3*). Here, without loss of generality, n is assumed to be odd. Each cell of the CA is assumed to have an unknown value, $x_i, 0 \le i \le n$ at the beginning. Boolean rules are set into the CA cells according to the CA configuration needed. Thus, each cell's output is determined by a corresponding local transition function f_i. Collectively, the functions are represented as F. The output bits of the CA are denoted by, $y_0, y_1, \ldots y_n$. The middle cell's output ($y_{\frac{n+1}{2}}$) is analyzed. Here, $f_{\frac{n+1}{2}}$ is the local transition function of the $\frac{n+1}{2}^{th}$ cell and $f_{\frac{n+1}{2}}^t$ is defined recursively as follows:

$$f_{\frac{n+1}{2}}^{t+1} = f_{\frac{n+1}{2}}(f_{\frac{n+1}{2}}^t)$$

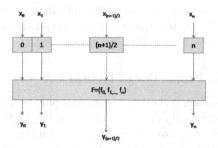

Fig. 3. Configurations of CA experimented

For that, we express the $\frac{n+1}{2}^{th}$ cell's output as a function of initial input unknowns, $x_i, 0 \le i \le n$. For a 3-neighbourhood CA.

$$y_{\frac{n+1}{2}} = f_{\frac{n+1}{2}}\left(x_{\frac{n+1}{2}-1}, x_{\frac{n+1}{2}}, x_{\frac{n+1}{2}+1}\right)$$

This process is iterated for multiple clock cycles, for the hybrid CA,

$$y^t_{\frac{n+1}{2}} = f^t_{\frac{n+1}{2}}\left(x_{\frac{n+1}{2}-t}, \ldots, x_{\frac{n+1}{2}}, \ldots, x_{\frac{n+1}{2}+t}\right)$$
$$y^t_{\frac{n+1}{2}} = f^t_{\frac{n+1}{2}}\left(x_{\frac{n+1}{2}-t}, \ldots, x_{\frac{n+1}{2}}, \ldots, x_{\frac{n+1}{2}+2t}\right)$$

Thus, it is clear that at t^{th} iteration, for a 3-neighbourhood CA, the output bit is a function of $2t+1$ bits. Beyond 3rd iteration, the Boolean function acts upon 10 or more variables and hence becomes unwieldy to analyze. In this paper, we have listed results of first 3 iterations only. We have chosen the $\frac{n+1}{2}^{th}$ cell for our analysis because it will be least affected by the boundary null values and more affected by the neighbouring cells and thus better charaterize the rule of the CA. However, in case of hybrid configurations, we have analyzed output of all nonuniform middle cells and have selected the best rule as the output.

Table 1. ANF of used 3-neighbourhood Rules

Type	Rule #	Nbd	ANF
	15	3	$\bar{x_1}$
	60	3	$x_1 \oplus x_2$
Linear	90	3	$x_1 \oplus x_3$
	150	3	$x_1 \oplus x_2 \oplus x_3$
	240	3	x_1
	30	3	$(x_2.x_3) \oplus x_1 \oplus x_2 \oplus x_3$
	45	3	$x_1 \oplus x_3 \oplus (x_2.x_3) \oplus 1$
	120	3	$x_1 \oplus (x_2.x_3)$
Non-linear	180	3	$x_1 \oplus x_2 \oplus (x_2.x_3)$
	210	3	$x_1 \oplus x_3 \oplus (x_2.x_3)$

Historically, researchers have studied balancedness, nonlinearity, resiliency and algebraic degree [7], [8] to explore CA as a crypto-primitive. Our emphasis is on a new cryptographic test called d-monomial test.

3.2   Cryptographic Properties of Hybrid CA

In this subsection we discuss the basic cryptographic properties of the rulesets mentioned above. The experiment is conducted using Mathematica 8 following the model described in the above subsection. It is seen that beyond 3-rd iteration these tests become practically impossible. So, we state results of first 3 iterations of the rulesets only. The values tabulated refers to the maximum obtainable among all bits of the output.

Balancedness of Hybrid CA. Balancedness is an important property of a primitive from cryptographic viewpoint. It demonstrates that no information can be obtained from the output bits in terms of bias of 0s and 1s. In table 2, we show the values of balancedness of different rulesets. Hence, even though rule 30

Table 2. Balancedness of the Rulesets

	Nonlinearity		
	Iterations		
Rules	1	2	3
Ruleset 1	Y	Y	Y
Ruleset 2	Y	Y	Y
Ruleset 3	Y	Y	Y
Ruleset 4	Y	Y	Y
Ruleset 5	Y	Y	Y
Ruleset 6	Y	Y	Y

uniform CA is not balanced for all three iterations, when it is alternated with rule 60, 90 cells it becomes balanced. Hence in respect of generating balanced functions with nonlinear rules we could use proper linear rules in alternate.

Nonlinearity of Hybrid CA. Nonlinearity of a crypto-primitive is also an important property. It measures the minimum distance of the output from linear functions. Since, a linear function is not cryptographically suitable, a highly nonlinear function implies stronger resistance against cryptographic analysis. In table 3, we show the results on the values of nonlinearity of the rulesets. Note that it is not possible to get nonlinearity more than 48 in this series of construction.

Resiliency of Hybrid CA. Resiliency measures a form of stronger balancedness of a crypto-primitive. It indicates the bias in change of output bits when input bits are changed. The results of resiliency of the rulesets is tabulated in 4. From the above observations we see that ruleset 5 provides best resiliency.

Table 3. Nonlinearity of the Rulesets

		Nonlinearity	
		Iterations	
Rules	1	2	3
Ruleset 1	2	8	32
Ruleset 2	2	8	48
Ruleset 3	2	8	48
Ruleset 4	2	8	48
Ruleset 5	2	8	32
Ruleset 6	2	2	48

Table 4. Resiliency of the Rulesets

		Resiliency	
		Iterations	
Rules	1	2	3
Ruleset 1	1	0	0
Ruleset 2	2	2	1
Ruleset 3	2	2	1
Ruleset 4	2	2	1
Ruleset 5	2	2	2
Ruleset 6	2	2	1

Algebraic Degree of Hybrid CA. Algebraic degree provides a crypto-primitive with algebraic strength against mathematical attacks such as Grobner basis, cube attack etc. In table 5, we gather the maximum algebraic degrees of the rulesets for the first three iterations.

Table 5. Algebraic Degrees of the Rulesets

		Algebraic Degree	
		Iterations	
Rules	1	2	3
Ruleset 1	2	2	3
Ruleset 2	2	2	3
Ruleset 3	2	3	3
Ruleset 4	2	3	4
Ruleset 5	2	3	4
Ruleset 6	2	3	4

***d*-Monomial Test of Hybrid CA [5].** *d*-monomial test results of the 6 hybrid CA are reproduced here from [5] in table 6.

Table 6. d-monomial Test of the Rulesets

Rules	Number of n-th degree terms			
	1	2	3	4
Ruleset 1	3,3,5	1,3,3	0,0,2	0,0,0
Ruleset 2	3,3,2	1,3,3	0,0,1	0,0,0
Ruleset 3	3,2,4	1,3,5	0,1,3	0,0,0
Ruleset 4	3,2,4	1,3,7	0,1,7	0,0,2
Ruleset 5	3,2,4	1,3,5	0,2,6	0,0,3
Ruleset 6	3,2,4	1,3,5	0,2,6	0,0,3

The table above shows that, rules 30, 60, ..., 240 and rules 30, 60, ..., 45 are better rules than all other combinations.

Distance. The rulesets are also tested for distance with input X and output Y where $|X| = |Y|$. We have randomly tested the rulesets for up to 3 iterations, with random length bit strings. It is seen that all the rulesets show an average distance of 2 over all the iterations. Thus leakage squeezing of order 1 are guaranteed for all six rulesets.

Considering other cryptographic properties, 3 iterations of the rulsets provides both cryptographic strength and shows order 1 leakage squeezing. The results show that any one among the six rulesets can be employed as squeezer. However, rulesets 5 or 6 are the best choice for the leakage squeezing applications.

4   Conclusion

In this paper, we have discussed the technique of leakage squeezing of orders 1 and 2. It is explained that although linear codes provide the required properties of leakage squeezing, they are weak with respect to cryptographic properties. We have explained that basic cryptographic properties are necessary for leakage squeezing applications. We have analyzed cryptographic properties of few hybrid nonlinear CA introduced in [5]. The distance of the rulesets is also explored. It is seen that the rulesets show average distance of 2, thus, guarantees order 1 leakage squeezing. It is seen that ruleset 5 and 6 are robust choices for first order leakage squeezing.

Acknowledgement. This work is partly supported by Microsoft India Research PhD Fellowship.

References

1. Carlet, C., Danger, J.-L., Guilley, S., Maghrebi, H.: Leakage squeezing of order two. Cryptology ePrint Archive, Report 2012/567 (2012), http://eprint.iacr.org/
2. Filiol, E.: A new statistical testing for symmetric ciphers and hash functions. In: Deng, R.H., Qing, S., Bao, F., Zhou, J. (eds.) ICICS 2002. LNCS, vol. 2513, pp. 342–353. Springer, Heidelberg (2002)
3. Gutowitz, H.: Cellular automata: Theory and experiment (1991)
4. Saarinen, M.J.O.: Chosen-iv statistical attacks on e-stream stream ciphers. eSTREAM, ECRYPT Stream Cipher Project, Report 2006/013, pp. 5–19 (2006)
5. Karmakar, S., Mukhopadhyay, D., Roy Chowdhury, D.: d-monomial Tests on Cellular Automata for Cryptographic Design. In: Bandini, S., Manzoni, S., Umeo, H., Vizzari, G. (eds.) ACRI 2010. LNCS, vol. 6350, pp. 261–270. Springer, Heidelberg (2010)
6. Maghrebi, H., Guilley, S., Danger, J.-L.: Leakage squeezing countermeasure against high-order attacks. In: Ardagna, C.A., Zhou, J. (eds.) WISTP 2011. LNCS, vol. 6633, pp. 208–223. Springer, Heidelberg (2011)
7. Martin, B., Sole, P.: Pseudo-random sequences generated by cellular automata. In: International Conference on Relations, Orders and Graphs: Interactions with Computer Science (2008)
8. Martin, B., Sole, P., Lacharme, P.: Pseudo-random sequences, boolean functions and cellular automata. Boolean Functions: Cryptography and Applications (2007)
9. Roy Chowdhury, D., Nandi, S., Chattopadhyay, S., Pal Chaudhuri, P.: Additive cellular automata - theory and applications (1997)
10. Wolfram, S.: Random sequence generation by cellular automata. In: Advances in Applied Mathematics, vol. 7, pp. 123–169 (1986)

1-Resiliency of Bipermutive Cellular Automata Rules

Alberto Leporati and Luca Mariot

Dipartimento di Informatica, Sistemistica e Comunicazione,
Università degli Studi Milano - Bicocca,
Viale Sarca 336/14, 20124 Milano, Italy
alberto.leporati@unimib.it, l.mariot@campus.unimib.it

Abstract. It is known that CA rules which are both leftmost and rightmost permutive (bipermutive rules) are expansively and mixing chaotic. In this paper, we prove that bipermutive rules also satisfy the condition of 1-resiliency (that is, balancedness and first order correlation-immunity), which is an important property used in the design of pseudorandom number generators for cryptographic purposes. We thus derive an enumerative encoding for bipermutive rules based on a graph representation, and we use it to generate all the 256 bipermutive rules of radius 2. Among these rules we select the ones which satisfy additional cryptographic properties: high nonlinearity and 2-resiliency. Finally, we assess the quality of the pseudorandom sequences generated by these remaining rules with the ENT and NIST statistical test suites, taking the elementary rule 30 as a benchmark.

Keywords: Cellular automata, boolean functions, pseudorandom number generators, stream ciphers, deterministic chaos, permutivity, resiliency, nonlinearity, Walsh transform, ENT test suite, NIST test suite.

1 Introduction

Cellular automata (CA) have widely been used in the past to define pseudorandom number generators (PRNG) for the design of stream ciphers. Starting with Wolfram [13], particular interest has been devoted to the study of CA rules of radius 1. Wolfram proposed to use a CA equipped with rule 30 and to sample the trace of its central cell as a pseudorandom sequence. Unfortunately, even if rule 30 is nonlinear and balanced, and even if it is chaotic with respect to Devaney's definition of topological chaos [4], it does not satisfy the property of *first order correlation-immunity*, introduced by Siegenthaler in [8]. More generally, Martin has pointed out in [6] that all nonlinear and balanced rules of radius 1 are not first order correlation-immune. As a consequence, a CA-based PRNG using these rules may pass classic statistical randomness tests, but it is susceptible to correlation attacks.

Cattaneo, Finelli and Margara showed in [2] that *bipermutive* rules (that is, rules which are both leftmost and rightmost permutive) are expansively chaotic, while in [3] it has been proved that rules which are either leftmost or rightmost permutive are mixing chaotic. Thus, bipermutive rules satisfy stronger definitions of topological chaos than the one given by Devaney.

J. Kari, M. Kutrib, and A. Malcher (Eds.): AUTOMATA 2013, LNCS 8155, pp. 110–123, 2013.

The aim of this paper is to study the class of bipermutive rules with respect to the cryptographic property of *resiliency*, which includes balancedness and correlation-immunity. In particular, we prove that bipermutive rules are 1-resilient, and we derive a graph-based encoding to enumerate all bipermutive rules of a given radius r. We then apply this encoding to generate all 256 bipermutive rules of radius 2, and compute their Walsh transforms to select only those which are nonlinear and 2-resilient (which is, by Tarannikov's bound [10], the best possible trade-off between these two properties in the case of boolean functions of 5 variables). We successively filter out the rules which do not generate sequences of 2^{16} bits that pass the statistical tests from the ENT suite, using rule 30 as a benchmark. Finally, we apply the more stringent NIST test suite to longer sequences (10^6 bits) produced by the remaining rules, observing that three of them pass all the tests, like rule 30.

The rest of this paper is organized as follows. Section 2 recalls basic definitions and theoretical results about cellular automata and the properties of nonlinearity and m-resilience a CA rule should satisfy for cryptographic applications. Section 3, after a brief introduction to topological chaos in CAs and permutive rules, reports the main theoretical contribution of the paper, namely the proof that bipermutive rules are also 1-resilient. Section 4 describes an enumerative encoding for bipermutive rules based on a graph representation and the application of this encoding to the generation of bipermutive rules of radius 2, in order to recover only those which are nonlinear and 2-resilient. Section 5 reports the results of the statistical tests of the ENT and NIST suites applied to the pseudorandom sequences generated by the rules found in Section 4. Finally, Section 6 sums up the results presented throughout the paper, and points out some possible future developments and improvements on the subject.

2 Cellular Automata and Cryptographic Properties of Boolean Functions

2.1 Cellular Automata

Cellular automata are a particular type of discrete dynamical systems, characterised by a regular lattice of *cells*. At each discrete time step, all the cells synchronously update their states by applying a *local rule*. Formally, we give the following definition of *finite one-dimensional cellular automaton*, which is the typical model of CA used in cryptographic applications.

Definition 1. *A* finite one-dimensional cellular automaton *is a 4-tuple* $\langle n, A, r, f \rangle$ *where* $n \in \mathbb{N}$ *is the number of cells, A is the set of local states, $r \in \mathbb{N}$ is the radius and* $f : A^{2r+1} \to A$ *is the local rule.*

Thus, essentially, a finite one-dimensional CA is composed by an array of n cells. In what follows, we assume $A = \mathbb{F}_2$: the CA, in this case, is called *boolean*. For all $i \in \{1, ..., n\}$ and $t \in \mathbb{N}$, we denote with c_i^t the state of the i-th cell at time t, and the next state is computed as $c_i^{t+1} = f(c_{i-r}^t, ..., c_i^t, ..., c_{i+r}^t)$. The *configuration* of the CA at time t is the binary vector $c^t = (c_1^t, ..., c_n^t)$. To update the cells at the boundaries, two approaches are possible: *null boundary conditions*, where r cells with constant states are added before the first cell and after the last one, and *periodic boundary conditions*, in which the array can be viewed as a ring, so that the last cell precedes the first one. For all radii $r \in \mathbb{N}$, each of the $2^{2^{2r+1}}$ local rules can be indexed by its *Wolfram code*, introduced in [12], which is basically the decimal representation of the binary string that encodes the truth table of the rule.

Wolfram extensively studied the 256 *elementary* rules (that is, rules of radius $r = 1$), and in [13] he proposed to use a CA with rule 30 as a pseudorandom number generator for cryptographic purposes, since it exhibits a chaotic behaviour when observing the sequence of configurations $\{c^t\}_{t \in \mathbb{N}}$. The CA is initialised with a random configuration c^0 (the seed), and at each time step the state of the central cell is taken as a new pseudorandom bit. Wolfram analysed this PRNG by applying several statistical tests, which suggested it could generate good pseudorandom sequences.

2.2   Cryptographic Boolean Functions

Boolean functions are fundamental in cryptography, in the design of both stream ciphers and block ciphers. Here we summarise the essential definitions and properties of the theory of cryptographic boolean functions applied in the rest of the paper to the local rules of CA. An excellent reference for cryptographic boolean functions is [1].

A *boolean function* in m variables is a mapping $f : \mathbb{F}_2^m \to \mathbb{F}_2$, which in the following we will identify by the 2^m-bit string representing its truth table. Given ω and x vectors of $\mathbb{F}_2^m$, by $\omega \cdot x$ we denote the *scalar product* between ω and x, computed as $\omega \cdot x = \bigoplus_{i=1}^{m} \omega_i \cdot x_i$. The polar value of $f(x)$ is $\hat{f}(x) = (-1)^{f(x)}$. The *Hamming weight* of a vector $x \in \mathbb{F}_2^m$, denoted by $w_H(x)$, is the number of nonzero coordinates in x. A boolean function $f : \mathbb{F}_2^m \to \mathbb{F}_2$ is called *balanced* if $|f^{-1}(0)| = |f^{-1}(1)| = 2^{m-1}$. Unbalanced functions are generally not desirable in cryptographic applications, since they present a statistical bias which can be exploited for linear and differential cryptanalysis.

We now recall the definition of the *Walsh Transform*, an essential tool used to characterise cryptographic properties of boolean functions.

Definition 2. *The* Walsh Transform *of a boolean function* $f : \mathbb{F}_2^m \to \mathbb{F}_2$ *is a function* $\hat{F} : \mathbb{F}_2^m \to \mathbb{R}$ *defined as follows:* $\forall \omega \in \mathbb{F}_2^m$

$$\hat{F}(\omega) = \sum_{x \in \mathbb{F}_2^m} \hat{f}(x) \cdot (-1)^{\omega \cdot x} \ . \tag{1}$$

The value $\hat{F}(\omega)$ is also called the *Walsh coefficient* of f with respect to the vector ω. A naive algorithm to compute the Walsh Transform of a boolean function having a truth table of $n = 2^m$ bits requires $O(n^2)$ operations. There is, however, a *Fast Walsh Transform* (FWT) algorithm, described in [1], which requires only $O(n \log_2 n)$ operations.

We describe some properties of the Walsh Transform which will be used extensively to prove the theoretical results of this paper:

Property 1.   Denoting by 0 the null vector of $\mathbb{F}_2^m$, it follows that $\hat{F}(0) = \sum_{x \in \mathbb{F}_2^m} \hat{f}(x)$.

Property 2.   From Property 1, it is obvious that a function f is balanced if and only if $\hat{F}(0) = 0$.

Property 3. If $w_H(\omega) = 1$, then $\hat{F}(\omega) = \sum_{x \in \mathbb{F}_2^m} \hat{f}(x) \cdot (-1)^{x_i}$, where i is the index of the nonzero coordinate of ω. Thus in this case the sign of the generic term in (1) is uniquely determined by the value of x_i.

Given a boolean function f, the maximum absolute value of its Walsh coefficients, $W_{\max}(f)$, is called the *spectral radius* of f. The spectral radius is useful to characterise the *nonlinearity* of a boolean function, which is formally defined as the Hamming distance from the set of affine functions: in [1] it is shown that given a boolean function $f : \mathbb{F}_2^m \to \mathbb{F}_2$ its nonlinearity is $Nl(f) = 2^{-1}(2^m - W_{\max}(f))$. In the design of stream or block ciphers, the nonlinearity of the boolean functions selected should be as high as possible, since it provides better confusion.

A second important property for cryptographic boolean functions is correlation-immunity, introduced by Siegenthaler in [8]. A boolean function f is said to be *k-th order correlation-immune* if the restrictions of f obtained by fixing k input coordinates of f all have the same Hamming weight. If a function used in a stream cipher does not satisfy this property, it is possible to apply a divide-and-conquer *correlation attack* described in [9] using k Linear Feedback Shift Registers, in order to recover the plaintext. A function which is both balanced and k-th order correlation-immune is called *k-resilient*. Xiao and Massey proved in [14] a necessary and sufficient condition for a boolean function to be k-th order correlation-immune, using its Walsh Transform.

Theorem 1. *A boolean function $f : \mathbb{F}_2^m \to \mathbb{F}_2$ is k-th order correlation-immune if and only if, $\forall \omega \in \mathbb{F}_2^m$ such that $1 \le w_H(\omega) \le k$, $\hat{F}(\omega) = 0$.*

Hence, in order to verify whether a given boolean function is k-resilient, by Property 2 and Theorem 1 it suffices to check that its Walsh Transform vanishes for all the input vectors having Hamming weight less than or equal to k, including the null vector.

The three properties of balancedness, nonlinearity and k-th order correlation-immunity induce a trade-off; in particular, Tarannikov [10] showed an upper bound on the maximum nonlinearity obtainable in k-resilient functions (with $k \le m - 2$), which is $2^{m-1} - 2^{k+1}$.

2.3 Correlation-Immunity of Elementary CA Rules

The local rule of a CA can be viewed as a boolean function (with an odd number of variables, since it is always defined on $2r + 1$ cells, where r is the radius), so it is possible to verify if it is suitable to design a CA-based PRNG by checking its balancedness, nonlinearity and correlation-immunity. Returning to Wolfram's PRNG, it turns out that rule 30 is both balanced and nonlinear (with $Nl(f_{30}) = 2$), but it is not first order correlation-immune. More generally, Martin has shown in [6] by an exhaustive search that, among the 256 elementary rules, only 8 *linear* rules are 1-resilient. This fact can also be interpreted as a corollary of Tarannikov's bound: if $r = 1$ then the local rule is defined over $m = 3$ variables, and the maximum nonlinearity for 1-resilient functions is $2^{3-1} - 2^{1+1} = 0$. The consequence is that elementary CA rules are not adequate for building a cryptographic PRNG or a stream cipher, so it is necessary to explore the spaces of rules having higher radii.

3 Bipermutive CA Rules

3.1 Symbolic Dynamics and Topological Chaos in Cellular Automata

The dynamics of one-dimensional CAs is generally studied on the space of *bi-infinite sequences* $A^{\mathbb{Z}} = \{c : \mathbb{Z} \to A\}$, since every finite CA is trivially periodic. In this case, a configuration c is a function which assigns to each integer number a symbol from the alphabet A. The set $A^{\mathbb{Z}}$ is usually endowed with the *Tychonoff distance*, which in the boolean case $A = \mathbb{F}_2$ is defined $\forall x, y \in A^{\mathbb{Z}}$ as

$$d(x,y) = \sum_{i=-\infty}^{+\infty} \frac{1}{2^{|i|}} |x(i) - y(i)| \ . \tag{2}$$

Under this distance, $A^{\mathbb{Z}}$ is a compact and perfect (i.e., without isolated points) metric space. Moreover, any global rule $F : A^{\mathbb{Z}} \to A^{\mathbb{Z}}$ induced by a CA local rule is a uniformly continuous function with respect to the Tychonoff distance. Thus a one-dimensional CA, now denoted by a triple $\langle A, r, f \rangle$, can be considered as a discrete time dynamical system (DTDS) $\langle X, F \rangle$, where the phase space is $X = A^{\mathbb{Z}}$ and the update function is the *global rule* $F : A^{\mathbb{Z}} \to A^{\mathbb{Z}}$ which applies at each time step the local rule f to all the cells $i \in \mathbb{Z}$.

The notion of *deterministic chaos* has been formalized in several rigorous definitions in the literature of dynamical systems. The most popular among them is perhaps the definition given by Devaney in [4], which uses a topological approach.

Definition 3. *A DTDS $\langle X, F \rangle$ is* Devaney-chaotic *(D-chaotic) if it satisfies the following conditions:*

1. Topological transitivity: *for all nonempty open subsets $U, V \subset X$, $\exists t \in \mathbb{N}$ such that $F^t(U) \cap V \neq \emptyset$.*
2. Topological regularity: *The set $Per(F) = \{x \in X : \exists p \in \mathbb{N} : F^p(x) = x\}$ of temporally periodic points is dense in X.*
3. Sensitivity to initial conditions: *there exists an $\varepsilon > 0$ such that $\forall x \in X$, $\forall \delta > 0$, $\exists y \in X$ with $d(x, y) < \delta$ and $\exists t \in \mathbb{N}$ such that $d(F^t(x), F^t(y)) \geq \varepsilon$.*

Other definitions of chaos have been introduced by substituting stronger conditions to the three proposed by Devaney. In particular, the definition of *expansive chaos* (E-chaos) in a perfect DTDS $\langle X, F \rangle$ reported in [2] substitutes sensitivity to initial conditions by *positive expansivity*: there exists an $\varepsilon > 0$ such that, $\forall x, y \in X$, $x \neq y$, $\exists t \in \mathbb{N}$ such that $d(F^t(x), F^t(y)) \geq \varepsilon$. In *mixing chaos* (M-chaos) [3] topological transitivity is replaced by *topological mixing*: for all nonempty open subsets $U, V \subset X$, $\exists t \in \mathbb{N}$ such that $\forall s \geq t$, $F^s(U) \cap V \neq \emptyset$.

3.2 Permutive Rules

We now turn to the *permutivity* property of a boolean function, successively applying it to CA local rules. Given $f : \mathbb{F}_2^m \to \mathbb{F}_2$, $x = (x_1, ..., x_{m-1}) \in \mathbb{F}_2^{m-1}$ and $\tilde{x} \in \mathbb{F}_2$, let us denote by $(x, \tilde{x}_{\{i\}})$, with $i \in \{1, ..., m\}$, the vector

$$(x, \tilde{x}_{\{i\}}) = (x_1, ..., x_{i-1}, \tilde{x}, x_i, ..., x_{m-1}) \in \mathbb{F}_2^m.$$

In other words, $(x, \tilde{x}_{\{i\}})$ is the vector of $\mathbb{F}_2^m$ created by inserting at position i in x the value $\tilde{x}$, and shifting to the right by one place all the components x_j with $j \geq i$.

Definition 4. *A boolean function $f : \mathbb{F}_2^m \to \mathbb{F}_2$ is called i-*permutive *(or* permutive in the i-th variable) *if, $\forall x = (x_1, ..., x_{m-1}) \in \mathbb{F}_2^{m-1}$, it results that*

$$f(x, 0_{\{i\}}) \neq f(x, 1_{\{i\}}) . \tag{3}$$

A function f which is 1-permutive is also called leftmost permutive *(or* L-permutive), *while a function which is m-permutive is called* rightmost permutive *(or* R-permutive). *We call* bipermutive *a function which is both L-permutive and R-permutive.*

In [2] and [3] two important relationships between permutive rules and chaotic CAs have been proved, which can be summarised as follows:

Theorem 2. *The following sufficient conditions hold:*

1. *A CA based on a local rule f which is bipermutive is E-chaotic.*
2. *A CA based on a local rule f which is either L-permutive or R-permutive is M-chaotic.*

Thus, bipermutive rules induce CAs which are strongly chaotic, since they satisfy both the definitions of M-chaos and E-chaos. In the case of elementary CAs, rule 30 is R-permutive (and so M-chaotic), while the bipermutive rules are 90, 105, 150 and 165, which are all linear.

3.3   Resiliency of Bipermutive Rules

We can now prove the following property: bipermutive rules, besides the chaotic behaviour they induce in CAs, are also 1-resilient. We begin by showing that if a boolean function is permutive in one of its variables, then it is balanced.

Lemma 1. *If $f : \mathbb{F}_2^m \to \mathbb{F}_2$ is i-permutive, then f is balanced.*

Proof. Considering Property 1, we rewrite the Walsh Transform of the null vector as follows:

$$\hat{F}(0) = \sum_{\{x \in \mathbb{F}_2^m : x_i = 0\}} \hat{f}(x) + \sum_{\{x \in \mathbb{F}_2^m : x_i = 1\}} \hat{f}(x) . \tag{4}$$

The function f is i-permutive, so $\forall x \in \mathbb{F}_2^{m-1}$, $\hat{f}(x, 1_{\{i\}}) = -\hat{f}(x, 0_{\{i\}})$. The second sum in (4) is exactly the opposite of the first sum, and $\hat{F}(0) = 0$. By Property 2, this means that f is balanced. ☐

Now we show that bipermutive rules are first order correlation-immune.

Lemma 2. *Let $f : \mathbb{F}_2^m \to \mathbb{F}_2$ be bipermutive. Then f is first order correlation-immune.*

Proof. Using the characterization of correlation-immunity given in Theorem 1, it is sufficient to show that $\forall \omega \in \mathbb{F}_2^m$ such that $w_H(\omega) = 1$, $\hat{F}(\omega) = 0$. Let ω be a generic *vector having Hamming weight 1. By Property 3, the Walsh Transform of* ω *can be computed as*

$$\hat{F}(\omega) = \sum_{x \in \mathbb{F}_2^m} \hat{f}(x) \cdot (-1)^{x_i} \ . \tag{5}$$

We distinguish two cases:

1. ω *has the nonzero coordinate in the first* $m-1$ *positions (there are* $m-1$ *vectors of such kind, from* $(1,0,...,0,0)$ *to* $(0,0,...,1,0)$*). We rewrite (5) as follows:*

$$\hat{F}(\omega) = \sum_{x \in \mathbb{F}_2^{m-1}} \hat{f}(x, 0_{\{m\}}) \cdot (-1)^{x_i} + \sum_{x \in \mathbb{F}_2^{m-1}} \hat{f}(x, 1_{\{m\}}) \cdot (-1)^{x_i} \tag{6}$$

where $i \in \{1,...,m-1\}$*. Since* f *is R-permutive,* $\hat{f}(x, 1_{\{m\}}) = -\hat{f}(x, 0_{\{m\}})$*. Moreover, since in (6)* x *varies in* $\mathbb{F}_2^{m-1}$*, the terms* $(-1)^{x_i}$ *are the same in both sums. Thus, it follows that*

$$\hat{F}(\omega) = \sum_{x \in \mathbb{F}_2^{m-1}} \hat{f}(x, 0_{\{m\}}) \cdot (-1)^{x_i} - \sum_{x \in \mathbb{F}_2^{m-1}} \hat{f}(x, 0_{\{m\}}) \cdot (-1)^{x_i} = 0 \ .$$

2. ω *has the nonzero coordinate in the last position, that is* $\omega = (0,0,...,1)$*. The Walsh Transform of* ω *is given by*

$$\hat{F}(\omega) = \sum_{x \in \mathbb{F}_2^m} \hat{f}(x) \cdot (-1)^{x_m} \ . \tag{7}$$

We observe that the substitution $\hat{f}(x, 1_{\{m\}}) = -\hat{f}(x, 0_{\{m\}})$ *used in the previous case does not work here, since the second sum in (6) would gather all the vectors with value 1 in the last coordinate, and the signs would all be changed* $((-1)^{x_m} = -1, \forall x \in \mathbb{F}_2^{m-1})$*. We thus rewrite (7) in the following way:*

$$\hat{F}(\omega) = \sum_{x \in \mathbb{F}_2^{m-1}} \hat{f}(x, 0_{\{1\}}) \cdot (-1)^{x_m} + \sum_{x \in \mathbb{F}_2^{m-1}} \hat{f}(x, 1_{\{1\}}) \cdot (-1)^{x_m} \ . \tag{8}$$

Now, f *is also L-permutive, so* $\hat{f}(x, 1_{\{1\}}) = -\hat{f}(x, 0_{\{1\}})$*. By using an argument analogous to the one used in case 1, it follows that*

$$\hat{F}(\omega) = \sum_{x \in \mathbb{F}_2^{m-1}} \hat{f}(x, 0_{\{1\}}) \cdot (-1)^{x_m} - \sum_{x \in \mathbb{F}_2^{m-1}} \hat{f}(x, 0_{\{1\}}) \cdot (-1)^{x_m} = 0 \ .$$

In conclusion, the Walsh Transform vanishes for all vectors of Hamming weight 1, thus the function f *is first order correlation-immune.* □

By combining Lemmas 1 and 2, we finally get the following

Theorem 3. *Let* $f : \mathbb{F}_2^m \to \mathbb{F}_2$ *be a bipermutive boolean function. Then,* f *is 1-resilient.*

4   Generating Bipermutive Rules of a Given Radius

Theorem 3 motivates the search for bipermutive boolean functions to be used in CA-based PRNGs, since they are both strongly chaotic and of cryptographic interest. The idea is to span the space of bipermutive functions of a given odd number of variables (or, equivalently, of a given radius) in order to check additional cryptographic properties, in particular, high nonlinearity and higher order of resiliency. We propose a simple enumerative encoding which allows us to represent a bipermutive function $f : \mathbb{F}_2^m \to \mathbb{F}_2$ as a string of 2^{m-2} bits, and then we apply it to exhaustively explore the set of bipermutive boolean functions defined on 5 variables.

4.1   An Enumerative Encoding for Bipermutive Functions

Let us denote by $\mathcal{F}_m = \{f : \mathbb{F}_2^m \to \mathbb{F}_2\}$ the space of boolean functions in $m \geq 2$ variables, and let $G = (V, E)$ be a graph where $V = \mathbb{F}_2^m$ is the set of vertices, and $E \subseteq V \times V$ is the set of edges defined by the following relation: for all $x = (x_1, \cdots, x_m)$ and $y = (y_1, \cdots, y_m) \in V$, the edge (x, y) is in E if and only if

$$(x_1 = \bar{y}_1 \wedge (\forall i \in \{2, \cdots, m\}\, x_i = y_i)) \bigvee (x_m = \bar{y}_m \wedge (\forall i \in \{1, \cdots, m-1\}\, x_i = y_i)) \ ,$$

where $\bar{y}_j$ is the complement of bit y_j. In other words, the edges in E connect those inputs in $\mathbb{F}_2^m$ which must have different output values in order to satisfy either L-permutivity or R-permutivity in a boolean function. The relation which defines E is symmetric, so the graph G is undirected. We now show some simple properties of G.

Property 4. The degree of each node $x \in V$ is 2. In fact, for all $x \in \mathbb{F}_2^m$, there exists a unique $x' \in \mathbb{F}_2^m$ such that $x_1 = \bar{x}_1'$ and $x_i = x_i'$ for all $i \in \{2, \cdots, m\}$. Similarly, there exists a unique $x'' \in \mathbb{F}_2^m$ such that $x'' \neq x'$ and $x_m = \bar{x}_m''$ and $x_i = x_i''$ for all $i \in \{1, \cdots, m-1\}$.

Property 5. Let x, y be vectors of $\mathbb{F}_2^m$ such that $x_1 = \bar{y}_1$, $x_m = \bar{y}_m$ and $x_i = y_i$ for all $i \in \{2, \cdots, m-1\}$. Then, the two adjacent nodes of x are the same as the adjacent nodes of y. In fact, let us suppose that $x', x'' \in \mathbb{F}_2^m$ are the two adjacent nodes of x, in particular that $x_1 = \bar{x}_1'$, $x_i = x_i'$ for all $i \in \{2, \cdots, m\}$ and $x_m = \bar{x}_m''$, $x_i = x_i''$ for all $i \in \{1, \cdots, m-1\}$. Then, $x_1' = y_1$ and $x_i' = y_i$ for all $i \in \{2, \cdots, m-1\}$. Since $x_m = x_m'$, it follows that $y_m = \bar{x}_m'$, so $(y, x') \in E$. A similar argument shows that $(y, x'') \in E$, so x', x'' are also the adjacent nodes of y.

Property 6. Since the relation which defines E is symmetric, from Property 5 we can deduce that the adjacent nodes of x' and x'' are exactly x and y, hence $\{x, x', x'', y\}$ is a connected component of G. There are 2^{m-2} pairs $(x, y) \in \mathbb{F}_2^m$ of vectors which differ in the leftmost and rightmost coordinates and are equal in the $m - 2$ central ones. Thus G is composed by 2^{m-2} disjoint connected components of this kind.

A boolean function $f \in \mathcal{F}_m$ can be represented as a label function $f : V \to \mathbb{F}_2$ on the vertices of G. If f is bipermutive then the label of each node x is different from the labels of its two adjacent nodes, while the labels of the nodes which are connected via a path of length 2 are the same. Considering Property 6, this means that the label of a single node uniquely determines the labels of the remaining nodes in the connected component where x resides. So, in the case of a bipermutive function, we can define the *configuration* of a generic connected component in G as the value of the label of one of its nodes x, called the *representative* of the connected component. The most natural choice is to select in each connected component the node x whose binary vector encodes the smallest integer number as representative, which is the one having value zero in the leftmost and rightmost coordinates. From a 2^{m-2}-bit string c we can thus recover the truth table of the corresponding bipermutive function $f : \mathbb{F}_2^m \to \mathbb{F}_2$ as follows: for all $j \in \{0, \cdots, 2^{m-2} - 1\}$, we label the representative r_j of the j-th connected component with the value c_j. The adjacent nodes of r_j are then labelled with $\bar{c}_j$, and the last node in the connected component (the one having nonzero value in the leftmost and rightmost coordinates) is labelled with c_j. Figure 1 reports an example of bipermutive rule represented on the graph G in the case of $m = 3$ variables. Given $m \in \mathbb{N}$, there are exactly $2^{2^{m-2}}$ bipermutive functions of m variables; moreover, by using this choice of representatives in G the truth tables of the functions can be enumerated in lexicographic order.

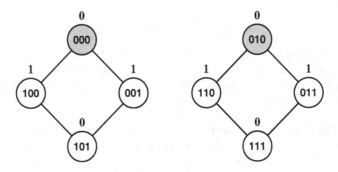

Fig. 1. Representation of the function 01011010 (rule 90) on the graph G. The representatives are shaded in gray, so this function corresponds to the string $c = 00$.

4.2   Application to the Case $r = 2$

It has already been observed that in the case of elementary CAs ($r = 1$) there are only four bipermutive rules which are all linear. We have thus used the enumerative encoding described in Section 4.1 to explore the set of $2^{2^3} = 256$ bipermutive rules of radius $r = 2$. The algorithm used to generate these functions is straightforward, since it simply loops on the set $\{0, \cdots, 255\}$, converts each integer i in the corresponding binary expansion c_i and instantiates the labels on the vertices of G according to the configurations of the connected components encoded by c_i.

By applying Tarannikov's bound to the case of boolean functions of 5 variables (which is exactly the set of CA rules of radius 2) we see that, with respect to the property of nonlinearity, there can be 1-resilient rules with $Nl = 12$ and 2-resilient rules with $Nl = 8$. For higher orders of resiliency, there are only linear functions. For each bipermutive rule generated by our algorithm, we computed its nonlinearity and checked if it was 2-resilient by using the Fast Walsh Transform. It turned out that all the rules were either nonlinear with $Nl = 8$ or linear. We thus selected the rules which were nonlinear and 2-resilient, since they can resist to second order correlation attacks. This left us, in total, with 56 rules.

5 Statistical Randomness Tests

Nonlinearity, resiliency and bipermutivity are not sufficient conditions to make a CA rule suitable for the design of a cryptographic PRNG: for this reason, we subjected the 56 2-resilient nonlinear bipermutive rules discovered by the method discussed in Section 4 to a series of statistical tests, in order to find which of them generate pseudorandom sequences at least as good as the ones produced by rule 30. We structured our analysis in two phases. First, we removed the rules which generated small pseudorandom sequences (2^{16} bits) that did not pass the tests of the ENT suite [11], using rule 30 as a benchmark. Then, we applied the NIST test suite [7] to longer sequences (10^6 bits) generated by the remaining rules. In both phases, we used Wolfram's method for pseudorandom generation. In particular, we employed a finite CA with periodic boundary conditions composed by $n = 64$ cells (since 64 bits is a common value for the length of the seed in many standard PRNGs, like ANSI X9.17) and we sampled the trace of the 32nd cell to generate the pseudorandom sequences.

5.1 ENT Tests Results

The ENT Test Suite, assembled by Walker and described in [11], is a battery of 5 statistical tests (Entropy, Chi-Square, Arithmetic Mean, Monte Carlo Value for π and Serial Correlation Coefficient) which can be used to check the quality of pseudorandom sequences. For each bipermutive 2-resilient nonlinear rule of radius 2 we generated a single sequence of length $l = 2^{16} = 65536$ bits, using as initial seed the configuration containing only a 1 in the 32nd cell. This method is similar to the one adopted by Koza in [5], where he evolved a CA-based PRNG by a genetic programming algorithm (even if, in that case, the fitness function was only the entropy of the generated sequence). Interestingly, the best rule found by Koza with his approach was rule 30.

As a first selection step, we discarded the rules which did not generate sequences that passed the Chi-Square test, since this is the most sensitive test in detecting deviations from randomness. As suggested in [11], a sequence passes the Chi-Square test if the corresponding p-value is included in the interval $[0.1, 0.9]$. After this selection, only 42 rules remained, and we subsequently compared their results with those obtained by rule 30, selecting only the ones with an error $err_\pi < 1\%$ in the approximation of π. The resulting 28 rules were similar or even better than rule 30 with respect to the other tests (entropy, arithmetic mean and serial correlation coefficient), so no further selection was performed.

We observed that 24 rules presented the same ENT results in couples. This fact was expected, since in each couple the rules are related by the *reflexive* transformation, mentioned in [6]. Given a binary vector $x \in \mathbb{F}_2^m$, with $x = (x_1, \cdots, x_m)$, the *mirror image* of x is defined as the vector $x_M = (x_m, \cdots, x_1)$. The *reflex* of a boolean function

$f : \mathbb{F}_2^m \to \mathbb{F}_2$ is the function f_R defined as $f_R(x) = f(x_M)$, $\forall x \in \mathbb{F}_2^m$. This transformation preserves the nonlinearity and resiliency of a function, since the spectral radius remains unaltered, and the Hamming weight of an input vector is the same as that of its mirror image. The remaining four rules not coupled are self-reflexive, that is $f_R(x) = f(x)$.

Considering our method of pseudorandom generation described earlier, two rules equivalent by reflexive transformation produce two sequences of configurations which are symmetric, thus the trace of the 32nd cell is the same. Table 1 shows the ENT results of the 28 final rules, grouped by reflection couples. The results of rule 30 are also reported for comparison.

Table 1. ENT tests results on the pseudorandom sequences generated by the 28 rules after the selection process. E_8 stands for the entropy computed on an 8-bit schema, χ^2 is the p-value of the Chi-Square test, μ_{dev} is the normalized deviation from the mean value $\mu = 127.5$, err_π is the error in the approximation of π and scc is the Serial Correlation Coefficient.

Rule - Reflected rule	E_8	χ^2	μ_{dev}	err_π	scc
1452976485 - 1717213605	7.979592	0.83	0.004848	0.37%	-0.002338
1453762905 - 1701485205	7.977838	0.56	0.008593	0.66%	0.002280
1453959510 - 1718196630	7.979487	0.85	0.000567	0.37%	-0.003930
1500161685 - 1516676505	7.978750	0.69	0.004215	0.75%	0.003161
1503307365 - 1784059305	7.976643	0.30	0.003097	0.01%	-0.012526
1516873110 (self-reflexive)	7.977783	0.57	0.003332	0.10%	0.003791
1520018790 - 1784255910	7.976146	0.32	0.001983	0.01%	0.015071
1705417305 (self-reflexive)	7.979135	0.82	0.006708	0.09%	0.001310
1705613910 - 1722128730	7.976625	0.34	0.008589	0.18%	0.017063
1772459610 (self-reflexive)	7.976147	0.27	0.004326	0.38%	0.002607
2509924965 - 2790676905	7.977823	0.52	0.005322	0.38%	-0.013957
2510907990 - 2791659930	7.976643	0.30	0.005385	0.55%	-0.025343
2526636390 - 2790873510	7.978825	0.73	0.000548	0.10%	-0.005077
2573821590 - 2590336410	7.978674	0.76	0.008456	0.57%	0.013556
2589549990 (self-reflexive)	7.979135	0.82	0.000952	0.75%	-0.010592
2778290790 - 2794805610	7.978866	0.83	0.007370	0.66%	0.011000
30 (benchmark)	7.979031	0.80	0.004169	0.66%	-0.013926

5.2   NIST Tests Results

To further investigate the randomness quality of the rules selected with the ENT suite, we applied the more stringent statistical tests devised by the NIST in [7] to longer generated sequences. For each couple of rules equivalent by reflexive transformation, we chose to test only the rule with the smallest Wolfram code (since the other is expected to show a similar pseudorandom behaviour), so in total we tested 12 rules plus the 4 self-reflexive ones.

The NIST suite includes 15 tests, some of which are repeated several times with different parameters and patterns: the total number of tests run on each sample of pseudorandom sequences is thus 187. The technical details of the tests can be found in [7].

For the sake of our discussion, it is sufficient to know that each test in the suite produces a p-value for each sequence in the sample, and that the sequence passes the test if its corresponding p-value is included in the confidence interval $[\alpha, 1 - \alpha]$, where α is the significance level. Then, the results of a test over the entire sample of sequences generated by a rule are interpreted using two approaches. First, the proportion of passing sequences is computed, and this proportion is considered acceptable if it lies above the *minimum pass rate*

$$mpr = \hat{p} - 3\sqrt{\frac{\hat{p}(1 - \hat{p})}{N}} \, , \qquad (9)$$

where $\hat{p} = 1 - \alpha$ and N is the sample size. Second, a Chi-Square test is performed to verify whether the p-values are well distributed, by dividing $[0, 1]$ in 10 subintervals.

To set up the parameters of the tests, we followed the recommendations suggested in [7]. In particular, for each rule we generated a sample of $N = 1000$ pseudorandom sequences of length $l = 10^6$ bits. The 1000 64-bit seeds for the CA have been created with the *HotBits* service (available at http://www.fourmilab.ch/hotbits/), which is a true random number generator (TRNG) based on the radioactive decays of a Caesium-137 source. The significance level adopted was $\alpha = 0.001$.

Table 2 reports the results of the 16 rules tested (along with rule 30, always used as a benchmark). For each rule, the value in the column "Approach 1" refers to the number of tests passed with respect to the proportions of passing sequences, while the value in "Approach 2" represents the number of tests passed with respect to the distribution of p-values. We can observe that, except for rule 1503307365, the worst results are

Table 2. NIST tests results on the pseudorandom sequences generated by the 16 final rules of radius 2 and the elementary rule 30, used as a benchmark.

Rule	Approach 1	Approach 2
1452976485	187/187	187/187
1453762905	186/187	186/187
1453959510	186/187	187/187
1500161685	184/187	186/187
1503307365	37/187	187/187
1516873110 (self-reflexive)	94/187	184/187
1520018790	187/187	187/187
1705417305 (self-reflexive)	25/187	186/187
1705613910	185/187	187/187
1772459610 (self-reflexive)	24/187	187/187
2509924965	186/187	187/187
2510907990	129/187	186/187
2526636390	187/187	186/187
2573821590	186/187	186/187
2589549990 (self-reflexive)	25/187	185/187
2778290790	187/187	187/187
30 (benchmark)	187/187	187/187

obtained by the self-reflexive rules, with very low pass rates concerning Approach 1. The reason could lie in the intrinsic symmetries of the space-time diagrams produced by this kind of rules, which are evident by using the pseudorandom generation method of Section 5.1 (initial configuration having only a 1 in the central cell).

The remaining rules all have pass rates close to the maximum, and three of them (1452976485, 1520018790 and 2778290790) pass all the tests with respect to both approaches, like rule 30. One could thus reasonably conclude that these three rules are at least as good as rule 30 for pseudorandom number generation, and moreover they satisfy an additional stronger definition of chaos (E-chaos) and 2-resiliency.

6 Conclusions

In this paper we showed that bipermutive rules, besides generating CAs which are expansive and mixing chaotic, are also 1-resilient, and thus potentially useful for the design of strong cryptographic PRNGs. We also derived an enumerative encoding for bipermutive rules based on a graph representation which groups the 2^m inputs of a boolean function $f : \mathbb{F}_2^m \to \mathbb{F}_2$ in 2^{m-2} disjoint connected components. Since it is already known by Tarannikov's bound that among the elementary CA rules there are no nonlinear resilient rules, we applied this encoding to generate the 256 bipermutive rules of radius 2, and used the Fast Walsh Transform to compute their nonlinearities and check whether they were 2-resilient.

We successively tested the resulting 56 nonlinear and 2-resilient rules with two batteries of statistical randomness tests, the ENT suite and the NIST suite. We used the former to discard the rules which did not generate good pseudorandom sequences of 2^{16} bits, and the latter to investigate more thoroughly the remaining 16 rules by sequences of 10^6 bits, taking in both phases the results obtained by rule 30 as a benchmark. The final results showed that rules 1452976485, 1520018790 and 2778290790 passed all the 187 NIST tests, like rule 30.

It is important to remark, however, that although these three rules are chaotic, 2-resilient, nonlinear, and generate good pseudorandom sequences, they cannot be used *alone* in the design of either a cryptographic PRNG or a stream cipher. In fact, there are many other properties of cryptographic boolean functions, described in [1], which we did not consider in this paper: propagation criterion, algebraic degree and algebraic immunity are some of the most important ones. An interesting direction for future research is thus to study the class of bipermutive rules with respect to these additional properties. We also saw that there are no bipermutive rules of radius 2 reaching the maximum nonlinearity allowed by Tarannikov's bound, even if they are not 2-resilient. Further investigation is needed to verify whether bipermutivity induces a stricter bound on the nonlinearity achievable by a boolean function.

The enumerative encoding described in Section 4.1 gives an effective mean to explore the spaces of rules having higher radii. The interest in doing such kind of search is twofold. The first motivation is practical: it is intuitive to think that, as the radius of the rules increases, the diffusion of a CA-based PRNG gets better. The second reason which motivates the exploration of rules with higher radii is to test conjectures about the aforementioned cryptographic properties, by finding counterexamples.

In the case of $r = 3$ and $r = 4$ there are $2^{2^5} = 4294967296$ and $2^{128} \approx 3.4 \cdot 10^{38}$ bipermutive rules, respectively; an exhaustive exploration as we did for $r = 2$ is thus infeasible. However, these search spaces could be reduced by improving our encoding in order to enumerate only those rules which are 2-resilient and highly nonlinear, using the Shannon decomposition. This approach will be pursued in future research. For all radii $r > 4$, instead, the set of possible rules is so large that heuristic methods would be necessary to efficiently visit the search space, even under the new encoding. For example, we observe that it would be straightforward to apply our enumerative encoding to evolve bipermutive rules by means of genetic algorithms.

Acknowledgements. We thank the anonymous referees for their suggestions on how to improve the current paper. This research was partially supported by Università degli Studi di Milano-Bicocca, Fondo di Ateneo (FA) 2011.

References

1. Carlet, C.: Boolean Functions for Cryptography and Error-Correcting Codes. In: Crama, Y., Hammer, P.L. (eds.) Boolean Models and Methods in Mathematics, Computer Science, and Engineering. Cambridge University Press, New York (2010)
2. Cattaneo, G., Finelli, M., Margara, L.: Investigating Topological Chaos by Elementary Cellular Automata Dynamics. Theor. Comput. Sci. 244(1-2), 219–244 (2000)
3. Cattaneo, G., Dennunzio, A., Margara, L.: Chaotic Subshifts and Related Languages Applications to One-Dimensional Cellular Automata. Fundam. Inform. 52(1-3), 39–80 (2002)
4. Devaney, R.L.: An Introduction to Chaotic Dynamical Systems. Addison-Wesley, Reading (1989)
5. Koza, J.R.: Genetic Programming: On the Programming of Computers by Means of Natural Selection. MIT Press, Cambridge (1992)
6. Martin, B.: A Walsh Exploration of Elementary CA Rules. J. Cell. Aut. 3(2), 145–156 (2008)
7. National Institute of Standards and Technology: A Statistical Test Suite for Random and Pseudorandom Number Generators for Cryptographic Applications. Special Publication 800-22, Revision 1a (2010)
8. Siegenthaler, T.: Correlation-Immunity of Nonlinear Combining Functions for Cryptographic Applications. IEEE Trans. Inf. Theory 30(5), 776–780 (1984)
9. Siegenthaler, T.: Decrypting a Class of Stream Ciphers Using Ciphertext Only. IEEE Trans. Comput. C-34(1), 81–85 (1985)
10. Tarannikov, Y.V.: On Resilient Boolean Functions with Maximal Possible Nonlinearity. In: Roy, B., Okamoto, E. (eds.) INDOCRYPT 2000. LNCS, vol. 1977, pp. 19–30. Springer, Heidelberg (2000)
11. Walker, J.: ENT Randomness Test Suite, http://www.fourmilab.ch/random/
12. Wolfram, S.: Statistical Mechanics of Cellular Automata. Rev. Mod. Phys. 55(3), 601–644 (1983)
13. Wolfram, S.: Random Sequence Generation by Cellular Automata. Adv. Appl. Math. 7(2), 123–169 (1986)
14. Xiao, G.-Z., Massey, J.L.: A Spectral Characterization of Correlation-Immune Combining Functions. IEEE Trans. Inf. Theory 34(3), 569–571 (1988)

On the Convergence of Boolean Automata Networks without Negative Cycles

Tarek Melliti[1], Damien Regnault[1], Adrien Richard[2], and Sylvain Sené[1,3]

[1] Laboratoire IBISC, EA4526, Université d'Évry Val-d'Essonne,
91000 Évry, France
{tarek.melliti,damien.regnault,sylvain.sene}@ibisc.univ-evry.fr
[2] Laboratoire I3S, UMR7271 CNRS et Université de Nice Sophia Antipolis,
06900 Sophia Antipolis, France
richard@i3s.unice.fr
[3] IXXI, Institut rhône-alpin des systèmes complexes,
69007 Lyon, France

Abstract. Since the 1980's, automata networks have been at the centre of numerous studies, from both theoretical (around the computational abilities) and applied (around the modelling power of real phenomena) standpoints. In this paper, basing ourselves on the seminal works of Robert and Thomas, we focus on a specific family of Boolean automata networks, those without negative cycles. For these networks, subjected to both asynchronous and elementary updating modes, we give new answers to well known problems (some of them having already been solved) about their convergence towards stable configurations. For the already solved ones, the proofs given are much simpler and neater than the existing ones. For the others, in any case, the proofs presented are constructive.

Keywords: Boolean automata networks, cycles, monotony, convergence and convergence time.

1 Introduction

Historically, the appearance of automata networks (ANs) in computer science flows from the works of McCulloch and Pitts on neural networks [14] and of von Neumann on cellular automata (CAs) [15], in the 1940's. In this way, they are amongst the first unconventional models of computation and constitute the origin of numerous key works in this domain, such as that of Kleene on finite automata [13] and of Elspas and Golomb on circuit theory [3, 7]. Then, in the 1980's, in a context at the frontier of discrete dynamical systems and models of computation, many researches were led on these objects that provided significant results on their dynamical behaviours and their expressiveness [4, 5, 10, 21]. Beyond these mostly theoretical works, the interest in ANs has been sustained through their application to biology. Since McCulloch and Pitts indeed, a thriving line of researches on ANs have been done about their ability to model biological regulation networks, with a special attention paid to

J. Kari, M. Kutrib, and A. Malcher (Eds.): AUTOMATA 2013, LNCS 8155, pp. 124–138, 2013.
© Springer-Verlag Berlin Heidelberg 2013

genetic networks. Amongst the best representative studies in this domain are those of Kauffman [11] and Thomas [26], from which high impact results on some governing laws of living systems have been obtained (we will evoke some of them later). Relying on both these computational and biological standpoints, which contribute equally to the motivations of the paper, the study developed further focuses on the convergence of ANs.

Before we give more details about the contents of the paper, let us give clarifications about ANs. From the most general point of view, an AN is a system of interacting computing units, the automata of the network, over a discrete time. Here, an automaton has to be considered as a discrete entity that computes a result, *i.e.* its updated state, according to a predetermined local transition function depending on the inputs it receives from other automata (possibly including itself) in the network, *i.e.* its neighbours. Thus, in some sense, an automaton can be viewed as a black box. The interactions between automata, that define the neighbourhood relations between them, are directed edges between automata. They can be of two sorts according to their activating ('+'-label) or inhibiting ('−'-label) nature. From this derives the fact that the architecture of an AN is captured by a digraph, classically called the interaction graph. Note that, in the specific context of CAs, the automata that are rather called cells share the same local transition function and are organised on a lattice graph. Let us highlight that, in this paper, we restrict ourselves to the study of finite ANs (*i.e.* of finite size, not to be confused with networks of finite automata). To go further, we speak of Boolean automata networks (BANs), meaning that automata states can only take Boolean values. From the computational point of view, it is well known that it is not a limitation [5, 24]. However, from the modelling point of view where automata can represent genes for instance, it is. But it is deliberate in the sense that such a limitation allows to focus on the state changes rather than on the states themselves.

Now that the static aspect of BANs has been presented, let us add that their study is classically dived into a dynamical dimension. Being given an arbitrary BAN, with the concept of a configuration that corresponds to the attribution of a state to every automaton, its dynamical behaviour can be studied by executing its local transition functions over time. In general, the behaviour of a BAN is also represented by a digraph, called the transition graph (in the context of CAs, we rather speak of space-time diagram). In the sequel, we pay particular attention to transient and asymptotic behaviours of BANs. The asymptotic behaviours of a BAN, its attractors, are the terminal strongly connected components of its transition graph. Note that to focus on the dynamical aspect of a BAN asks for choosing an updating mode (*e.g.* a non-deterministic one [28], a deterministic one [21] or a probabilistic one [23]). In this work, we selected the (perfectly) asynchronous one, that gives non-deterministically from each configuration the ability of updating every automaton[1].

---

[1] Nevertheless, notice that the results extend naturally to the elementary updating mode [17, 16], unless an explicit mention is given.

Some peculiar architectural patterns of BANs, namely the cycles, are known to play a major role in their dynamical behaviours. Two kinds of cycles are distinguished: the positive and the negatives ones, the former being composed of an even number of negative arcs, the latter of an odd number of negative arcs. Let us now recall three results that constitute the basis of our study: (i) the Robert's theorem – if the interaction graph of a BAN does not contain any cycle, its dynamical behaviour is "trivial", $i.e.$ it admits a unique attractor that is a stable configuration [21]; (ii) the first Thomas' rule – the presence of a positive cycle in a BAN is necessary for it to admit several stable configurations and (iii) the second Thomas' rule – the presence of a negative cycle is necessary for it to admit a stable oscillation [18–20, 27]. From these, the general aim of this paper is to address the problem of the convergence (and the convergence time) of BANs with no negative cycles in their architecture. As a result, with n denoting the number of automata ($i.e.$ the size) of such a BAN, the main contributions are:

- a result showing that the absence of negative cycles in BANs implies Boolean monotonicity;
- a new proof of the second Thomas' rule, much simpler and neater;
- a result showing that, for any configuration, there exists a path of length at most n in the transition graph from this configuration to a stable configuration.

In Section 2 are given the main definitions and notations used in the paper. Section 3 presents the results discussed above about the convergence of BANs with no negative cycles, before Section 4 concludes the paper and provides some relevant perspectives of this work.

2   Definitions and Notations

This section gives the classical definitions and notations in the context of BANs. Those that are more specific will be given when they will prove to be useful.

2.1   BANs

Let $\mathbb{B} = \{0,1\}$ and let $V = \{1,\ldots,n\}$ denote a set of $n \in \mathbb{N}$ Boolean automata such that $\forall i \in V$, $x_i \in \mathbb{B}$ is the $state$ of automaton i. A $configuration$ of $\mathcal{N}$ is a vector $x \in \mathbb{B}^n$ that instantiates the state of each automaton of V (a configuration can be denoted by either a vector or a binary word). Because special attention is paid to automata switches in this paper, we introduce the following notations:

$\forall x \in \mathbb{B}^n$,

1. $\forall i \in V$, $\overline{x}^i = (x_1, \ldots, x_{i-1}, \neg x_i, x_{i+1}, \ldots, x_n)$, and
2. $\forall W = W' \uplus \{i\} \subseteq V$, $\overline{x}^W = \overline{(\overline{x}^i)}^{W'} = \overline{(\overline{x}^{W'})}^i$.

Furthermore, let $\mathbb{1} = \{-1, +1\}$ and $s : \mathbb{B} \to \mathbb{1}$ be the function that switches from Boolean values to signed values such that $s(b) = b - \neg b$. In order to compare two

$$\mathscr{N}_1 = \begin{cases} f_1(x) = x_3 \\ f_2(x) = x_1 \vee x_3 \\ f_3(x) = x_2 \wedge \neg x_4 \\ f_4(x) = \neg x_1 \end{cases}$$

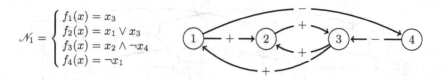

Fig. 1. A BAN $\mathscr{N}_1$ of size 4 and its signed interaction graph G_1

configurations $x, y \in \mathbb{B}^n$, we use $D(x,y) = \{i \in V \mid x_i \neq y_i\}$ and the Hamming distance $d(x,y) = |D(x,y)|$.

A BAN $\mathscr{N}$ whose automata set is V is a set of n Boolean functions such that $\mathscr{N} = \{f_i : \mathbb{B}^n \to \mathbb{B} \mid i \in V\}$. Given $i \in V$, f_i is called the *local transition function* of automaton i. It predetermines its behaviour depending on the states of other automata that influence it and that appear consequently as literals in the Boolean expression of f_i. More precisely, it predetermines its behaviour for every configuration $x \in \mathbb{B}^n$, meaning that if i is updated in x, its state switches from x_i to $f_i(x)$. We introduce now the *sign of an interaction* (*i.e.* an influence) from j to i, both in V, in configuration $x \in \mathbb{B}^n$ with:

$$\mathrm{sign}_x(j,i) = s(x_j) \cdot (f_i(x) - f_i(\overline{x}^j)).$$

From this, the set of interactions that are effective in x is defined as $A(x) = \{(j,i) \in V^2 \mid \mathrm{sign}_x(j,i) \neq 0\}$. And we derive directly the *interaction graph*, or *architecture*, of $\mathscr{N}$ by defining the digraph $G = (V, A)$, where $A = \bigcup_{x \in \mathbb{B}^n} A(x)$ is the set of interactions (cf. Figure 1) and $|A| = m$. We add that automata of V that influence i are called the *neighbours* of i, and that the neighbourhood of $i \in V$ in G is denoted by $V^-(i)$. In this paper, we consider BANs whose interaction graphs are *simple*, *i.e.* if there exists $(j,i) \in A$, it is unique and such that $\forall x \in \mathbb{B}^n, \mathrm{sign}_x(j,i) \neq 0$ and is constant, and thus denoted simply by $\mathrm{sign}(j,i) \in \mathbb{1}$. Remark that if $\mathrm{sign}(j,i) = +1$ (resp. $\mathrm{sign}(j,i) = -1$), (j,i) is an activating (resp. inhibiting) interaction so that the state of i tends to mimic (resp. negate) that of j. The digraph obtained by labelling each arc $(i,j) \in A$ with $\mathrm{sign}(i,j)$ is the *signed interaction graph* of $\mathscr{N}$. We also denote it by G, in order not to burden the reading. To finish on BANs, we add that the sign of a path in G equals the product of the signs of its arcs, which leads us to define positive and negative cycles in G. Abusing notations, a *cycle* C of G is *positive* (resp. *negative*) if $\mathrm{sign}(C) = +1$ (resp. $\mathrm{sign}(C) = -1$). Note that this paper only deals with BANs whose signed interaction graphs do not contain any negative cycle.

2.2   Transition Graphs

In a BAN $\mathscr{N}$, we call *elementary transition* a couple of configurations $(x,y) \in \mathbb{B}^n \times \mathbb{B}^n$, such that y is obtained by updating automata of x, meaning that $\exists W \neq \emptyset \subseteq V, \forall i \in V, y_i = x_i$ if $i \in V \setminus W$ and $y_i = f_i(x)$ if $i \in W$. If

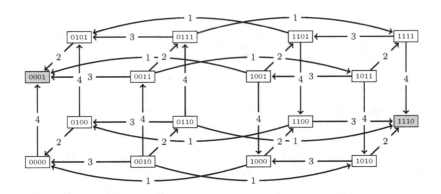

Fig. 2. The asynchronous transition graph $\mathscr{G}_1$ of $\mathscr{N}_1$, defined in Figure 1, and its two attractors, the stable configurations 0001 and 1110 (ineffective transitions have been omitted)

$x = y$ (*i.e.* $\mathrm{d}(x,y) = 0$), then transition (x,y) is said to be *ineffective*. Conversely, if $0 < \mathrm{d}(x,y) \le n$, it is *effective*. As evoked, a transition (x,y) can induce the updating of automata of a subset $W \ne \emptyset \subseteq V$. If $|W| > 1$, (x,y) is *synchronous*. Otherwise, if $|W| = 1$, (x,y) is *asynchronous* and is denoted by $x \longrightarrow y$, which implies that $\mathrm{d}(x,y) \le 1$. Let $T = \{x \longrightarrow y \mid x,y \in \mathbb{B}^n\}$ be the set of asynchronous transitions of $\mathscr{N}$. Digraph $\mathscr{G} = (\mathbb{B}^n, T)$ is then the *asynchronous transition graph* of $\mathscr{N}$ (cf. Figure 2). In other words, $\mathscr{G}$ represents the discrete dynamical system associated to $\mathscr{N}$ when the latter is governed by the *non-deterministic "perfectly" asynchronous updating mode*. In this paper, as said before, results presented are for BANs subjected to this specific updating mode. However, unless we mention it, they trivially extend to the *elementary (also called general) updating mode*, that considers both synchronous and asynchronous transitions [17], to which we associate an *elementary transition graph* whose T is then the set of all possible elementary transitions. Notice that the reason for which the results about convergence times presented in this paper apply to the elementary updating mode directly comes from the nature of elementary transition graphs. Indeed, an asynchronous transition graph is a subgraph of the related elementary transition graph. As a consequence, a path in the former also is a path in the latter, and thus, the upper bound results are valid in both cases.

Let $\mathscr{N}$ be an arbitrary BAN of size n and let $\mathscr{G} = (\mathbb{B}^n, T)$ its associated asynchronous transition graph. Let $x \in \mathbb{B}^n$ be any configuration of $\mathscr{N}$. We define as a *trajectory* of x any path in $\mathscr{G}$ that starts in x. A strongly connected component (SCC) of $\mathscr{G}$ that does not admit any outgoing transition is a *terminal strongly connected component* (TSCC). An *attractor* of $\mathscr{N}$ is a TSCC of $\mathscr{G}$, that corresponds thus to an asymptotic behaviour of $\mathscr{N}$. The *size of an attractor* is defined as the number of configurations it contains. An attractor of size 1 (resp. of size greater than 1) is a *stable configuration* (resp. a *stable oscillation*).

Finally, we call *convergence time of a configuration* x the length of the shortest trajectory that leads it to an attractor and *convergence time of a BAN* the biggest convergence time of all configurations in $\mathbb{B}^n$.

3   Results

This section aims at presenting the main results obtained on BANs with no negative cycles: a relationship with the Boolean monotonicity, a new simple and neat proof of the Thomas' second rule and a result about the linear convergence time of such BANs depending on their sizes.

3.1   Negative Cycles and Monotonicity

The *global transition function* of a BAN $\mathcal{N} = \{f_i : \mathbb{B}^n \to \mathbb{B} \mid i \in V\}$ is the map $f : \mathbb{B}^n \to \mathbb{B}^n$ such that, for all $x \in \mathbb{B}^n$ and $i \in V$, $f(x)_i = f_i(x)$. We say that $\mathcal{N}$ is *monotone* if

$$\forall x, y \in \mathbb{B}^n, \ x \leq y \implies f(x) \leq f(y),$$

where $\leq$ is the usual partial order on $\mathbb{B}^n$. Equivalently, $\mathcal{N}$ is monotone if its signed interaction graph has only positive arcs. For all $W \subseteq V$, the *W-switch* of $\mathcal{N}$ is the BAN $\mathcal{N}^W = \{f_i^W : \mathbb{B}^n \to \mathbb{B} \mid i \in V\}$ such that

$$\forall x \in \mathbb{B}^n, \ f^W(x) = \overline{f(\overline{x}^W)}^W.$$

In other words, $\mathcal{N}^W$ is obtained from $\mathcal{N}$ by replacing, for automata in W, ones by zeros and zeros by ones. By doing this operation, a lot of properties are preserved. In particular, the asynchronous transition graph of $\mathcal{N}^W$ is isomorphic to that of $\mathcal{N}$ (the isomorphism being $x \mapsto \overline{x}^W$). Besides, the signed interaction graph G^W of $\mathcal{N}^W$ is obtained from the signed interaction graph G of $\mathcal{N}$ by: *(i)* kipping exactly the same vertices and the same arcs, and *(ii)* changing the sign of ingoing and outgoing arcs of W, *i.e.* arcs (j, i) such that $j \in W$ and $i \notin W$ and arcs (j, i) such that $j \notin W$ and $i \in W$. So G and G^W have the same cycles, and these cycles have the same signs, even if the repartition of signs on arcs may differ. These similarities lead us to say that a BAN $\mathcal{N}'$ is *equivalent* to $\mathcal{N}$ if $\mathcal{N}'$ is the W-switch of $\mathcal{N}$ for some $W \subseteq V$ (cf. Figure 3).

Proposition 1. *Let $\mathcal{N}$ be a BAN and let G be its signed interaction graph. If G is strongly connected and has no negative cycles, then $\mathcal{N}$ is equivalent to a monotone BAN.*

Proof. The proof is based on arguments that we can find in [1, 8]. First of all, let us note that if G has no negative arcs, it is monotone by definition. So, let us admit that G has negative arcs.

Pick any vertex $i \in V$ of G. For any vertex $j \in V$, G has at least one path from i to j (since G is strongly connected), and all paths from i to j have the same sign (since otherwise G would have a negative cycle). Let us denote by

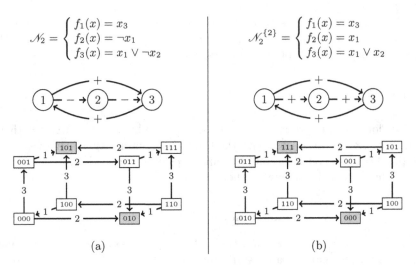

Fig. 3. (a) A BAN $\mathcal{N}_2$ of size 3, its signed interaction graph G_2 and its asynchronous transition graph $\mathscr{G}_2$; (b) the monotone BAN $\mathcal{N}_2^{\{2\}}$ equivalent to $\mathcal{N}_2$ (its $\{2\}$-switch actually) and its associated asynchronous transition graph $\mathscr{G}_2^{\{2\}}$

$\text{sign}_{ij} \in \mathbb{1}$ this sign, and let W be the set of vertices j such that $\text{sign}_{ij} = +1$. We shall prove that an arc $(k,l) \in A$ of G is negative if and only if it is entering or leaving W. Let (k,l) be any arc of G.

If $k,l \in W$ then G has a positive path from i to k and from i to l. Thus, if (k,l) is negative, then together with the positive path from i to k, it gives a negative path from i to l, which is a contradiction. Thus (k,l) is positive, and we prove in a similar way that (k,l) is positive if $k,l \notin W$.

If (k,l) is an outgoing arc of W ($k \in W$ and $l \notin W$) then G has a positive path from i to k and a negative path from i to l. Thus if (k,l) is positive, then together with the positive path from i to k it gives a positive path from i to l, which is a contradiction. Thus (k,l) is negative, and we prove in a similar way that (k,l) is negative if it is an ingoing arc of W.

Hence, an arc of G is negative if and only if it is an ingoing or an outgoing arc of W. Let $\mathcal{N}^W$ be the W-switch of $\mathcal{N}$, and let G^W be its signed interaction graph. As said above, G^W is obtained from G by changing the signs of ingoing and outgoing arcs of W. We deduce that G^W has only positive arcs, so that $\mathcal{N}^W$ is monotone (cf. Figure 3). □

Actually, it is possible to characterise BANs that are equivalent to a monotone BAN in terms of undirected negative cycle. To do so, we need the following characterisation of Harary [8]: *An arc-signed undirected graph has no negative cycles if and only if there exists a set of vertices W such that an edge of the graph is negative if and only if it has one end in W and another outside W.* Now, let $\mathcal{N}$ be a BAN with signed interaction graph G, and let U(G) be the undirected arc-signed graph obtained from G by forgetting directions (U(G) may have loops, and U(G) has both a positive arc and a negative arc between two vertices if G has a negative cycle of length two between these vertices). Using the characterisation of Harary, we can obtain the following characterisation: *A BAN $\mathcal{N}$ is equivalent to a monotone BAN if and only if $U(G)$ has no negative cycle.* The previous proposition (which is enough for our purpose) follows from the fact that if G is strongly connected, then $U(G)$ has no negative cycles if and only if G has no negative cycles. Analogues of this characterisation are well known in the context of differential systems, see [9, 25] for instance.

3.2   Stable Configurations and Stable Oscillations

In this section, we show how to recover known results about stable configurations and oscillations from the previous proposition and the following two easy results on monotone BANs.

Proposition 2. *Suppose that $\mathcal{N}$ is monotone and such that, $\forall i \in V$, $f_i \neq cst$. Then, configurations $0\ldots0$ and $1\ldots1$ are stable configurations.*

Proof. Let f be the global transition function of $\mathcal{N}$. If $f(0\ldots0) \neq 0\ldots0$ then $f_i(0\ldots0) = 1$ for some $i \in V$. Let $x \in \mathbb{B}^n$. Since $0\ldots0 \leq x$ and $\mathcal{N}$ is monotone, we have $f_i(0\ldots0) \leq f_i(x)$ so $f_i(x) = 1$. Thus $f_i(\cdot) = cst = 1$, which is a contradiction. As a consequence, $f(0\ldots0) = 0\ldots0$ and configuration $0\ldots0$ is stable. We prove in a similar way that $f(1\ldots1) = 1\ldots1$.   □

Proposition 3. *Suppose that $\mathcal{N}$ is monotone. For all $x \in \mathbb{B}^n$, the asynchronous transition graph of $\mathcal{N}$ has a path of length at most $2n$ from x to a stable configuration.*

Proof. Let $\mathcal{G}$ be the asynchronous transition graph of $\mathcal{N}$ whose global transition function is f. Let $P = x^0 x^1 \ldots x^p$ be a decreasing path of $\mathcal{G}$ starting from $x = x^0$, and of maximal length for this property, *i.e.*

$$x^0 \geq x^1 \geq \cdots \geq x^p \quad \text{and} \quad x^p \leq f(x^p).$$

Let $Q = y^0 y^1 \ldots y^q$ be an increasing path of $\mathcal{G}$ starting from $y^0 = x^p$, and of maximal length for this property, *i.e.*

$$y^0 \leq y^1 \leq \cdots \leq y^q \quad \text{and} \quad y^q \geq f(y^q).$$

Let $k < q$. If $y^k \leq f(y^k)$ then $y^k \leq y^{k+1} \leq f(y^k)$, and since $\mathcal{N}$ is monotone, $f(y^k) \leq f(y^{k+1})$. Thus:

$$y^k \leq f(y^k) \implies y^{k+1} \leq f(y^{k+1}).$$

Since $y^0 = x^p$, we have $y^0 \leq f(y^0)$ and we deduce that $\forall 0 \leq k \leq q$, $y^k \leq f(y^{k+1})$. In particular, $y^q \leq f(y^q)$, and we deduce that $y^q = f(y^q)$. Thus the concatenation of P and Q gives a path from x to the stable configuration y^q. Since P and Q are decreasing and increasing, we have $p, q \leq n$. As a consequence, the concatenation of P and Q is of length at most $2n$.   □

Let $\mathcal{N}$ be BAN and let G be its signed interaction graph. Aracena [1] (see also [2]) proved the following: *If G is strongly connected and has no negative cycles (and at least one arc) then the global transition function has at least two stable configurations.* This is an immediate consequence of Propositions 1 and 2. Actually, all the arguments of the original proof are more or less contained in the proof of these two propositions, so we cannot speak about a proof simplification here. However, the interest in Proposition 1, which gives a new relationship between monotonicity and negative cycles, is clearly visible with the following second application.

In [19], the following discrete version of the second Thomas' rule has been established, with a quite complex proof: *If G has no negative cycles, then the asynchronous transition graph of $\mathcal{N}$ has no stable oscillations.* Actually, a very easy proof results directly from Propositions 1 and 3. Indeed, suppose that G has no negative cycles, and suppose first that G is strongly connected. Then $\mathcal{N}$ is equivalent to a monotone BAN $\mathcal{N}'$ by Proposition 1. And we deduce from Proposition 3 that, in the asynchronous transition graph $\mathcal{G}'$ of $\mathcal{N}'$, a stable configuration can be reached from every initial configuration. Since the asynchronous transition graph $\mathcal{G}$ of $\mathcal{N}$ is isomorphic to $\mathcal{G}'$, we have proven the following: *If G has no negative cycles and is strongly connected, then, in $\mathcal{G}$, a stable configuration can be reached from any initial configuration* $(*)$. Now, suppose that G is not strongly connected. Then, by applying $(*)$ on the SCCs of G, proceeding from the initial ones to the terminal ones (according to the underlying topological ordering of the SCCs), we obtain the same conclusion: a stable configuration can be reached from any initial configuration. As a consequence, $\mathcal{G}$ has no stable oscillations, which had to be proven.

3.3   More Precisions about Convergence Times

In this part, for a given monotone BAN $\mathcal{N}$ of size n and an arbitrary initial configuration $x \in \mathbb{B}^n$, we interest in the set $\mathcal{A}(x)$ of stable configurations reachable from x. We will show the followings results:

– there exist two stables configurations $a^+(x)$ and $a^-(x)$ of $\mathcal{A}(x)$ such that for any $a \in \mathcal{A}(x)$, $a^-(x) \le a \le a^+(x)$;
– $a^-(x)$ and $a^+(x)$ are reachable from x in less than $2n - 4$ transitions and, in some cases, this bound is tight;
– there exists a configuration $a \in \mathcal{A}(x)$ such that a is reachable from x in at most n transitions.

To compute $a^-(x)$, we will proceed as in the proof of Proposition 3, by using a decreasing path from x of maximal length and, then, an increasing path of maximal length. The computation of $a^+(x)$ is done symmetrically. Let us denote by $\mathbf{0}(x)$ (resp. $\mathbf{1}(x)$) a configuration (which can be proven to be unique) resulting from following a decreasing path P of maximal length (resp. an increasing path Q of maximal length).

Lemma 1. *Let $\mathcal{N}$ be a monotone BAN and $\mathcal{G}$ its associated asynchronous transition graph. Consider a configuration $x \in \mathbb{B}^n$ of $\mathcal{N}$. If there exists an automaton i such that $\mathbf{0}(x)_i = 1$, then the configurations where the state of automaton i equals 0 are not reachable from x. Conversely, if there exists an automaton i such that $\mathbf{1}(x)_i = 0$, the configurations where the state of automaton i equals 1 are not reachable from x.*

Proof. Let $x \in \mathbb{B}^n$. First, let us prove the first part of the lemma. Consider an automaton i such that $\mathbf{0}(x)_i = 1$, and let us suppose that there exists a configuration $y \in \mathbb{B}^n$ reachable from x such that $\mathrm{f}_i(y) = 0$. Without loss of generality, we suppose that y is the closest configuration to x with an automaton k such that $\mathrm{f}_k(y) = 0$ and $\mathbf{0}(x)_k = 1$ (in $\mathcal{G}$). Since $\mathrm{f}_i(y) = 0$, $\mathrm{f}_i(\mathbf{0}(x)) = 1$ and f_i is monotone, there exists at least one automaton $j \in V^-(i)$ such that $y_j = 0$ and $\mathbf{0}(x)_j = 1$. Now, since $\mathbf{0}(x)_j = 1$, we have $x_j = 1$ and thus j switches from state 1 to state 0 along the path from x to y, which is a contradiction with the fact that y is the closest configuration to x with an automaton k such that $\mathrm{f}_k(y) = 0$ and $\mathbf{0}(x)_k = 1$. We prove in a similar way the second part of the lemma. $\square$

Corollary 1. *Let $\mathcal{N}$ be a monotone BAN and $\mathcal{G}$ its associated asynchronous transition graph. Consider a configuration $x \in \mathbb{B}^n$ of $\mathcal{N}$. For any configuration y reachable from x, $\mathbf{0}(x) \leq \mathbf{0}(y)$.*

Lemma 2 below gives a mean to detect *irreversible transitions*, i.e. transitions that make an automaton stable in the sense that its state cannot change anymore.

Lemma 2. *Let $\mathcal{N}$ be a monotone BAN and $\mathcal{G}$ its associated asynchronous transition graph. Consider a configuration $x \in \mathbb{B}^n$ of $\mathcal{N}$. If there exists an automaton $i \in V$ such that $x_i = 0$ and $f_i(\mathbf{0}(x)) = 1$, configurations with automaton i in state 0 are not reachable from a configuration reachable by x with automaton i in state 1.*

Proof. Consider a configuration $x \in \mathbb{B}^n$ of $\mathcal{N}$ with an automaton $i \in V$ such that $x_i = 0$ and $\mathrm{f}_i(\mathbf{0}(x)) = 1$. Let $y \in \mathbb{B}^n$ be a configuration with $y_i = 1$ that is reachable from x, and $z \in \mathbb{B}^n$ a configuration reachable from y. By Corollary 1, $\mathbf{0}(x) \leq \mathbf{0}(y)$ and $\mathrm{f}_i(\mathbf{0}(y)) = 1$. Configuration $\mathbf{0}(y)$ is reachable from y by a decreasing path and, since f_i is monotone, $\mathbf{0}(y) = 1$. By Corollary 1, $\mathbf{0}(y) \leq \mathbf{0}(z) \leq z$ and, necessarily, $z_i = 1$. $\square$

Let us denote by $a^-(x)$ (resp. $a^+(x)$) the configuration $\mathbf{1}(\mathbf{0}(x))$ (resp. $\mathbf{0}(\mathbf{1}(x))$). Note that both these configurations are reachable from x.

Theorem 1. *Let $\mathcal{N}$ be a monotone BAN of size n and $\mathcal{G}$ its associated asynchronous transition graph. Consider an arbitrary configuration $x \in \mathbb{B}^n$ of $\mathcal{N}$. Configurations $a^-(x)$ and $a^+(x)$ are stable and $\forall a \in \mathscr{A}(x)$, $a^-(x) \leq a \leq a^+(x)$.*

Proof. From the proof of Proposition 3, $a^-(x)$ is stable. Symmetrically, it is easy to show that $a^+(x)$ is too.

Consider any $a \in \mathscr{A}(x)$. Since a is reachable from x, by Lemma 1 we have $\mathbf{0}(x) \leq a$. Now, consider a minimal increasing path from $\mathbf{0}(x)$ to $a^-(x)$. Suppose (for a contradiction) that there is an automaton $i \in V$ such that $a_i = 0$ and $a^-(x)_i = 1$. Without loss of generality, we suppose that i is the first that is updated along the path with this property $(*)$. Then, let $y \in \mathbb{B}^n$ be the configuration reached from $\mathbf{0}(x)$ just before the updating of i. Thus we have $f_i(y) = 1$. Since $a \geq \mathbf{0}(x)$ and since i respects $(*)$, $a \geq y$ holds. Moreover, since f_i is monotone, $f_i(a) = 1$, which is a contradiction with the fact that a is a stable configuration. Thus $a^-(x) \leq a$ and we prove with similar arguments that $a \geq a^+(x)$. $\qquad\square$

Let $\mathcal{O}(f)$ be the time complexity for evaluating the local transition functions. Remark that the computation time to find $a^+(x)$ and $a^-(x)$ is $\mathcal{O}(n + m + f)$. Despite this time complexity in the general case, genetic regulation networks are known to have a connectivity (*i.e.* the average in-degree of G) $2 \leq K \leq 3$ [12]. As a consequence, we can assume that the time complexity in real-life examples is $\mathcal{O}(n)$.

Let us now give an upper bound (only valid for the asynchronous updating mode) on the convergence time from x to $a^-(x)$ (and conversely for $a^+(x)$), *i.e.* an upper bound on the length of shortest paths from x to $a^-(x)$. More precisely, let us prove that the convergence time from x to $a^-(x)$ is at most $2n - 4$ (for $n \geq 3$). Suppose first that no local update functions are constant, so that $1\dots1$ and $0\dots0$ are stable configurations. Consider that x is not $1\dots1$ (otherwise $x = a^-(x)$ and there is nothing to prove). If $\mathbf{0}(x) = 0\dots0$ then $a^-(x) = \mathbf{0}(x)$ and the convergence time is $d(x, 0\dots0) < n$. So, suppose that $\mathbf{0}(x)$ is not $0\dots0$. Then the convergence time from x to $\mathbf{0}(x)$ is at most $n - 2$, and the convergence time from $\mathbf{0}(x)$ to $a^-(x) = \mathbf{1}(\mathbf{0}(x))$ is at most $n - 1$. Now, suppose (for a contradiction) that the convergence time from x to $a^-(x)$ is $2n-3$. Then the convergence time from x to $\mathbf{0}(x)$ is $n - 2$ and the convergence time from $\mathbf{0}(x)$ to $a^-(x)$ is $n-1$. We deduce that, in configuration x, there is a unique automaton, let us call it i, whose state is 0, and we deduce that $a^-(x) = 1\dots1$. Since there are no transitions from x to $a^-(x)$ (otherwise the convergence time is 1) and since the network is monotone, we deduce that for all $y \in \mathbb{B}^n$, if $y_i = 0$ then $f_i(y) = 0$. But it means that configuration $1\dots1$ cannot be reached from x, which is a contradiction. As a consequence, the convergence time from x to $a^-(x)$ is at most $2n - 4$. Now, from this, it is easy to see that if the network contains k constant local update function, then the convergence time from x to $a^-(x)$ is at most $k + 2(n - k) - 4$, so that $2n - 4$ is a correct bound in every case. Now, studying the dynamics of networks defined as

$$\begin{cases} f_1(x) = x_1 \vee x_n \\ \forall i \in \{2, \dots, n - 1\}, \ f_i(x) = x_{i-1} \\ f_n(x) = x_{n-1} \wedge x_n \end{cases}$$

evidences that the bound is obtained (it is easy to show it with $n = 3$ by computing the convergence time of $x = 101$ to $a^-(x) = 110$).

Also, notice that if a stable configuration a verifies $a^-(x) \leq a \leq a^+(x)$, we cannot conclude that $a \in \mathscr{A}(x)$. The simplest example is the BAN of size 3 defined as

$$\begin{cases} f_1(x) = x_2 \wedge x_3 \\ \forall i \in \{2,3\}, \; f_i(x) = x_{i-1} \vee x_i \end{cases}.$$

Consider the initial configuration $x = 100$. We have $a^-(x) = 000$ and $a^+(x) = 111$. Furthermore, $a^-(x) \leq a = 001 \leq 111$ is stable but is not reachable from x.

Now, we show that every configuration can converge in no more than n transitions.

Theorem 2. *Let $\mathscr{N}$ be a monotone BAN of size n and $\mathscr{G}$ its associated asynchronous transition graph. Consider an arbitrary configuration $x \in \mathbb{B}^n$ of $\mathscr{N}$. There exists a stable configuration $a \in \mathscr{A}(x)$ such that a is reachable in at most n transitions from x without switching the state of an automaton twice.*

Proof. Consider an arbitrary configuration $x \in \mathbb{B}^n$ of $\mathscr{N}$ and the following algorithm that returns a couple of configurations $(y, z) \in \mathbb{B}^n \times \mathbb{B}^n$:

```
// Input: N and x ∈ B^n.
y ← x
z ← 0(y)
while ∃i ∈ V s.t. f_i(z) = 1 ∧ z_i = 0 do
    y_i ← 1
    z ← 0(y)
end
return y, z
```

Consider an automaton i such that $z_i = 1$. Since $z = \mathbf{0}(y)$, $f_i(z) = 1$. Now, consider an automaton j such that $z_j = 0$. Suppose that $f_j(z) = 1$. In this case, either $y_j = 0$, which is a contradiction because the algorithm should have switched its state to 1, or $y_j = 1$, and, since $z = \mathbf{0}(y)$, this contradicts the monotonicity of f_j. Thus, z is a stable configuration.

Now, let us prove that z is reachable from x. Consider the following invariant: When an automaton i of y is switched from 0 to 1, $f_i(y) = 1$. Since $y \geq \mathbf{0}(y)$, $f_i(\mathbf{0}(y)) = 1$ and f_i is monotone, then $f_i(y) = 1$. Thus, y is reachable from x. And since $z = \mathbf{0}(y)$, z is reachable from x.

By Lemma 2, there is a path of irreversible transitions from x to y. Since $z = \mathbf{0}(y)$, there is a decreasing path from y to z. Thus, z is reachable in no more than n transitions from x without switching the state of an automaton twice. And we deduce that the convergence time of x is at most n.   □

4   Conclusion and Perspectives

In this paper, we have focused on BANs without negative cycles and have shown (or given new neater proofs of) pertinent results in a context at the frontier of theoretical computer science and theoretical biology. Notice once again that, although proofs are given in the framework of BANs subjected with the asynchronous updating mode (for easing the reading), they remain valid for the much more complicated elementary updating mode. Of course, this is due to the restriction we did on BANs themselves, by considering only those with no negative cycles that are known to admit no stable oscillations as asymptotic behaviours. Rather than recalling now the results presented in the previous lines, we prefer drawing some perspectives that we believe relevant for further works.

The first perspective directly comes from the last result presented. It shows that, in a monotone BAN of size n (and its equivalent BANs), any configuration can reach dynamically a stable configuration in at most n transitions. A natural question that remains to be answered to in the same framework as that used in this paper is the following: are the stable configurations that are reachable from a given arbitrary initial configuration all reachable in $2n - 4$ transitions? If not, are they in a polynomial number of transitions according to n? Furthermore, this study allows to give, for each configuration of monotone(-equivalent) BANs, a basic representation of its set of attractors, and thus, of the attraction basins of the underlying dynamical systems. However, it should be possible to go further and give more precisions about these sets, as it has been done in the case of Minority in [22]. Also, of course, it would be interesting to characterise BANs of size n inducing negative cycles in their architecture which would not break the convergence time property in at most n transitions.

Moreover, following [6, 17, 16, 21], we know that the choice of the updating mode is crucial for the dynamical behaviour of a BAN, even a monotone one, to have certain properties. For instance, although monotone BANs admit only stable configurations as asymptotic behaviours according to both the asynchronous and elementary updating modes, that is not the case if they are subjected to the parallel updating mode. For instance, consider a monotone positive cycle of size n evolving in parallel, it admits stable oscillations (or limit cycles) and, consequently, does not converge necessarily. As a consequence, it would be of interest to dive this study and its associated perspectives into the context of deterministic updating modes, such as the block-sequential ones.

Finally, on the basis of the present work, the last perspective that seems amongst the most relevant according to us would be to work on the discrete version of the monotone function theory on Banach spaces notably developed by Hirsch and Smith in [9, 25]. This would lead us to obtain a better understanding of the common properties of such continuous and discrete objects and, possibly, to highlight fundamental properties they do not share.

Acknowledgements. This work has been supported by the ANR projects BioTempo (ANR-10-BLAN-0218), Synbiotic (ANR-10-BLAN-0307) and QuasiCool (ANR-12-JS02-011-01), and by Bottollier Motoculture through a working group organised in Sallanches at the beginning of 2013 and we are particularly grateful to Pascal Bottollier for having fostered us during a week.

References

1. Aracena, J.: Maximum number of fixed points in regulatory Boolean networks. Bulletin of Mathematical Biology 70, 1398–1409 (2008)
2. Aracena, J., Demongeot, J., Goles, E.: Positive and negative circuits in discrete neural networks. IEEE Transactions on Neural Networks 15, 77–83 (2004)
3. Elspas, B.: The theory of autonomous linear sequential networks. IRE Transactions on Circuit Theory 6, 45–60 (1959)
4. Goles, E.: Fixed point behavior of threshold functions on a finite set. SIAM Journal on Algebraic and Discrete Methods 3, 529–531 (1982)
5. Goles, E., Martínez, S.: Neural and automata networks: dynamical behaviour and applications. Kluwer Academic Publishers (1990)
6. Goles, E., Salinas, L.: Sequential operator for filtering cycles in Boolean networks. Advances in Applied Mathematics 45, 346–358 (2010)
7. Golomb, S.W.: Shift register sequences. Holden-Day (1967)
8. Harary, F.: On the notion of balance of a signed graph. Michigan Mathematical Journal 2, 143–146 (1953)
9. Hirsch, M.W., Smith, H.: Monotone maps: a review. Journal of Difference Equations and Applications 11, 379–398 (2005)
10. Hopfield, J.J.: Neural networks and physical systems with emergent collective computational abilities. Proceedings of the National Academy of Sciences of the USA 79, 2554–2558 (1982)
11. Kauffman, S.A.: Metabolic stability and epigenesis in randomly constructed genetic nets. Journal of Theoretical Biology 22, 437–467 (1969)
12. Kauffman, S.A.: Origins of order: self-organization and selection in evolution. Oxford University Press (1993)
13. Kleene, S.C.: Representation of events in nerve nets and finite automata. In: Automata studies, Annals of Mathematics Studies, vol. 34, pp. 3–41. Princeton Universtity Press (1956)
14. McCulloch, W.S., Pitts, W.H.: A logical calculus of the ideas immanent in nervous activity. Bulletin of Mathematical Biophysics 5, 115–133 (1943)
15. von Neumann, J.: Theory of self-reproducing automata. University of Illinois Press (1966)
16. Noual, M.: Synchronism vs. asynchronism in Boolean automata networks. Tech. rep., Laboratoire I3S, UMR UNS CNRS (2012), arXiv:1104.4039
17. Noual, M.: Updating automata networks. Ph.D. thesis, École normale supérieure de Lyon (2012), tel-00726560
18. Remy, É., Ruet, P., Thieffry, D.: Graphic requirement for multistability and attractive cycles in a Boolean dynamical framework. Advances in Applied Mathematics 41, 335–350 (2008)
19. Richard, A.: Negative circuits and sustained oscillations in asynchronous automata networks. Advances in Applied Mathematics 44, 378–392 (2010)
20. Richard, A., Comet, J.P.: Necessary conditions for multistationarity in discrete dynamical systems. Discrete Applied Mathematics 155, 2403–2413 (2007)
21. Robert, F.: Discrete iterations: a metric study. Springer (1986)
22. Rouquier, J.B., Regnault, D., Thierry, É.: Stochastic minority on graphs. Theoretical Computer Science 412, 3947–3963 (2011)
23. Saint Savage, N.: The effects of state dependent and state independent probabilistic updating on Boolean network dynamics. Ph.D. thesis, University of Manchester (2005)

24. Smith, A.R.: Simple computation-universal cellular spaces. Journal of the ACM 18, 339–353 (1971)
25. Smith, H.L.: Monotone dynamical systems: an introduction to the theory of competitive and cooperative systems, Mathematical surveys and monographs, vol. 41. American Mathematical Society (1995)
26. Thomas, R.: Boolean formalization of genetic control circuits. Journal of Theoretical Biology 42, 563–585 (1973)
27. Thomas, R.: On the relation between the logical structure of systems and their ability to generate multiple steady states or sustained oscillations. In: Numerical Methods in the Study of Critical Phenomena. Springer Series in Synergetics, vol. 9, pp. 180–193. Springer (1981)
28. Thomas, R.: Regulatory networks seen as asynchronous automata: a logical description. Journal of Theoretical Biology 153, 1–23 (1991)

Color Blind Cellular Automata*

Ville Salo and Ilkka Törmä

TUCS – Turku Centre for Computer Science, Finland
University of Turku, Finland
{vosalo,iatorm}@utu.fi

Abstract. We introduce the classes of color blind and typhlotic cellular automata, that is, cellular automata that commute with all symbol permutations and all symbol mappings, respectively. We show that color blind cellular automata form a relatively large subclass of all cellular automata which contains an intrinsically universal automaton. On the other hand, we give simple characterizations for the color blind CA which are also group homomorphisms, and for general typhlotic CA, showing that both must be trivial in most cases.

Keywords: cellular automata, commutation, symbol permutations, homomorphisms.

1 Introduction

Suppose we wish to study a cellular automaton f, that is, a continuous shift invariant function from $S^{\mathbb{Z}}$ to itself, where S is a finite alphabet. A natural direction of study would be to consider its relation to some other cellular automata, for example to find the commutator of f, the set of all cellular automata it commutes with. This is known as the *commuting block maps problem*, and it has a long history, dating back to the 70s [2]. Algebraically, the commutator of f can also be viewed as the set of homomorphisms of the unary algebra $(S^{\mathbb{Z}}, f)$ that are also cellular automata. To generalize this notion, one defines the commutator of a whole family of cellular automata as the set of those CA that commute with all of them.

In this article, we study so-called color blind (typhlotic) cellular automata, that is, automata which commute with all symbol permutations (all symbol mappings, respectively), on full shifts and their subshifts. In other words, color blind cellular automata form the commutator of the family of all cellwise permutations. They are interesting mainly from the mathematical point of view, as the commutator of a simple but nontrivial class of CA. We give a natural logical characterization of color blind cellular automata and show that there exists an intrinsically universal color blind CA. Perhaps somewhat surprisingly, we show that intrinsic universality is also possible in typhotic CA if the full shift is binary, but that every typhlotic CA must be a shift map on other full shifts. We also

---

* Research supported by the Academy of Finland Grant 131558.

J. Kari, M. Kutrib, and A. Malcher (Eds.): AUTOMATA 2013, LNCS 8155, pp. 139–154, 2013.

show that in a quantitative sense, the class of color blind cellular automata is relatively as large as possible in the class of all cellular automata.

We then consider the case of full shifts over a finite group alphabet. The natural self-maps of such objects are the cellular automata that are also group homomorphisms for the product group structure, and we call them homomorphic cellular automata. We investigate cellular automata that are both color blind and homomorphic. This turns out to be very restrictive, and the situation is similar to that of typhlotic CA without the group structure: if the alphabet group is sufficiently simple ($\mathbb{Z}_2$, $\mathbb{Z}_3$, or $\mathbb{Z}_2^2$), then there exist nontrivial color blind homomorphic CA, but on more complicated full group shifts, all color blind homomorphic CA are shift maps.

2   Definitions

Let S be a finite set, called the *alphabet*. The *full shift* is the space $S^{\mathbb{Z}}$ of infinite configurations over S endowed with the product topology. For $x \in S^{\mathbb{Z}}$ and $n \in \mathbb{Z}$, we denote by x_n the symbol of x at coordinate n. For a word $w \in S^*$ and $s \in S$, we denote by $|w|$ the length of w, and by $|w|_s$ the number of occurrences of s in w. For a configuration $x \in S^{\mathbb{Z}}$, we say w *occurs in* x if $w = x_{[n,n+|w|-1]}$ for some $n \in \mathbb{Z}$.

A subset $X \subset S^{\mathbb{Z}}$ is called a *subshift* if it is closed in the topology and invariant under the *shift map* $\sigma : S^{\mathbb{Z}} \to S^{\mathbb{Z}}$, defined by $\sigma(x)_n = x_{n+1}$. Alternatively, a subshift X is defined by a set $\mathcal{F} \subset S^*$ of *forbidden words* as the set of configurations in which no $w \in \mathcal{F}$ occurs. If $\mathcal{F}$ can be taken finite, X is a *subshift of finite type* (SFT for short). A configuration $x \in S^{\mathbb{Z}}$ is *spatially periodic* if $\sigma^p(x) = x$ for some $p > 0$.

A continuous mapping $f : X \to X$ in a subshift that commutes with σ is called a *cellular automaton*. All cellular automata f are defined by *local functions* $F : S^N \to S$, where $N \subset \mathbb{Z}$ is the finite *neighborhood* of f, by the formula $f(x)_n = F(x_{n+N})$ for all $n \in \mathbb{Z}$ [4]. We usually define $N = [-r, r]$ for some $r \in \mathbb{N}$, called the *radius* of f. To each CA f we associate a local function f_{loc}, which in general is not uniquely defined, but this should not cause any confusion. A configuration $x \in X$ is called *temporally periodic (with respect to f)* if $f^p(x) = x$ for some $p > 0$. A symbol mapping $\pi : S \to S$ can also be seen as a cellular automaton on $S^{\mathbb{Z}}$ by $\pi(x)_n = \pi(x_n)$.

Let S be a finite algebra. Then, $S^{\mathbb{Z}}$ becomes an algebra when the operations are applied cellwise. We say a CA $f : S^{\mathbb{Z}} \to S^{\mathbb{Z}}$ is *homomorphic* (with respect to the algebraic structure of S) if it is a homomorphism of $S^{\mathbb{Z}}$. From the results of [10] we know that this is the case exactly if the local rule $F : S^N \to S$ is a homomorphism. If S is an abelian group and f is of the form $\sum_{i=0}^{k-1} \sigma^{n_i}$ for some $n_i \in \mathbb{Z}$, we say f is a *sum of shifts*, and if the n_i are pairwise distinct, f is a *sum of distinct shifts*.

Let X be a nonempty set, and let $Q \subset 2^X$. If $\emptyset \notin Q$ and for all $A, B \in Q$ we have $A \subset C \implies C \in Q$ and $A \cap B \in Q$, then Q is a *filter* on X. If additionally $Q \subset Q' \implies Q = Q'$ for all filters Q' of X, then Q is an *ultrafilter*.

Remark 1. In the literature, the terminology related to cellular automata that are also group homomorphisms varies wildly. For example, in [7], the authors use the terms additive CA and group CA for cellular automata that are homomorphic with respect to an abelian group alphabet, and the term k-rule for CA that are sums of k distinct shifts. In [8] the term linear CA is used for homomorphic cellular automata. On the other hand, in [6] and many subsequent articles, the term linear CA refers to cellular automata on $\mathbb{Z}_p^{\mathbb{Z}}$ that we would call sums of shifts. Of course, over the alphabet $\mathbb{Z}_p$ the notions of homomorphic CA and sum of shifts coincide, but not over general abelian group alphabets. Even worse, the term linear is sometimes used to refer to *one-dimensional* CA. We have chosen our terminology in the hope of being as unambiguous as possible.

3   Color Blind Cellular Automata

We begin with the definition of our objects of interest, the color blind cellular automata.

Definition 1. *Let $f : S^{\mathbb{Z}} \to S^{\mathbb{Z}}$ be a CA such that for all symbol permutations $\pi : S \to S$ we have $f \circ \pi = \pi \circ f$. Then we say f is* color blind. *If f commutes with all symbol mappings, we say f is* typhlotic.

In other words, the set of color blind (typhlotic) cellular automata on $S^{\mathbb{Z}}$ is exactly the commutator of the set of all permutations on S (functions from S to itself, respectively). Another way to express this is that the set of spacetime diagrams of a color blind CA is closed under permuting the colors. We use the somewhat obscure term typhlotic, meaning blind, to avoid cluttering the global namespace of cellular automata: we will soon see that these automata are rather trivial (Theorem 2), and presumably do not have much theory beyond what we prove in this article.

Example 1. The radius-1 cellular automaton f on $\{0, 1, 2\}^{\mathbb{Z}}$ defined by

$$f_{\text{loc}}(a, b, c) = \begin{cases} c, \text{ if } a = b \neq c, \\ a, \text{ if } a \neq b = c, \\ b, \text{ otherwise} \end{cases}$$

is clearly color blind. It always chooses the symbol in its neighborhood that is in the minority, or acts as the identity CA if such a symbol does not exist. A portion of a spacetime diagram of f is shown in Figure 1.

A CA f on $S^{\mathbb{Z}}$ is called *captive* if the local rule f_{loc} satisfies $f_{\text{loc}}(a_1, \dots, a_n) \in \{a_1, \dots, a_n\}$ for all $a_1, \dots, a_n \in S$. Color blind CA are 'almost captive' in the following sense.

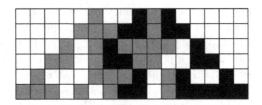

Fig. 1. A sample spacetime diagram of the cellular automaton of Example 1, with time advancing downward. The labels of the colors are unimportant, since any symbol permutation of a spacetime diagram of a color blind CA is also its spacetime diagram.

Lemma 1. *Let* $f : S^{\mathbb{Z}} \to S^{\mathbb{Z}}$ *be a color blind CA. Then* $f_{\mathrm{loc}}(a_1, \ldots, a_n) \in \{a_1, \ldots, a_n\}$ *whenever* $|\{a_1, \ldots, a_n\}| < |S| - 1$.

Proof. Suppose that we have $|\{a_1, \ldots, a_n\}| < |S| - 1$, but $a = f_{\mathrm{loc}}(a_1, \ldots, a_n) \notin \{a_1, \ldots, a_n\}$. Then, there exists

$$b \in S \setminus \{a, a_1, \ldots, a_n\}.$$

Now, f does not commute with the transposition $(a\ b)$. □

The automaton of Example 1 is captive by definition. However, not all color blind automata are captive, since the local rule may output the 'last remaining color' unambiguously when all but one color appear in the neighborhood, as the alphabet size is known. The following is an example of this phenomenon.

Example 2. The radius-1 cellular automaton f on $\{0, 1, 2\}^{\mathbb{Z}}$ defined by

$$f_{\mathrm{loc}}(a, b, c) = \begin{cases} d, & \text{if } |\{a, b, c\}| = 2 \text{ and } d \notin \{a, b, c\}, \\ b, & \text{otherwise} \end{cases}$$

is color blind. It always chooses the unique symbol that does not appear in its neighborhood, or acts as the identity CA if such a symbol does not exist. It is clearly not captive. A portion of a spacetime diagram of f is shown in Figure 2.

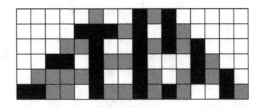

Fig. 2. A sample spacetime diagram of the cellular automaton of Example 2, with time advancing downward

Typhlotic CA are in fact captive, which we will obtain as a corollary of Theorem 2. We continue with a simple logical characterization of color blind cellular automata which motivates their definition.

Definition 2. *Fix a set of variables $V = \{v_1, \ldots, v_n\}$. A color blind equation over V is a boolean combination of basic equations of the form $v_i = v_j$. For a symbol equation E over V, an alphabet S and a word $w \in S^n$, we denote by $E(w)$ the equation obtained by replacing each v_i by w_i in E. The equation E defines a set of words $E(S) \subset S^n$ by $E(S) = \{w \in S^n \mid E(w) \text{ holds}\}$. We say E is* captive *on S if the last letter of w occurs at least twice in w for all $w \in E(S)$, and* captive, *if it is captive on S for all finite S. If $n = 2r+2$ and $E(S)$ defines a function from S^{2r+1} to S, we let $f_E^S : S^{\mathbb{Z}} \to S^{\mathbb{Z}}$ be the cellular automaton whose local function it is. We say f_E^S is* defined by a color blind equation.

Lemma 2. *A set of words $W \subset S^n$ is defined by a color blind equation if and only if it is closed under symbol permutations.*

Proof. First, let $W = E(S)$ for an equation E, and consider an arbitrary symbol permutation $\pi : S \to S$. It is clear that if $E(w)$ holds for a word $w \in S^n$, then so does $E(\pi(w))$, and thus W is closed under symbol permutations.

Suppose then that W is closed under symbol permutations. For all $w \in W$, define the equation $E_w = \bigwedge_{i,j \in [0, n-1]} t(i, j)$, where $t(i, j)$ is $v_i = v_j$ if $w_i = w_j$, and $\neg(v_i = v_j)$ otherwise. We let $E = \bigvee_{w \in W} E_w$. Now, it is clear that $W \subset E(S)$. On the other hand, let $v \in E(S)$. This means that $v \in E_w(S)$ for some $w \in W$. It is easy to see that there then exists a symbol permutation $\pi : S \to S$ with $\pi(w) = v$, and since W is closed under symbol permutations, we have $v \in W$. □

As a cellular automaton commutes with symbol permutations if and only if its local rule does, we obtain the following corollary.

Corollary 1. *A CA $f : S^{\mathbb{Z}} \to S^{\mathbb{Z}}$ is (captive and) color blind if and only if it is defined by a (captive and) color blind equation.*

Example 3. The cellular automaton of Example 1 is defined by the captive and color blind equation

$$(v_1 = v_2 \wedge v_2 \neq v_3 \wedge v_3 = v_4) \vee (v_1 \neq v_2 \wedge v_2 = v_3 \wedge v_1 = v_4) \vee (v_2 = v_4),$$

where v_1, v_2, v_3 and v_4 correspond to a, b, c and $f_{\text{loc}}(a, b, c)$ in the definition, respectively.

The characterization essentially says that a cellular automaton is color blind if and only if it can be defined without referring to any particular colors, but only their arrangements on the neighborhood. If we restrict to captive color blind cellular automata, the equation defining the color blind CA can be chosen so that it defines a CA on any subshift containing the original. This is essentially the content of Proposition 1. To prove it, we need a few definitions and lemmas.

Definition 3. *Let $X \subset Y \subset S^{\mathbb{Z}}$ be subshifts. If $X = Y \cap Z$ for some SFT $Z \subset S^{\mathbb{Z}}$, we say X is a subSFT of Y.*

Lemma 3. *If X is a subSFT of Y and $X = \bigcap_{i \in \mathbb{N}} X_i$ for some subshifts X_i of Y such that $X_{i+1} \subset X_i$ for all $i \in \mathbb{N}$, then $X = X_i$ for some i.*

Proof. Let $X = Y \cap Z$ where Z is an SFT. Then, $\bigcap_{i \in \mathbb{N}} X_i = X \subset Z$, so $X_i \subset Z$ for all large enough i, since Z is an SFT (all the finitely many forbidden patterns of Z must be absent in some X_i). But $X_i = X$ for all such i.

Definition 4. *Let $X \subset S^{\mathbb{Z}}$ be a subshift, and let $f : X \to X$ be a CA. Suppose that whenever $\pi : S \to S$ is a symbol permutation and $x \in X$ satisfies $\pi(x) \in X$, then $\pi(f(x)) = f(\pi(x))$. Then we say f is color blind on X. If there exists $r \in \mathbb{N}$ such that for all $x \in X$ there exists $k \in [-r, r]$ such that $f(x) = x_k$, we say f is captive on X.*

Proposition 1. *Let $X \subset S^{\mathbb{Z}}$ be a subshift. Then a CA $f : X \to X$ is captive and color blind on X iff $f = f_E^S|_X$ for a captive color blind equation E.*

Proof. If $f = f_E^S|_X$ for some captive color blind equation E and $\pi : S \to S$ is any symbol permutation, then $\pi(f_E^S(x)) = f_E^S(\pi(x))$ for all $x \in S^{\mathbb{Z}}$, so in particular this is the case when $x, \pi(x) \in X$. In this case f is also clearly captive on X.

For the other direction, the idea is to take the subshift

$$Y = \{(x, y) \in X^2 \mid f(x) = y\},$$

and define a decreasing sequence of subshifts $Y_i \subset (S^2)^{\mathbb{Z}}$ such that $Y = \bigcap_{i \in \mathbb{N}} Y_i$, and the Y_i are all defined by color blind equations of a certain form. Since the subshift Y is a subSFT of $Z = X^2$ and $Y_i \subset Z$, Lemma 3 implies that $Y = Y_i$ for some $i \in \mathbb{N}$.

So suppose that $f : X \to X$ is captive and color blind on X, and let $[-r, r]$ be the neighborhood of f. For all $i \in \mathbb{N}$, define $W_i = \{x_{[-r-i, r+i]} \cdot f(x)_0 \mid x \in X\}$. Let E_i be a set of equations defined by the W_i, as in Lemma 2, so that $E_i(v \cdot a)$ holds if and only if there is a permutation $\pi : S \to S$ and some $w \cdot b \in W_i$ with $\pi(w \cdot b) = v \cdot a$. For large enough i the E_i are captive, since f is captive on X. Define then

$$Y_i = \{(x, y) \in X^2 \mid \forall j \in \mathbb{Z} : E_i(x_{[j-r-i, j+r+i]} \cdot y_j)\} \subset (S^2)^{\mathbb{Z}}.$$

Now, we claim that $Y = \{(x, y) \in X^2 \mid f(x) = y\} = \bigcap_{i \in \mathbb{N}} Y_i$. Clearly, $Y \subset Y_i$ for all $i \in \mathbb{N}$, so suppose $(x, y) \in \bigcap_{i \in \mathbb{N}} Y_i$ but $(x, y) \notin Y$. We may assume $f(x)_0 \neq y_0$. Now, as $E_i(x_{[-r-i, r+i]} \cdot y_0)$ holds for all i, there exist symbol permutations $\pi_i : S \to S$ and words $w_i \cdot b_i \in W_i$ such that $\pi_i(w_i \cdot b_i) = x_{[-r-i, r+i]} \cdot y_0$.

Take an infinite subsequence where the π_i and b_i are fixed, and denote these by π and b. Then, extract a subsequence where the w_i converge to some configuration $z \in S^{\mathbb{Z}}$. Now we have $z \in X$, $\pi(z) = x \in X$, $f(z)_0 = b$ and thus $\pi(f(z))_0 = \pi(b) = y_0$, but $f(\pi(z))_0 = f(x)_0$. This is a contradiction, and thus $Y = \bigcap_{i \in \mathbb{N}} Y_i$.

Since Y is a subSFT of X^2 and the sequence $(Y_i)_{i \in \mathbb{N}}$ is decreasing, we have $Y = Y_i$ for some $i \in \mathbb{N}$ by Lemma 3, and the captive color blind equation E_i thus defines a local function $f_{\mathrm{loc}} : \mathcal{B}_{2(r+i)+1}(X) \to S$ for f. Let F be the equation defined by $\mathcal{B}_{2(i+r)+1}(X)$ and let

$$E = E_i \vee (\neg F \wedge v_{\mathrm{out}} = v_1),$$

where $v_{\mathrm{out}} = v_{2(r+i)+2}$ denotes the output value of the function defined by E. Then, f_E^R is a captive color blind cellular automaton for any alphabet R: If the input of the local function is a word of X up to renaming the symbols, then f_E^R chooses the output from the inputs as f would. Otherwise, the word does not satisfy F, and f_E^R chooses the leftmost input as the output.   □

Example 4. The restriction of captivity in the above result is necessary: the symbol permutation $(0\ 1)$ on $\{0,1\}^{\mathbb{Z}}$ cannot be extended, as a cellular automaton, to a color blind cellular automaton on $\{0,1,2\}^{\mathbb{Z}}$.

We also show by another example that the color blind equation defined by f_{loc} may not be sufficient even if it is captive in the sense that it always outputs a symbol seen in the neighborhood. Let X consist of the configurations $x = {}^{\infty}(0122)^{\infty}$ and $y = {}^{\infty}(0022)^{\infty}$ and their shifts, and define $f_{\mathrm{loc}} : \{0,1,2\}^3 \to \{0,1,2\}$ by $f_{\mathrm{loc}}(a,b,c) = b$, except for $f_{\mathrm{loc}}(0,1,2) = 0$. Now, f is captive and color blind on X (the only symbol permutation we need to check is $(0\ 2)$). However, the color blind equation defined by f_{loc} does not extend to a cellular automaton on $\{0,1,2\}^{\mathbb{Z}}$, since $f_{\mathrm{loc}}(012) = 0 = f_{\mathrm{loc}}(201)$. One can check that the local rule with neighborhood $N = [-1, 2]$ suffices though.

4   Constructing Color Blind Cellular Automata

In this section, we give concrete examples of color blind cellular automata, and prove some results that require explicit construction of such objects.

Definition 5. *Let $f : S^{\mathbb{Z}} \to S^{\mathbb{Z}}$ be a cellular automaton with neighborhood size n. We say f is a* majority CA *if, whenever $f_{\mathrm{loc}}(s_1, \ldots, s_n) = s$, we have $|\{i \in [1, n] \mid s_i = s\}| \geq |\{i \in [1, n] \mid s_i = s'\}|$ for all $s' \in S$.*

This means that the local rule of a majority CA always outputs a symbol that occurs a maximal number of times in the input. All majority CA are of course captive. In the binary case, there is a unique majority CA for each odd neighborhood size, and this CA is color blind. In other cases, the CA must have a tie-breaking rule. To make such a CA color blind we can, for example, always choose the leftmost input symbol s_m that maximizes $|\{i \in [1, n] \mid s_i = s_m\}|$.

Of the 256 elementary cellular automata (see [12] for the definitions and the numbering scheme), 16 rules are color blind. The even-numbered rules are summarized in Table 1, while the odd-numbered rules are obtained by subtracting their numbers from 255, effectively composing them with the symbol permutation $(0\ 1)$. We show the even-numbered color blind rules, as they are exactly the

Table 1. The even-numbered color blind elementary CA. The variables v_1, v_2 and v_3 denote inputs to the local rule, and v_4 is its output.

CA	Color blind equation	Description
142	$(v_4 \neq v_2) \iff (v_1 = v_2 \neq v_3)$	Left shift with 'barriers'
150	$(v_1 = v_2) \iff (v_4 = v_3)$	Sum of neighborhood mod 2
170	$v_4 = v_3$	Left shift
178	$(v_4 = v_2) \iff (v_1 = v_2 = v_3)$	Flip unless all inputs equal
204	$v_4 = v_2$	Identity
212	$(v_4 \neq v_2) \iff (v_1 \neq v_2 = v_3)$	Mirrored 142
232	$(v_4 \neq v_2) \iff (v_1 \neq v_2 \neq v_3)$	Majority
240	$v_4 = v_1$	Right shift

captive ones. Of these 8 elementary automata, the most interesting ones are 150 and 142. Rule 150 is a sum of three distinct shifts, and some properties of rule 142 are studied in at least [3].

In the next result, *intrinsic universality* is understood with respect to simulation by injective bulking. In this formalism, a cellular automaton $f : S^{\mathbb{Z}} \to S^{\mathbb{Z}}$ *simulates* another automaton $g : T^{\mathbb{Z}} \to T^{\mathbb{Z}}$ if there exists an injective function $\phi : T \to S^{m \times n}$ from T-symbols to S-rectangles such that for every spacetime diagram x of g, the configuration $\phi(x)$ is a spacetime diagram of f. An intrinsically universal automaton is then one that simulates any other CA. See [9] for the precise definitions; the main message of the theorem is that captive color blind cellular automata can be very complex both from the computational and the dynamical points of view.

Theorem 1. *For any alphabet S with $|S| \geq 2$, there exists an intrinsically universal captive color blind cellular automaton on $S^{\mathbb{Z}}$.*

Proof. It is enough to show that any single CA can be simulated by a captive color blind automaton, as there exists an intrinsically universal CA and injective simulations are composable. Let thus $g : [1, n-1]^{\mathbb{Z}} \to [1, n-1]^{\mathbb{Z}}$ be any cellular automaton, choose distinct symbols $a, b \in S$ and for all $i \in [1, n-1]$, let $w_i = a^i b^{2n-i}$. Define the injection $h : [1, n-1]^{\mathbb{Z}} \to S^{\mathbb{Z}}$ by

$$h(x) = w_{x_{-2}} w_{x_{-1}} . w_{x_0} w_{x_1} \dots .$$

Let $Z = h([1, n-1]^{\mathbb{Z}})$ and $Y = \bigcup_{i=0}^{2n-1} \sigma^i(Z)$. It is easy to see that $Y \subset S^{\mathbb{Z}}$ is an SFT, since its configurations are exactly the infinite concatenations of the finitely many words $w_i \in a^+ b^+$. Define $f : Z \to Z$ by $f \circ h = h \circ g$. Now, f has a unique shift-commuting extension to a function $\hat{f} : Y \to Y$, which is then a cellular automaton simulating g. We may assume $\hat{f}$ has neighborhood $[-r, r]$ for some $r > 2n$. Then $\hat{f}$ is trivially captive and commutes with all symbol permutations of Y, since both symbols are always visible in the neighborhood, and no nontrivial symbol permutation keeps any configuration of Y inside it. Thus, $\hat{f}$ has a color blind extension to $S^{\mathbb{Z}}$ by Proposition 1. □

In [1], the set $\mathrm{Aut}(X)$ of bijective cellular automata on a mixing SFT $X \subset S^{\mathbb{Z}}$ is considered (see the article for the precise definition). The *symmetry of X* is defined as the relative asymptotic density of $\mathrm{Aut}(X)$ in the set of all cellular automata on X: $s(X) = \limsup_{n \to \infty} \frac{1}{n} \log\log |\mathrm{Aut}(X)_n|$, where $\mathrm{Aut}(X)_n$ denotes the set of bijective cellular automata on X that can be defined on the neighborhood $[-\lfloor n/2 \rfloor, \lceil n/2 \rceil]$. Inspired by this, we define the following.

Definition 6. *Let $\mathcal{C}$ be a family of cellular automata on $S^{\mathbb{Z}}$. The density of $\mathcal{C}$ is defined as*

$$d(\mathcal{C}) = \limsup_{n \to \infty} \frac{1}{n} \log_{|S|} \log_{|S|} |\mathcal{C}_n|, \tag{1}$$

where $\mathcal{C}_n$ denotes the set of cellular automata in $\mathcal{C}$ that can be defined on the neighborhood $[-\lfloor n/2 \rfloor, \lceil n/2 \rceil]$.

We now show that color blind cellular automata are abundant in the sense of the previous definition. Note that the set $\mathcal{CA}$ of all cellular automata on $S^{\mathbb{Z}}$ has density 1, as $|\mathcal{CA}_n| = |S|^{|S|^n}$ for all $n \in \mathbb{N}$.

Proposition 2. *Denote by $\mathcal{CB}$ the set of captive color blind cellular automata on $S^{\mathbb{Z}}$. Then $d(\mathcal{CB}) = 1$.*

Proof. Let $S = \{s_1, \ldots, s_{|S|}\}$, and let $n \in \mathbb{N}$ be arbitrary. We define an injective map $\phi : \mathcal{CA}_n \to \mathcal{CB}_{n+|S|}$, which shows that $|\mathcal{CA}_n| \le |\mathcal{CB}_{n+|S|}|$. For that, let $f \in \mathcal{CA}_n$ have neighborhood size n. The local function $\phi(f)_{\mathrm{loc}} : S^{n+|S|} \to S$ works as follows on the inputs $a_1, \ldots, a_{n+|S|} \in S$. If the symbols $a_{n+1}, \ldots, a_{n+|S|}$ are pairwise distinct, we let $\pi : S \to S$ be the symbol permutation that maps each a_{n+i} to s_i. The local function then returns $\pi^{-1}(f_{\mathrm{loc}}(\pi(a_1), \ldots, \pi(a_n)))$. If the symbols $a_{n+1}, \ldots, a_{n+|S|}$ are not pairwise distinct, $\phi(f)_{\mathrm{loc}}$ returns a_1. Then $\phi(f)$ is captive and color blind, and ϕ is injective.

Now, we calculate

$$\frac{1}{n+|S|} \log_{|S|} \log_{|S|} |\mathcal{CB}_{n+|S|}| \ge \frac{1}{n+|S|} \log_{|S|} \log_{|S|} |\mathcal{CA}_n|$$
$$= \frac{1}{n+|S|} \log_{|S|} \log_{|S|} |S|^{|S|^n} = \frac{n}{n+|S|} \xrightarrow{n \to \infty} 1,$$

which proves the claim. $\qquad\square$

We remark here that our definition of density measures the asymptotic growth rate of a set of cellular automata on a given alphabet, when the radius increases. An alternative perspective is taken in [11], where the radius $r \in \mathbb{N}$ is fixed, and the density of a set $\mathcal{C}$ is cellular automata is defined as the limit of $|\mathcal{C}^n|/|\mathcal{CA}^n|$, when it exists, where $\mathcal{C}^n$ is the set of CA in $\mathcal{C}$ with radius r on an alphabet of size n. Interestingly, it is shown in particular that the density of the set of all captive cellular automata is 0, so the *opposite* of the analogue of Proposition 2 holds in this formalism.

5   Typhlotic Cellular Automata

We now turn our attention to typhlotic cellular automata, and start with the observation that they are not necessarily trivial. For example, the intrinsically universal CA given in Theorem 1 is in fact typhlotic in the case $|S| = 2$. Furthermore, every binary majority CA is typhlotic. These CA are already color blind, so we only need to check that they commute with the symbol maps that are not permutations, namely the constant maps $s \mapsto 0$ and $s \mapsto 1$. But this easily follows from the fact that both the intrinsically universal CA and majority CA are captive.

Somewhat curiously, if the alphabet S has more than two elements, the situation changes drastically. For example, as a corollary of Theorem 2, a ternary color blind majority CA can not be typhlotic unless it has a neighborhood of size 1. The proof of Theorem 2 follows from some rather general set theory. Namely, we show that a typhlotic CA is defined by an ultrafilter on its neighborhood, and ultrafilters on finite sets are very simple. We note that we do not need any hard set theoretic results on ultrafilters: they just happen to provide convenient terminology for the proof.

We start with two characterizations of ultrafilters. The first one is just the observation that the well-known partition property of ultrafilters characterizes them, as also the filter axioms follow from it. This result has already appeared in at least [5]. The second one is rather specific to typhloticity, and is in fact just the first part of Theorem 2 in thin disguise.

Lemma 4 (Corollary 1.6 of [5]). *Let X be a nonempty set, let $k \in \mathbb{N}$ with $k \geq 3$, and let $Q \subset 2^X$ have the property that for all partitions $(A_1, \ldots, A_k)$ of X, exactly one A_i is in Q. Then Q is an ultrafilter. Furthermore, every ultrafilter satisfies the property for every $k \geq 1$.*

Proof. First, from the partition $(X, \emptyset, \ldots, \emptyset)$ we deduce that $\emptyset \notin Q$ and $X \in Q$. Now, Q cannot contain two disjoint subsets $A, B \subset X$, as otherwise the partition $(A, B, X \setminus (A \cup B), \emptyset, \ldots, \emptyset)$ would contradict the assumptions. Thus, if $A \subset X$, then exactly one of A and $X \setminus A$ is in Q, by the partition $(A, X \setminus A, \emptyset, \ldots, \emptyset)$.

Suppose then that $A \in Q$ and $A \subset B$. The partition $(X \setminus B, A, B \setminus A, \emptyset, \ldots, \emptyset)$ proves that $X \setminus B \notin Q$, so by the above $B \in Q$. Finally, if $A, B \in Q$, then neither of $A \setminus B$ or $B \setminus A$ can be in Q, and then the partition $(A \setminus B, B \setminus A, A \cap B, \emptyset, \ldots, \emptyset)$ shows that $A \cap B \in Q$.

The converse claim is a well known property of ultrafilters. $\qquad\qquad\square$

For the next lemma, we define a more general definition of typhloticity.

Definition 7. *Let S and T be sets with S finite, and let $f : S^T \to S$ be a function. Then we say f is typhlotic if for every function $g : S \to S$, we have $f \circ g = g \circ f$, where g is applied coordinatewise on the left side of the equation.*

Lemma 5. *Let T be a set, and S a finite set with $|S| \geq 3$. Then the map $f \mapsto \{\{i \in T \mid x_i = f(x)\} \mid x \in S^T\}$ is a bijection from the set of typhlotic maps $f : S^T \to S$ to the set of ultrafilters on T.*

Proof. Without loss of generality, let $S = [1, k]$. For all $x \in S^T$ and $s \in S$ we define $x|_s = \{i \in T \mid x_i = s\}$.

Let first $f : S^T \to S$ be typhlotic, and denote by $Q \subset 2^T$ the image of f under the mapping. By Lemma 4, we need to show that if (A_1, A_2, A_3) is a partition of T, then exactly one of the A_i is in Q, that is, of the form $x|_{f(x)}$ for some $x \in S^T$. First, since $k \geq 3$, there exists $x \in S^T$ such that $x|_i = A_i$ for all $i \in \{1, 2, 3\}$. Then $f(x) \in \{1, 2, 3\}$, for otherwise, letting $\pi : S \to S$ be the symbol map that sends $f(x)$ to 1 and otherwise acts as the identity, we would have $1 = \pi(f(x)) = f(\pi(x)) = f(x)$, a contradiction. Thus at least one of the A_i is in Q.

Suppose then that, for example, $A_1 = x|_{f(x)}$ and $A_2 = y|_{f(y)}$ for some $x, y \in S^T$, where we may assume $f(x) = 1$ and $f(y) = 2$ by applying symbol permutations. Let $z \in S^T$ be defined by $z|_i = A_i$ for all $i \in \{1, 2, 3\}$. If $f(z) = 1$, define the symbol map $\pi : S \to S$ by $\pi(2) = 2$ and $\pi(s) = 3$ for all $s \in S \setminus \{2\}$. Then

$$3 = \pi(f(z)) = f(\pi(z)) = f(\pi(y)) = \pi(f(y)) = \pi(2),$$

a contradiction. A symmetric argument shows that $f(z) \neq 1$ is likewise impossible. Thus exactly one of the A_i is in Q, and Q is a ultrafilter.

Conversely, let Q be an ultrafilter on T, and define $f : S^T \to S$ by $f(x) = a$ iff $\{i \in T \mid x_i = a\} \in Q$. Again by Lemma 4 (the converse direction), f is then well-defined. Since ultrafilters are closed under supersets, f is easily seen to be typhlotic. As the ultrafilter corresponding to f is Q, this concludes the claim. □

The following is also a well known property of ultrafilters (for instance, it appears as Example 1.3 in [5]).

Lemma 6. *Let T be finite and let Q be an ultrafilter on T. Then Q is principal, that is, $Q = \{A \subset T \mid j \in A\}$ for some $j \in T$.*

Proof. Since T is finite, we can take a minimal set A in Q. If A is a singleton, we are done. If A is not a singleton, Q is not a maximal filter. □

Theorem 2. *If $|S| \geq 3$, the typhlotic CA $f : S^{\mathbb{Z}} \to S^{\mathbb{Z}}$ are exactly the shift maps. If $|S| = 2$, they are exactly the captive color blind CA.*

Proof. First, suppose $|S| \geq 3$, and let $N \subset \mathbb{Z}$ be the neighborhood of f. The local rule $f_{\text{loc}} : S^N \to S$ is typhlotic since f is. Let Q be the ultrafilter on N that defines it, given by Lemma 5. Since N is finite, $Q = \{A \subset N \mid j \in A\}$ for some $j \in N$ by Lemma 6, which means

$$f(x)_0 = a \iff \{i \in N \mid x_i = a\} \in Q \iff x_j = a.$$

Thus f is a shift map.

In the case $|S| = 2$, a CA is captive if and only if it commutes with constant maps, and all symbol maps are either permutations or constant maps. This concludes the proof. □

6   Homomorphic Color Blind Automata

In Section 4, we saw that color blind cellular automata can do almost anything a general cellular automaton can do, with any alphabet size. On the other hand, typhlotic cellular automata turned out to be almost the same objects as color blind CA in the binary case, but shift maps for larger alphabets. In this section, we show that cellular automata that are color blind and *homomorphic* satisfy a similar property: if the group is very simple, the color blind homomorphic CA form a large subclass of all homomorphic CA, but when the group is larger, they are all shift maps.

Color blindness of homomorphic CA was also studied in [7], and there, the term k-rule was used for a sum of k distinct shifts. In the article, two particular cases of our main result Theorem 3 were proven. We prove Theorem 3 in a long series of simple lemmas, starting with the fact that every CA that is a group homomorphism is a sum of symbol endomorphisms. For simplicity, we use additive notation for all groups, as we will see very soon, in Lemma 10, that a full group shift that admits a color blind homomorphic CA must be abelian.

Lemma 7. *Let G be a finite group and let $f : G^{\mathbb{Z}} \to G^{\mathbb{Z}}$ be a homomorphic CA with neighborhood $N = [-r, r]$. For all $i \in N$, there exists a group endomorphism $f_i : G \to G$ such that*

- $f_i(g) + f_j(h) = f_j(h) + f_i(g)$ *whenever* $h, g \in G$ *and* $i \neq j \in N$, *and*
- $f_{\mathrm{loc}}(g_1, \ldots, g_n) = f_1(g_1) + f_2(g_2) + \cdots + f_n(g_n)$ *for all* $g_1, \ldots, g_n \in G$.

Note that the order of summation in the above formula for f_{loc} is irrelevant by the first item.

Proof. For all $i \in N$, define the function $f_i : G \to G$ by

$$f_i(g) = f_{\mathrm{loc}}(\underbrace{1, \ldots, 1}_{i-1}, g, \underbrace{1, \ldots, 1}_{m-i}),$$

and note that this is an endomorphism of G. Let $i < j \in N$ and $g, h \in G$. Since f_{loc} is a homomorphism, we have

$$
\begin{aligned}
f_i(g) + f_j(h) &= f_{\mathrm{loc}}(1, \ldots, g, \ldots, 1, \ldots, 1) + f_{\mathrm{loc}}(1, \ldots, 1, \ldots, h, \ldots, 1) \\
&= f_{\mathrm{loc}}(1, \ldots, g, \ldots, h, \ldots, 1) \\
&= f_{\mathrm{loc}}(1, \ldots, 1, \ldots, h, \ldots, 1) + f_{\mathrm{loc}}(1, \ldots, g, \ldots, 1, \ldots, 1) \\
&= f_j(h) + f_i(g),
\end{aligned}
$$

and for all $g_1, \ldots, g_n \in G$,

$$
\begin{aligned}
f_{\mathrm{loc}}(g_1, \ldots, g_n) &= \sum_{i=-r}^{r} f_{\mathrm{loc}}(\underbrace{1, \ldots, 1}_{i-1}, g_i, \underbrace{1, \ldots, 1}_{m-i}) \\
&= f_1(g_1) + f_2(g_2) + \cdots + f_n(g_n).
\end{aligned}
$$

This concludes the proof.   □

We call the endomorphisms f_i the *symbol endomorphisms of f*. If $n \geq 1$, all endomorphisms of $\mathbb{Z}_n$ are multiples of the identity map, so we have the following.

Lemma 8. *Let G be a finite abelian group with decomposition $G = \prod_{i=1}^{m} \mathbb{Z}_{p_i^{m_i}}$, where the p_i are prime numbers and $m_i \geq 1$. Then every homomorphic cellular automaton on $G^{\mathbb{Z}}$ is a sum of shifts if and only if the primes p_i are distinct.*

Thus, in general every group homomorphic CA is a *sum of shifted endomorphisms*, and for certain abelian groups the endomorphisms can be taken to be identity maps. Note that the fact that the images of distinct symbol endomorphisms commute means that the local rule of a homomorphic cellular automaton first projects its inputs to subgroups of G which commute with each other, and then multiplies them together. In particular, we have the following.

Lemma 9. *Let G be a group and let the CA $f : G^{\mathbb{Z}} \to G^{\mathbb{Z}}$ be homomorphic. If at least two of the symbol endomorphisms of f are surjective, then G is abelian.*

We now see that in the case of color blind homomorphic CA, there is no loss of generality in retricting to the abelian case.

Lemma 10. *Let G be a finite group and let the CA $f : G^{\mathbb{Z}} \to G^{\mathbb{Z}}$ be color blind and homomorphic with minimal neighborhood size at least 2. Then G is abelian, and if $|G| \geq 4$, then f is a sum of distinct shifts.*

Proof. All groups of order at most 3 are abelian, so we may assume $|G| \geq 4$. Let $1 \neq g \in G$, and consider the configuration $z(g) = {}^{\infty}1g1^{\infty}$. Since the local rule sees at most two distinct symbols in its neighborhood, the image $f(z(g))$ must also be a configuration over $\{1, g\}$ by Lemma 1. Since f commutes with the transposition $(g\ h)$, we have $I = \{i \in \mathbb{Z} \mid f(z(g))_i = g\} = \{i \in \mathbb{Z} \mid f(z(h))_i = h\}$ for all $1 \neq h \in G$. From this we deduce that the symbol endomorphisms of f are either trivial or identity maps, and since at least two of them must be nontrivial, G is abelian by Lemma 9. Also, we clearly have $f = \sum_{i \in N} \sigma^i$, where $N \subset \mathbb{Z}$ is the set of those i for which the symbol endomorphism f_i is nontrivial, so f is a sum of distinct shifts. $\qquad\square$

From now on, all alphabets will be abelian groups. Lemma 8 and Lemma 10 now give us the following.

Corollary 2. *Let G be a finite abelian group and $f : G^{\mathbb{Z}} \to G^{\mathbb{Z}}$ a color blind homomorphic CA. Then f is a sum of shifts, which are distinct if $|G| \geq 4$.*

The radius-1 CA f with local rule $(a, b, c) \mapsto a + 2b + c$ is an example of a color blind homomorphic CA on $\mathbb{Z}_3^{\mathbb{Z}}$ which is not a sum of distinct shifts.

Lemma 11. *Let G be a finite abelian group and $f : G^{\mathbb{Z}} \to G^{\mathbb{Z}}$ a homomorphic CA. The f commutes with the symbol permutation $\phi_g(h) = h + g$ if and only if $f({}^{\infty}g^{\infty}) = {}^{\infty}g^{\infty}$.*

Proof. Having $f(^\infty g^\infty) = {}^\infty g^\infty$ is equivalent to $f(x) + {}^\infty g^\infty = f(x) + f(^\infty g^\infty)$ for all $x \in G^{\mathbb{Z}}$, which is simply commutation with ϕ_g, since $f(x) + f(^\infty g^\infty) = f(x + {}^\infty g^\infty)$. □

We now proceed with a case analysis on the small groups $\mathbb{Z}_2$, $\mathbb{Z}_3$ and $\mathbb{Z}_2^2$.

Lemma 12. *Let the CA $f : \mathbb{Z}_2^{\mathbb{Z}} \to \mathbb{Z}_2^{\mathbb{Z}}$ be homomorphic with minimal neighborhood size $m \in \mathbb{N}$. Then f is color blind if and only if f fixes $^\infty 1^\infty$, if and only if m is odd.*

Proof. The only nontrivial permutation of $\mathbb{Z}_2$ is ϕ_1, so it follows from Lemma 11 that f is color blind if and only if it fixes $^\infty 1^\infty$. Since f is a sum of shifts by Corollary 2, and the shifts are trivially distinct, this is the case if and only if m is odd. □

Lemma 13. *Denote $G = \mathbb{Z}_2^2$, and let the CA $f : G^{\mathbb{Z}} \to G^{\mathbb{Z}}$ be homomorphic. Then f is color blind iff it is a sum of an odd number of distinct shifts.*

Proof. The proof relies on the facts that $2ng = 0$ for all $g \in G$ and $n \in \mathbb{N}$, and if $G = \{a, b, c, d\}$ then $a + b + c = d$.

Suppose first that f is color blind. Corollary 2 applies, so that f is a sum of m distinct shifts for some $m \in \mathbb{N}$. This means that $X = \{(0,0), (0,1)\}^{\mathbb{Z}} \cong \mathbb{Z}_2^{\mathbb{Z}}$ is closed under f, and the restriction of f to X is also a sum of shifts. If $f|_X$ were not color blind then f would not be either, so m must be odd by Lemma 12.

On the other hand, let f be a sum of m distinct shifts for odd m, and consider an arbitrary transposition $\phi = (g\ h)$. Denote $G = \{a, b, g, h\}$. Let $g_1, \ldots, g_m \in G$, and for $c \in G$, let n_c be the number of $i \in \{1, \ldots, m\}$ such that $g_i = c$.

If both n_g and n_h are even, then exactly one of n_a and n_b is odd, let us say n_a. Then $f_{\text{loc}}(\phi(g_1), \ldots, \phi(g_m)) = a = \phi(f_{\text{loc}}(g_1, \ldots, g_m))$. If both n_g and n_h are odd, we may again assume n_a is odd and n_b is even, so that $f_{\text{loc}}(\phi(g_1), \ldots, \phi(g_m)) = a + g + h = \phi(f_{\text{loc}}(g_1, \ldots, g_m))$, since $a + g + h = b \notin \{g, h\}$ is a fixed point of ϕ.

If $n_g + n_h$ is odd, we may assume n_g is odd and n_h is even. Then, $n_a + n_b$ is even, and the cases left to consider are that both n_a and n_b are odd or both are even. If n_a and n_b are both odd, then $f_{\text{loc}}(g_1, \ldots, g_m) = a + b + g = h$, which implies $f_{\text{loc}}(\phi(g_1), \ldots, \phi(g_m)) = a + b + h = g$ and $\phi(f_{\text{loc}}(g_1, \ldots, g_m)) = \phi(h) = g$. If both are even, then $f_{\text{loc}}(\phi(g_1), \ldots, \phi(g_m)) = h = \phi(g) = \phi(f_{\text{loc}}(g_1, \ldots, g_m))$. This finishes the proof since transpositions generate the group of permutations. □

Lemma 14. *Let the CA $f : \mathbb{Z}_3^{\mathbb{Z}} \to \mathbb{Z}_3^{\mathbb{Z}}$ be homomorphic. Then f is color blind if and only if it fixes $^\infty 1^\infty$, if and only if it is a sum of $3k + 1$ shifts for some k.*

Proof. By Lemma 11, f fixes $^\infty 1^\infty$ if and only if it commutes with the symbol permutation ϕ_1. We prove that all such homomorphic CA are color blind, for which it is enough to show that they also commute with the transposition $(1\ 2)$.

By Corollary 2, f is a sum of shifts $\sum_{i=1}^{m} \sigma^{k_i}$ for some $m \in \mathbb{N}$ and $k_i \in \mathbb{Z}$. For all $x \in \mathbb{Z}_3^{\mathbb{Z}}$, we then have

$$((1\ 2) \circ f)(x) = (1\ 2) \left(\sum_{i=1}^{m} \sigma^{k_i}(x) \right) = \sum_{i=0}^{m} (1\ 2)(\sigma^{k_i}(x)))$$

$$= \sum_{i=0}^{m} \sigma^{k_i}((1\ 2)(x)) = (f \circ (1\ 2))(x),$$

where the second equality follows from the fact that $(1\ 2)$ is an automorphism of $\mathbb{Z}_3$ and the third one directly from the fact that $(1\ 2)$ is a cellular automaton.

Finally, it is easy to see that a sum of m shifts on $\mathbb{Z}_3^{\mathbb{Z}}$ fixes the point $^{\infty}1^{\infty}$ if and only if $m \equiv 1 \bmod 3$. □

Finally, we handle the remaining cases in a single lemma.

Lemma 15. *Let G be a finite abelian group such that $|G| > 3$ and $G \not\cong \mathbb{Z}_2^2$, and let the CA $f : G^{\mathbb{Z}} \to G^{\mathbb{Z}}$ be homomorphic. Then f is color blind if and only if it is a shift map.*

Proof. First, a shift map is trivially a color blind homomorphic CA for any group alphabet.

As for the nontrivial direction, Corollary 2 again applies, so that f_{loc} returns the sum of the values in the neighborhood N of f. If $|N| = 0$, then f does not commute with symbol permutations, as it sends everything to $^{\infty}0^{\infty}$. Assume then that $|N| \geq 2$.

We first suppose $|G| > 4$. In this case, we take $0 \neq g \in G$ and $h \in G$ such that $h \notin \{0, g, -g\}$. Now, $g + h \notin \{0, g, h\}$, so that $f_{\mathrm{loc}}(g, h, 0, \ldots, 0) = g + h \notin \{0, g, h\}$, which is a contradiction by Lemma 1. Now, let $|G| = 4$, so by the assumption that $G \not\cong \mathbb{Z}_2^2$, we have that $G \cong \mathbb{Z}_4$. But now $f_{\mathrm{loc}}(1, 1, 0, \ldots, 0) = 2$, again contradicting Lemma 1.

Of course, in the remaining case that $|N| = 1$, f is a shift map. □

We collect the results of this section into a single statement.

Theorem 3. *Let G be a finite group, and let $f : G^{\mathbb{Z}} \to G^{\mathbb{Z}}$ be a homomorphic cellular automaton. Then, f is color blind iff one of the following (partially overlapping) conditions holds.*

- *$G = \mathbb{Z}_2$, $G = \mathbb{Z}_2^2$ or $G = \mathbb{Z}_3$, and f fixes unary points,*
- *$G = \mathbb{Z}_2$ or $G = \mathbb{Z}_2^2$, and f is a sum of an odd number of distinct shifts,*
- *$G = \mathbb{Z}_3$, and f is a sum of $3k + 1$ shifts for some k,*
- *$|G| > 4$ or $G = \mathbb{Z}_4$, and f is a shift map.*

Proof. If G is not abelian, then f is a shift map by Lemma 10. In the converse case, Lemma 12, Lemma 13, Lemma 14 and Lemma 15 give the claim. □

This gives a complete characterization of homomorphic color blind cellular automata on full shifts whose alphabet is a finite group. We also note that in our arguments we mainly manipulated the local functions of cellular automata, so the result should hold as such for multidimensional automata with exactly the same proofs. Thus Theorem 3 is a generalization of the results of [7], which state that for all dimensions $d \geq 1$, any sum of 4 distinct shifts on $\mathbb{Z}_3^{\mathbb{Z}^d}$ is color blind, and no sum of m distinct shifts on $\mathbb{Z}_n^{\mathbb{Z}^d}$ is color blind if $n \geq m > 1$.

References

1. Boyle, M., Lind, D., Rudolph, D.: The automorphism group of a shift of finite type. Transactions of the American Mathematical Society 306(1), 71–114 (1988)
2. Coven, E.M., Hedlund, G.A., Rhodes, F.: The commuting block maps problem. Trans. Amer. Math. Soc. 249(1), 113–138 (1979)
3. Fukś, H.: Dynamics of the cellular automaton Rule 142. Complex Systems 16(2), 123–138 (2005)
4. Hedlund, G.A.: Endomorphisms and automorphisms of the shift dynamical system. Math. Systems Theory 3, 320–375 (1969)
5. Leinster, T.: Codensity and the ultrafilter monad. ArXiv e-prints (September 2012)
6. Martin, O., Odlyzko, A.M., Wolfram, S.: Algebraic properties of cellular automata. Comm. Math. Phys. 93(2), 219–258 (1984)
7. Miller, N.R., Bardzell, M.J.: The evolution homomorphism and permutation actions on group generated cellular automata. Complex Systems 15(2), 121–136 (2004)
8. Moore, C., Boykett, T.: Commuting cellular automata. Complex Systems 11(1), 55–64 (1997)
9. Ollinger, N.: Intrinsically universal cellular automata. In: Neary, T., Woods, D., Seda, A.K., Murphy, N. (eds.) CSP. EPTCS, vol. 1, pp. 199–204 (2008)
10. Salo, V., Törmä, I.: Geometry and Dynamics of the Besicovitch and Weyl Spaces. ArXiv e-prints (April 2012)
11. Theyssier, G.: How common can be universality for cellular automata? In: Diekert, V., Durand, B. (eds.) STACS 2005. LNCS, vol. 3404, pp. 121–132. Springer, Heidelberg (2005)
12. Wolfram, S.: Statistical mechanics of cellular automata. Rev. Modern Phys. 55(3), 601–644 (1983)

Commutators of Bipermutive and Affine Cellular Automata*

Ville Salo and Ilkka Törmä

TUCS – Turku Centre for Computer Science, Finland
University of Turku, Finland
{vosalo,iatorm}@utu.fi

Abstract. We discuss bipermutive cellular automata from a combinatorial and topological perspective. We prove a type of topological randomizing property for bipermutive CA, show that the commutator of a bipermutive CA is always small and that bipermutive affine CA have only affine CA in their commutator. We show the last result also in the multidimensional case, proving a conjecture of [Moore-Boykett, 97].

Keywords: cellular automata, bipermutivity, commutation, affine cellular automata.

1   Introduction

Bipermutive cellular automata, that is, CA which are permutive in the left- and rightmost coordinates of their neighborhood, have been investigated in great detail in the literature. Most of the work has been in the ergodic theory of cellular automata, as this is a natural framework for studying the randomizing nature of bipermutive automata. We refer to [5] for a survey of this theory.

We take a more combinatorial approach, and study the topological dynamics of bipermutive cellular automata and their commutators in the monoid of cellular automata. On the side of topological dynamics, we obtain some basic results about orbits of one-dimensional configurations and subshifts. We prove a simple lemma stating that every pattern is self-replicating on a periodic background. We use this to show that every SFT with sufficient mixing properties becomes a full shift in the limit in the action of the CA, and we say the CA topologically randomizes such SFTs, as this is a kind of topological analogue of asymptotic randomization in ergodic theory. For bipermutive CA and a mixing SFT, topological randomization turns out to be equivalent to the existence of a transitive point. We also present a particular case of asymptotic randomization in the multidimensional setting, for a natural generalization of bipermutivity, which we call total extremal permutivity.

Our results about orbits are purely qualitative: while we prove that certain subshifts tend to the full shift, we do not obtain any sensible bounds for when a pattern first appears. One can extract such bounds from our proofs, but they are

---
* Research supported by the Academy of Finland Grant 131558.

J. Kari, M. Kutrib, and A. Malcher (Eds.): AUTOMATA 2013, LNCS 8155, pp. 155–170, 2013.
© Springer-Verlag Berlin Heidelberg 2013

not very good: For example, we can prove that the golden mean shift X tends to the full shift in the action of the binary XOR automaton f. However, the bounds directly obtained fall short of showing that all binary words of length n appear in $f^{a^{(n)}}(X)$ where $a^{(n)} = a^{a^{\cdot^{\cdot^{a}}}}$ denotes tetration and a is the size of the alphabet.

Interestingly, we obtain rather strong quantitative results on the commutator using the purely qualitative results on orbits: Our main result on the commutator of a totally extremally permutive CA is that for any radius, it contains only exponentially many cellular automata with that radius, while the number of cellular automata of a given radius in general is doubly exponential.

We then move on to totally extremally permutive affine self-maps of group shifts, where affine means homomorphic up to the addition of a constant. Our main result here extends the result of [4] that affine bipermutive CA have only affine CA in their commutator to all dimensions, which was conjectured in [4]. In fact, we show that the multidimensional case rather directly reduces to the one-dimensional case, so that the first proof is just an application of the result of [4]. The second proof is based directly on the lemma that all patterns self-replicate on a periodic background, as we can use this to superpose two patterns. In the case of a *homomorphic* totally extremally permutive CA on $\mathbb{Z}_p^{\mathbb{Z}^d}$, and considering only CA with 0 as a quiescent state, we give a third proof which shows that the commutator is exactly the set of all homomorphisms. This in turn is a direct consequence of our results on orbits of subshifts.

2 Definitions

Let S be a finite set, called the *alphabet*. For $d \in \mathbb{N}$, the *d-dimensional full shift* is the space $S^{\mathbb{Z}^d}$ of infinite configurations over S endowed with the product topology. For $x \in S^{\mathbb{Z}^d}$, we denote by x_n the symbol of x at coordinate n. For any $s \in S$, when the dimension d is clear from context, we define $c(s) \in S^{\mathbb{Z}^d}$ as the configuration with $c(s)_n = s$ for all $n \in \mathbb{Z}^d$. A one-dimensional configuration $x \in S^{\mathbb{Z}}$ is *spatially periodic* if $x_{i+p} = x_i$ for some $p > 0$ and all $i \in \mathbb{Z}$.

A subset $X \subset S^{\mathbb{Z}^d}$ is called a *subshift* if it is closed in the topology and invariant under all *shift maps* $\sigma^m : S^{\mathbb{Z}^d} \to S^{\mathbb{Z}^d}$ for $m \in \mathbb{Z}^d$, defined by $\sigma^m(x)_n = x_{n+m}$. A *pattern* is a pair (N, w), where $w \in S^N$, for a finite domain $N \subset \mathbb{Z}^d$. We denote $\mathcal{B}_N(X) = \{(N, x_N) \mid x \in X\}$, and define the *language* of X as $\mathcal{B}(X) = \{(N, x_N) \mid N \subset \mathbb{Z}^d \text{ finite}, x \in X\}$. In the one-dimensional case, patterns are replaced by words in these definitions. Since a subshift is uniquely defined by its language, and every extendable and factor-closed language defines a one-dimensional subshift [3], we may write $X = \mathcal{B}^{-1}(L)$, if $\mathcal{B}(X)$ is the set of factors of the extendable language $L \subset S^*$. The *entropy* of a subshift $X \subset S^{\mathbb{Z}^d}$ is defined as $h(X) = \lim_{n \to \infty} \frac{1}{n^d} \log |\mathcal{B}_{[0,n-1]^d}(X)|$.

Alternatively, a subshift is defined by a set $F \in S$ of *forbidden patterns* as the set of configurations $\mathcal{X}_F = \{x \subset S^{\mathbb{Z}^d} \mid \forall (N, w) \in F, n \in \mathbb{Z}^d : x_{n+N} \neq w\}$. If F is finite, then $\mathcal{X}_F$ is *of finite type* (SFT for short). Once a finite set of forbidden patterns is chosen in the one-dimensional case, the length of the longest pattern is called the *window size* of the corresponding SFT. We say an SFT $X \subset S^{\mathbb{Z}}$ is *mixing* if there exists $n \in \mathbb{N}$, called its *mixing distance*, such that for all $u, w \in \mathcal{B}(X)$ and $m \geq n$ there exists $v \in \mathcal{B}_n(X)$ such that $uvw \in \mathcal{B}(X)$.

A continuous mapping $f : X \to X$ in a subshift that commutes with all shift maps is called a *cellular automaton*. All cellular automata f are defined by *local functions* $F : S^N \to S$, where $N \subset \mathbb{Z}^d$ is the finite *neighborhood* of f, by the formula $f(x)_n = F(x_{n+N})$ for all $n \in \mathbb{Z}^d$ [2]. A configuration x of X is called *temporally periodic (with respect to f)* if $f^p(x) = x$ for some p. If $X = S^{\mathbb{Z}^d}$, we denote by f_{loc} the local function of f with the minimal neighborhood.

A CA f with minimal neighborhood N is *permutive* in a coordinate $n \in N$ if for all $x \in S^N$, permuting the symbol of x at n permutes the image $f_{\mathrm{loc}}(x)$. We say a CA $f : S^{\mathbb{Z}^d} \to S^{\mathbb{Z}^d}$ is *totally extremally permutive* if $|N| \geq 2$, and f_{loc} is permutive in every coordinate that is also a vertex of the convex hull of N. Here, the convex hull of N is a polygon in $\mathbb{R}^d$, and the word 'vertex' refers to any corner of this polygon. We define a *bipermutive* CA as a totally extremally permutive CA in dimension one. It is easy to see that our definition of bipermutivity coincides with the usual definition.

Function composition $\circ$ gives the set of all CA (on a fixed subshift) the structure of a monoid. The *commutator* of the CA $f : X \to X$ is then naturally defined as

$$C(f) = \{g : X \to X \mid g \text{ is a CA}, f \circ g = g \circ f\}.$$

Let G be a finite group. Then applying the operations of G cellwise gives rise to a natural group structure on $G^{\mathbb{Z}^d}$. A cellular automaton which is a group homomorphism of $G^{\mathbb{Z}^d}$ is said to be *homomorphic*. We avoid the commonly used terms 'linear' and 'additive' as the first can also refer to one-dimensional cellular automata, and both terms are sometimes used to refer to cellwise sums of shift maps. If $f : G^{\mathbb{Z}^d} \to G^{\mathbb{Z}^d}$ satisfies $f(x) = g(x) \cdot c(C)$ for all x, for some $C \in G$ and some homomorphic CA g, then we say f is *affine*.

We denote by $SL_d(\mathbb{Z})$ the restriction of $SL_d(\mathbb{R})$ to those functions that map $\mathbb{Z}^d$ bijectively to itself. For a configuration $x \in S^{\mathbb{Z}^d}$ and $A \in SL_d(\mathbb{Z})$, we define $A(x) \in S^{\mathbb{Z}^d}$ by $A(x)_n = x_{A(n)}$ for all $n \in \mathbb{Z}^d$, and for a subshift $X \subset S^{\mathbb{Z}^d}$, we define $A(X) = \{A(x) \mid x \in X\}$. Here, the choice of A over A^{-1} in $x_{A(n)}$ is by analogy with how shift maps are defined: we always transform the view, not the configuration. From the linearity of A it follows that $A(X)$ is also a subshift. For a cellular automaton $f : X \to X$, we define $A(f) : A(X) \to A(X)$ by $A(f)(x) = A(f(A^{-1}(x)))$ for all $x \in X$. It is easy to see that $A(f)$ is a cellular automaton, and if $N \subset \mathbb{Z}^d$ is the neighborhood of f, then $A^{-1}(N)$ is that of $A(f)$. Moreover, $A(f)$ is totally extremally permutive, homomorphic or affine if and only if f is, and if $g : X \to X$ is another CA, we have $A(f \circ g) = A(f) \circ A(g)$.

Multi-dimensional and one-dimensional full shifts have a natural connection through the following definitions. Let

$$X_p^d = \{x \in S^{\mathbb{Z}^d} \mid \forall i \in \{2, \dots, d\} : \sigma^{pe_i}(x) = x\},$$

where $(e_i)_i$ are the natural basis of $\mathbb{Z}^d$. That is, X_p^d is the d-dimensional full shift restricted to points with period $p \in \mathbb{N}$ in all but the first dimension. There is a natural bijection between X_p^d and $(S^{p^{d-1}})^{\mathbb{Z}}$, which we call ρ_p (the dimension will always be clear from context).

3   Self-replication in Bipermutive CA

In this section, we study the behavior of individual configurations under the action of bipermutive CA. We give some examples, and prove Lemma 1 which states that every pattern, when surrounded by temporally and spatially periodic content, eventually self-replicates in the orbit of a bipermutive cellular automaton. All of the results of this article are, to some extent, based on this observation.

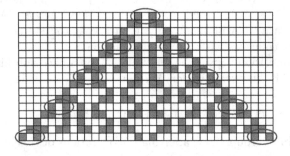

Fig. 1. An illustration of the elementary CA 150 running from the initial pattern 101 for 16 generations. The red ellipses show that the initial pattern repeats periodically at the borders.

We start with an illustration of this fundamental property of bipermutive CA for a particularly simple example: the binary CA with local rule $g_{\text{loc}}(a, b, c) = a + b + c \bmod 2$ and neighborhood $\{-1, 0, 1\}$. This is the elementary cellular automaton number 150, see Figure 1 for a sample spacetime diagram. In addition to being permutive in each coordinate, this CA exemplifies many other interesting properties (for example, it is homomorphic and totalistic). We illustrate how one can build an arbitrary pattern from restricted (sparse) input using only its bipermutivity in Figure 2.

Let f be bipermutive, and let $a \in S$ be such that $f^p(^\infty a^\infty) = {}^\infty a^\infty$. Then, as we outlined above, any word $w \in S^n$, when superposed on the periodic background $^\infty a^\infty$, is a kind of self-replicating pattern: Copies of w periodically appear on both borders of the light cone starting from w. See Figure 1 for a concrete illustration. The precise statement is formulated in Lemma 1. The proof is straightforward.

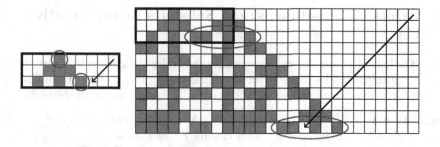

Fig. 2. We illustrate the general idea of building patterns from sparse configurations using the CA 150. We show how to systematically use its bipermutivity to build the pattern 111 while keeping the starting configuration sparse (although it 'accidentally' appears already on the first step). In the figure on the left, we show an initial part of the spacetime diagram of the configuration with a single 1, until the 1 reappears sufficiently far to the right, indicated by the red circles. The arrow indicates that by permuting the upper right coordinate, we simultaneously permute the cell it points to. In the figure on the right, we have permuted said coordinate so that the prefix 11 of 111 is obtained. We then repeat the procedure by waiting for the (arbitrary) data to the right of 11 to repeat sufficiently far away, and locating a suitable coordinate a that can be used to extend the repeated 11 into 111.

Lemma 1. *Let $f : S^{\mathbb{Z}} \to S^{\mathbb{Z}}$ be a left permutive CA with neighborhood $[-r, r']$, and let $y \in S^{\mathbb{Z}}$ be temporally and spatially periodic with periods t and p, respectively. Let $x \in S^{\mathbb{Z}}$ be such that $x_i = y_i$ for all $i > 0$, and let $n \in \mathbb{N}$. Then, denoting $C = pt(|S|^n)!$ and $I = [-n+1, 0]$, for all $\ell \in \mathbb{N}$, we have*

$$f^{\ell C}(x)_{I+\ell rC} = x_I.$$

Proof. We begin with an auxiliary observation. Let $A = (Q, \Sigma, \delta)$ be a reversible DFA, and let $q \in Q$ and $w \in \Sigma^*$ be arbitrary. Then $\delta(q, w^{\ell \cdot |Q|!}) = q$ for all $\ell \in \mathbb{N}$, which follows from the fact that the function $\delta(\cdot, w)$ is a bijection from Q to itself.

Then, let $Q = S^n$ and $\Sigma = S^{r+r'}$, and let $\delta : (Q \times \Sigma) \to Q$ be defined by $\delta(q, w) = f(qw)$. We claim that $A = (Q, \Sigma, \delta)$ is a reversible DFA. That it is a DFA is trivial, so let $q, q' \in Q$ and $w \in \Sigma$ with $q_i \neq q'_i$, where $i \in [0, n-1]$ is maximal. Since f is left permutive, we have $\delta(q, w)_i \neq \delta(q', w)_i$, and thus A is reversible.

Consider the words $q_i = f^i(x)_{I+ri} \in Q$ and $w_i = f^i(x)_{[1, r+r']+ri} \in \Sigma$ for $i \in \mathbb{N}$. Since r is the right 'speed of light' for f, we actually have $w_i = f^i(y)_{[1, r+r']+ri}$ for all $i \in \mathbb{N}$, and thus the sequence $(w_i)_{i \in \mathbb{N}}$ is periodic with period pt. Furthermore, we see that $\delta(q_i, w_i) = q_{i+1}$ holds for all i. Denoting $w = w_0, \ldots, w_{pt-1} \in \Sigma^{pt}$, we have $\delta(q_0, w^{\ell \cdot |Q|!}) = q_0$ for all $\ell \in \mathbb{N}$ by the above discussion on reversible DFAs, and expanding the definitions gives the claim. □

The lemma states that the pattern x_I is repeated on every Cth step on the right border of the light cone. Of course, in the right (or bi-) permutive case, a symmetric result holds. We refer to both results as Lemma 1.

4 Orbits of One-dimensional Subshifts in Bipermutive CA

With the help of Lemma 1, we now consider the orbits of *subshifts* in bipermutive cellular automata. The focus is on their long-term (asymptotic) dynamics, in particular the set of patterns that will eventually appear during the evolution.

Definition 1. *Let X be a subshift, $f : X \to X$ a cellular automaton and $Y \subset X$ a subshift of X. We define the f-orbit closure Y^f of Y to be the set $\overline{\bigcup_{i \in \mathbb{N}} f^i(Y)}$. We also define the* asymptotic set *of Y as $\omega_f(Y) = \bigcap_{n \in \mathbb{N}} \overline{\bigcup_{i \geq n} f^i(Y)}$.*

Clearly, we always have $\omega_f(Y) \subset Y^f$, and $Y^f = Y^{\sigma^m \circ f}$ for all $m \in \mathbb{Z}$.

The first nontrivial result that follows from Lemma 1 is a generalization of the ideas in the caption of Figure 2. Namely, the property of a bipermutive cellular automaton $f : S^{\mathbb{Z}} \to S^{\mathbb{Z}}$ that every word is self-replicating can be used to show that every word occurs in some image $f^n(X)$ if the SFT $X \subset S^{\mathbb{Z}}$ satisfies certain mixing properties. In fact, an SFT X satisfying the assumptions of the following theorem will even contain a transitive point for f by a slightly more involved proof, but we do not need this result.

Theorem 1. *Let $f : S^{\mathbb{Z}} \to S^{\mathbb{Z}}$ be a bipermutive CA and $X \subset S^{\mathbb{Z}}$ a nontrivial mixing SFT with window size m. If there exists $v_1 \in \mathcal{B}_{m-1}(X)$ such that $v_1 s \in \mathcal{B}_m(X)$ for all $s \in S$, then $\omega_f(X) = S^{\mathbb{Z}}$.*

Proof. Suppose that such a v_1 exists. Without loss of generality we can assume that $^{\infty}v_1^{\infty} \in X$, and that m is also a mixing distance for X. Namely, since periodic points are dense in X, we have $^{\infty}vv_1^{\infty} \in X$ for some $v \in \mathcal{B}(X)$, and then we can simply replace v_1 by vv_1. Also, it is clear that m can be replaced by a larger value. Let then $w \in S^*$ be arbitrary. We will show, by induction on $|w|$, that there exist arbitrarily large $n \in \mathbb{N}$ such that $w \in \mathcal{B}(f^n(X))$, from which the claim then follows. The case $|w| = 0$ is trivial.

Suppose then that the claim holds for $w \in S^*$, and let $s \in S$. We will prove the claim for the word ws. Figure 3 illustrates the proof. Let r and r' be the left and right radii of f, respectively. By the induction hypothesis, for arbitrarily large $n \in \mathbb{N}$, there exists a word $u \in \mathcal{B}_{|w|+n(r+r')}(X)$ such that $f^n(u) = w$. We can take n so large that $f^n(^{\infty}v_1^{\infty}) = {}^{\infty}v_2^{\infty}$ has the property that $f^p(^{\infty}v_2^{\infty}) = {}^{\infty}v_2^{\infty}$ for some $p \in \mathbb{N}$, where $|v_2| = m - 1$.

For all $k \in [m, 2m - 2]$ we choose a mixing word $z_k \in \mathcal{B}_k(X)$ and an arbitrary left extension $y_k \in S^{-\mathbb{N}}$ such that $x_k = y_k.uz_kv_1^{\infty} \in X$. Now, $f^n(x_k)_{[rn,\infty)} = wz_k'v_2^{\infty}$ for some $z_k' \in \mathcal{B}_{k+n(r+r')}(X)$. Then, by Lemma 1, there exists $t_k > k + n(r + r') + |v_1|$ such that

$$f^{n+\ell t_k}(x_k)_{[r(n+\ell t_k),\infty)} = wz_k'v_2^{\infty}$$

for all $\ell \in \mathbb{N}$. Let $h = \mathrm{lcm}\{t_k \mid k \in [m, 2m - 2]\}$, so that

$$f^{n+h}(x_k)_{[r(n+h),\infty)} = wz_k'v_2^{\infty},$$

for all k.

Let now k be such that

$$a = (r + r')(n + h) + |w| + 1 \equiv |u| + k \bmod (m - 1). \tag{1}$$

We can permute the coordinate a of x_k (and choose a new right tail arbitrarily), because (1) and the fact that $h > k + n(r + r') + |v_1|$ imply that it is preceded by the word v_1, and m is the window size of X. Permuting the coordinate a in x_k (point A in Figure 3) permutes the coordinate $a - r'(n + h) = r(n + h) + |w| + 1$ in $f^{n+h}(x_k)$ (point B in Figure 3) without affecting any coordinate to the left of it, and thus all the words ws for $s \in S$ occur in $f^{n+h}(X)$. Since n may be chosen arbitrarily large, this concludes the induction step.   □

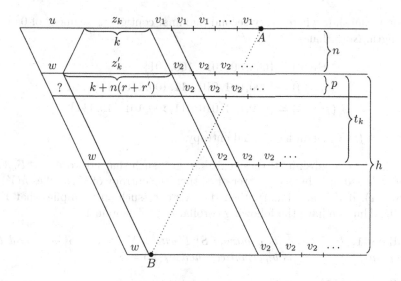

Fig. 3. A schematic diagram of the proof of Theorem 1. The coordinate A may be changed to any symbol without changing the left part, and by permuting A, we also permute B.

Note that in the proof of Theorem 1, both left and right permutivity are needed: As the CA is left permutive, Lemma 1 guarantees that w repeats on the right border of the light cone. Right permutivity on the other hand guarantees that the permutation applied to the coordinate a of x_k propagates along the left side of the light cone to a permutation of the $(n + h)$th image.

Also, we note that if X is a proper subshift of $S^{\mathbb{Z}}$, then $\bigcup_{n \in \mathbb{N}} f^n(X)$ is not actually equal to $S^{\mathbb{Z}}$. In fact, for all n, the subshift $f^n(X)$ has the same entropy as X, since a bipermutive CA is finite-to-one [3], and thus cannot contain a transitive point (a configuration in which every finite pattern occurs). This means that the appearance of all words of S^k for larger and larger k in $f^n(X)$ is somehow compensated by having these words appear in only a small number of different contexts.

Example 1. Let $X \subset \{0,1\}^{\mathbb{Z}}$ be the golden mean shift (the SFT with forbidden pattern 11), and let $f : \{0,1\}^{\mathbb{Z}} \to \{0,1\}^{\mathbb{Z}}$ be the binary XOR automaton, which is bipermutive. Then

$$f(X) = \mathcal{B}^{-1}((0^*(11)^*)^*).$$

Thus, $f(X)$ is conjugate to the even shift $\mathcal{B}^{-1}((1^*(00)^*)^*)$ by the CA that applies the permutation (0 1) cellwise, and it is indeed well known that the golden mean shift and the even shift have equal entropy. However, $\mathcal{B}_2(X) = \{00, 01, 10\}$, while $\mathcal{B}_2(f(X)) = \{00, 01, 10, 11\}$.

We continue one more step:

$$f^2(X) = \mathcal{B}^{-1}((0^*10(00)^*1)^*),$$

the binary subshift where every second maximal contiguous segment of 0s is of odd length. Note that

$$\mathcal{B}_3(X) = \{000, 001, 010, 100, 101\},$$
$$\mathcal{B}_3(f(X)) = \{000, 001, 010, 011, 100, 110, 111\}, \text{and}$$
$$\mathcal{B}_3(f^2(X)) = \{000, 001, 010, 011, 100, 101, 110, 111\},$$

but X and $f^2(X)$ again have equal entropy.

Let $Y \subset S^{\mathbb{Z}}$ be a subshift. If these exists $m \in \mathbb{N}$ such that no word $w \in \mathcal{B}_m(Y)$ can be followed in Y by every letter of S, then the entropy of Y satisfies $h(Y) \leq \log(|S| - 1)$. If Y is also binary, then the existence such an m implies that Y is periodic. Thus we have the following corollaries to Theorem 1.

Corollary 1. *If $Y \subset S^{\mathbb{Z}}$ is a mixing SFT with $h(Y) > \log(|S| - 1)$ and the automaton $f : S^{\mathbb{Z}} \to S^{\mathbb{Z}}$ is bipermutive, then $\omega_f(Y) = S^{\mathbb{Z}}$.*

Corollary 2. *If $Y \subset \{0,1\}^{\mathbb{Z}}$ is a nontrivial mixing SFT and the automaton $f : \{0,1\}^{\mathbb{Z}} \to \{0,1\}^{\mathbb{Z}}$ is bipermutive, then $\omega_f(Y) = \{0,1\}^{\mathbb{Z}}$.*

In the special case that the alphabet is a group of prime order and the cellular automaton is a homomorphism, we can relax our assumptions on the SFT X. We only sketch the proof of the following result, as it is mostly the same as that of Theorem 1.

Theorem 2. *Let $p \in \mathbb{N}$ be a prime, let $S = \mathbb{Z}_p$, let the CA $f : S^{\mathbb{Z}} \to S^{\mathbb{Z}}$ be a group homomorphism with at least two neighbors, and let $Y \subset S^{\mathbb{Z}}$ be a nontrivial mixing SFT. Then $\omega_f(Y) = S^{\mathbb{Z}}$.*

Proof (Sketch). First, note that f is automatically bipermutive. Since X is nontrivial, there exists a long word $v_1 \in \mathcal{B}(X)$ such that $v_1 a, v_1 b \in \mathcal{B}(X)$ for some $a \neq b \in \mathbb{Z}_p$. Let $wc \in \mathcal{B}(\omega_f(X))$ for some $c \in \mathbb{Z}_p$, and as in the proof of Theorem 1, there exist $k \in \mathbb{N}$ and $u \in \mathcal{B}(X)$ such that $uv_1 a$ is an f^{pk}-preimage of wc. Then $uv_1 b$ is an f^{pk}-preimage of wd, where $d = c + b - a$ in $\mathbb{Z}_p$ by the linearity of f. After p such operations, we see that $we \in \mathcal{B}(\omega_f(X))$ for all $e \in \mathbb{Z}_p$. $\qquad\square$

Theorem 2 can be thought of as a kind of topological analogue of Theorem 5.3 in [5] (proved in [6]), which in particular states that the ergodic averages of any Markov measure with full support converge to the uniform Bernoulli measure in the weak-star topology, under the action of a bipermutive homomorphic CA on $\mathbb{Z}_p^{\mathbb{Z}}$. The automaton is said to *asymptotically randomize* such a measure. Using analogous terminology, we can say that a CA f *topologically randomizes* a subshift X if $\omega_f(X) = S^{\mathbb{Z}}$, and Theorem 2 then states that a bipermutive homomorphic CA topologically randomizes every nontrivial mixing SFT $X \subset \mathbb{Z}_p^{\mathbb{Z}}$. Theorem 1 can of course also be phrased in terms of topological randomization, but the class of subshifts randomized is not quite as natural (see Question 1).

There is also a more familiar meaning to these results, as topological randomization for a left (or right) permutive cellular automaton in fact corresponds to the existence of a transitive point.

Theorem 3. *Let $f : S^{\mathbb{Z}} \to S^{\mathbb{Z}}$ be a left permutive CA with neighborhood $[-r, r']$, where $r > 0$, and let $X \subset S^{\mathbb{Z}}$ a mixing SFT such that $\omega_f(X) = S^{\mathbb{Z}}$. Then X contains a transitive point for f.*

Proof. We show that given any $w \in \mathcal{B}_p(X)$ and $v \in S^p$, there exist $x \in X$ and $N \in \mathbb{N}$ such that $x_{[0,p-1]} = w$ and $f^N(x)_{[0,p-1]} = v$. We may assume without loss of generality that $^{\infty}w.w^{\infty} \in X$, and then there exist $m, t \in \mathbb{N}$ such that $f^m(^{\infty}w.w^{\infty}) = f^{t+m}(^{\infty}w.w^{\infty}) = {}^{\infty}u.u^{\infty}$ for some $u \in \mathcal{B}(X)$. Since $\omega_f(X) = S^{\mathbb{Z}}$, there exists $M \geq m$ and $v_1, v_2 \in \mathcal{B}(X)$ such that $f^M(v_1 v_2) = v$ and $|v_1| = rM$. Define $y = zv_1.v_2 w'w^{\infty}$, where $z \in S^{-\mathbb{N}}$ and $w' \in \mathcal{B}(X)$ are chosen such that $y \in X$ and p divides $|v_2 w'|$. Now, $f^M(y) = z'.vw''u'^{\infty}$ for some $z' \in S^{-\mathbb{N}}$, $w'' \in (S^p)^*$ and $u' \in S^p$. Lemma 1 now implies that for $C = pt(|S|^p)!$ and all $\ell \in \mathbb{N}$, we have $f^{M+\ell C}(y)_{\ell rC+[0,p-1]} = v$. Since $y_{\ell rC+[0,p-1]} = w$ for large enough ℓ, some translate of y can be chosen as x.   □

The next (rather trivial) example shows that the restriction to a group of prime order is necessary in Theorem 2, that just mixing does not suffice for proving Theorem 1, and that entropy $h(Y) \geq \log(|S|/2)$ is not enough for Corollary 1.

Example 2. Let $f : \{0,1\}^{\mathbb{Z}} \to \{0,1\}^{\mathbb{Z}}$ be the elementary cellular automaton number 150, $X = (\{0,1\} \times \{0\})^{\mathbb{Z}} \subset (\{0,1\}^2)^{\mathbb{Z}} = Y$ and $g = f \times f$. Then X is a mixing SFT with $h(X) = \log 2$, g is homomorphic and bipermutive, and $h(Y) = \log 4$, but $g(X) = X$.

Here, the CA g is a group homomorphism, and $\mathcal{B}_1(X)$ is a subgroup of the full group that g cannot expand. We do not know whether such cheating is the only way to guarantee that a mixing SFT does not expand to the full shift. In fact, we do not know whether a bipermutive CA randomizes every mixing SFT that uses the full alphabet.

Question 1. Let $f : S^{\mathbb{Z}} \to S^{\mathbb{Z}}$ be a bipermutive cellular automaton, and $Y \subset S^{\mathbb{Z}}$ a nontrivial mixing SFT with $\mathcal{B}_1(Y) = S$. Do we then have $\omega_f(Y) = S^{\mathbb{Z}}$?

A positive solution to Question 1 seems plausible, especially if f is also a group homomorphism, and would extend Theorem 1 to a much more natural class of topologically randomized subshifts.

Definition 2. *Let* $0 \in S$ *and* $d, k \geq 1$. *The* k-*sparse subshift of dimension* d *is the SFT* $X \subset S^{\mathbb{Z}^d}$ *defined by the forbidden patterns*

$$\{P \in S^{[1,k]^d} \mid |P|_0 \leq k^d - 2\}.$$

For example, the one-dimensional binary 2-sparse subshift is just the golden mean shift, since it is defined by the set of forbidden patterns

$$\{w \in \{0, 1\}^2 \mid |w|_0 \leq 0\} = \{11\}.$$

We can apply Theorem 1 to such subshifts to obtain concrete examples of simple subshifts that bipermutive automata take to the full shift in the limit, as the k-sparse subshift obviously satisfies the assumption of Theorem 1. This observation (and especially its generalization Proposition 1) is useful in the study of commutation of cellular automata, as we will see in the next section.

Corollary 3. *Let* $f : S^{\mathbb{Z}} \to S^{\mathbb{Z}}$ *be a bipermutive CA,* $k \in \mathbb{N}$, *and* $X \subset S^{\mathbb{Z}}$ *the* k-*sparse subshift. Then* $\omega_f(X) = S^{\mathbb{Z}}$.

5   Orbits of Multidimensional k-sparse Shifts in Totally Extremally Permutive CA

In this section, we extend Corollary 3 to higher dimensions. The proof is essentially the same as that of Theorem 1, but we use some additional tricks to make the argument cleaner. Namely, we apply a certain transformation of $SL_d(\mathbb{Z})$ to make the neighborhood shape more suitable, and then use a similar shoot-and-reperiodize technique as in [7] to partially reduce the problem to the one-dimensional case.

Definition 3. *For* $\mathbf{n} = (x_1, \ldots, x_d) \in \mathbb{Z}^d$, *denote* $\pi(\mathbf{n}) = x_1$. *A set* $N \subset \mathbb{Z}^d$ *is* pointy, *if*

$$|N \cap \pi^{-1}(\min \pi(N))| = |N \cap \pi^{-1}(\max \pi(N))| = 1.$$

Lemma 2. *Let* $f : S^{\mathbb{Z}^d} \to S^{\mathbb{Z}^d}$ *be a cellular automaton. Then, there exists* $A \in SL_d(\mathbb{Z})$ *such that* $A(f)$ *has a pointy neighborhood.*

Proof. For all $n \in \mathbb{N}$, define the *shear map* $A_n \in SL_d(\mathbb{Z})$ by

$$A_n(x_1, x_2, \ldots, x_d) = (x_1 + n \sum_{i=2}^{d} x_i, x_2, \ldots, x_d).$$

Let $N \subset \mathbb{Z}^d$ be the neighborhood of f. Then for $n = \max \pi(N) - \min \pi(N) + 1$, the image $A_n(N)$ is pointy, so $A_n(f)$ has a pointy neighborhood. $\square$

The usefulness of pointy neighborhoods comes from the following observation.

Lemma 3. *Let $f : S^{\mathbb{Z}^d} \to S^{\mathbb{Z}^d}$ be a totally extremally permutive CA with a pointy neighborhood. Then for all p, the automaton $f' = \rho_p(f) : (S^{p^{d-1}})^{\mathbb{Z}} \to (S^{p^{d-1}})^{\mathbb{Z}}$ defined by $f' = \rho_p \circ f \circ \rho_p^{-1}$ is bipermutive.*

Proposition 1. *If the CA $f : S^{\mathbb{Z}^d} \to S^{\mathbb{Z}^d}$ is totally extremally permutive with quiescent state 0, then $\omega_f(X) = S^{\mathbb{Z}^d}$, where X is the d-dimensional k-sparse subshift.*

Proof. We prove here the case $d = 2$. The general case follows similarly, but is notationally more complex. We first ensure that the neighborhood is pointy (the first axis is the horizontal one) and is located at the west border of the east half-plane, so that on points with a vertical period, a one-dimensional bipermutive CA with right speed of light 0 is simulated. The general idea is to successively draw larger and larger patterns at the origin as follows: As vertically periodic configurations are in a sense just one-dimensional horizontal configurations, we can apply Lemma 1 to any vertically periodic and horizontally 0-finite configuration to obtain that any finite set of columns repeats infinitely many times in the orbit. Now, as in the proof of Theorem 1, we carefully shoot a signal in the right cell at the right time, and add a huge vertical period to conclude the induction step.

Let us make this precise. We may assume without loss of generality that the lexicographically minimal element in the neighborhood of f is $(0,0)$, and that the maximal is (m_1, m_2) with $m_1 > 0$. We may also assume that f has a pointy neighborhood by Lemma 2. Let $n \geq k$, and let $P \in S^{n \times n}$ be arbitrary. We inductively construct vertically periodic configurations $x^i \in X$ such that the lexicographical prefix of P of size i occurs in some $f^t(x^i)$ at the origin, and $x^i_{(a,b)} = 0$ for all $b \in \mathbb{Z}$ for large enough $a \in \mathbb{Z}$. For x^1, we choose $x^1_{(0,nm)} = P_{(0,0)}$ for all $m \in \mathbb{Z}$, and $x^1_n = 0$ for all other $n \in \mathbb{Z}^2$.

Suppose then that x^i has already been constructed, and let $p \in \mathbb{N}$ be its vertical period. By Lemma 3, when restricted to the set X^2_p, f simulates a bipermutive one-dimensional CA $g : (S^p)^{\mathbb{Z}} \to (S^p)^{\mathbb{Z}}$ through the bijection ρ_p. Denote $H = \{(a,b) \mid a \geq 0\} \subset \mathbb{Z}^2$. Since $\rho_p(x^i)_\ell = 0^p$ for all large enough $\ell \in \mathbb{Z}$ and the left radius of g is 0, we can use Lemma 1 to conclude that there exist arbitrarily large $t > 0$ such that $x^i|_H = f^t(x^i)|_H$.

Now, there are arbitrarily large $t \in \mathbb{N}$ such that $f^t(x^i)$ contains the lexicographical prefix of P of size i at the origin. Let thus t be larger than the maximal $a \in \mathbb{Z}$ with $x^i_{(a-k,b)} \neq 0$ for some $b \in \mathbb{Z}$. Let (c,d) be the lexicographically $(i+1)$th coordinate of P. We let $y(s)^i \in X$ be as x^i, but with the coordinate $(tm_1 + c, tm_2 + d)$ containing $s \in S$. Now, permuting s in $y(s)^i$ permutes $f^t(y(s)^i_{(c,d)})$, so we can choose s so that $f^t(y(s)^i_{(c,d)}) = P_{(c,d)}$, and denote $y^i = y(s)^i$.

Since (m_1, m_2) is the lexicographically maximal vector in the neighborhood of f, (c,d) is the lexicographically minimal coordinate which can change in $f^t(y(s)^i)$, when we permute s. Thus, $f^t(y^i)$ contains the lexicographical prefix of P of size $i+1$ at the origin. We obtain x^{i+1} from y^i by adding any sufficiently large vertical period. □

Similarly to how Theorem 1 could be generalized to Theorem 2, we can generalize Proposition 1 to Proposition 2. We omit the proof.

Proposition 2. *Let $p \in \mathbb{N}$ be a prime, let $S = \mathbb{Z}_p$, let $f : S^{\mathbb{Z}^d} \to S^{\mathbb{Z}^d}$ be a group homomorphism with at least two neighbors, and let $Y \subset S^{\mathbb{Z}}$ be a the k-sparse shift. Then $\omega_f(\{0,1\}^{\mathbb{Z}^d} \cap Y) = S^{\mathbb{Z}}$.*

6   Commutation

In this section, we discuss the commutator of a totally extremally permutive cellular automaton. First, we consider the size of such a commutator, and then look at what happens when the totally extremally permutive CA is also an affine map on a full shift with cellwise defined group structure.

6.1   Size of the Commutator of a Totally Extremally Permutive CA

In this section, we prove a strong upper bound on the number of commuting cellular automata of any radius. This result is based on the following lemma, which relates the commutator of a given CA f to the f-closures of subshifts.

Lemma 4. *Let $X \subset S^{\mathbb{Z}^d}$ be a subshift, let $f : X \to X$ be a CA and let $Y \subset X$ with $Y^f = X$. Then the map $\phi : C(f) \to X^Y$ defined by $\phi(g) = g|_Y$ is injective.*

Proof. Let $g, h \in C(f)$ be such that $g|_Y = h|_Y$, and let $x \in X$ be arbitrary. Let $r \in \mathbb{N}$ be a common radius for g and h, and let $y \in Y$ and $i \in \mathbb{N}$ be such that $f^i(y)_{[-r,r]^d} = x_{[-r,r]^d}$. Then, since $g, h \in C(f)$, we have

$$g(x)_0 = g(f^i(y))_0 = f^i(g(y))_0 = f^i(h(y))_0 = h(f^i(y))_0 = h(x)_0.$$

Since x was arbitrary, we have $g = h$. □

Proposition 3. *Let $f : S^{\mathbb{Z}^d} \to S^{\mathbb{Z}^d}$ be a totally extremally permutive CA with a quiescent state $0 \in S$. For all $n \in \mathbb{N}$, define*

$$C_n(f) = \left\{ g \in C(f) \mid [0, n-1]^d \text{ is a neighborhood for } g \right\}.$$

Then $|C_n(f)| \leq |S|^{1+n^d(|S|-1)}$. If $S = \mathbb{Z}_p$ for a prime $p \in \mathbb{N}$ and f is a group homomorphism, then $|C_n(f)| \leq |S|^{1+n^d}$.

Proof. Let $X \subset S^{\mathbb{Z}^d}$ be the n-sparse shift. Proposition 1 and Lemma 4 together imply that $|C_n(f)|$ is at most the number of local maps $\mathcal{B}_{[0,n-1]^d}(X) \to S$. Since we have $|\mathcal{B}_{[0,n-1]^d}(X)| = 1 + n^d(|S| - 1)$, the number of such maps is $|S|^{1+n^d(|S|-1)}$. In the homomorphic case, apply Proposition 2 to replace X with $Y = X \cap \{0,1\}^{\mathbb{Z}^d}$, where we have $|\mathcal{B}_{[0,n-1]^d}(Y)| = 1 + n^d$. □

The upper bound, reached for example by the identity CA, is $|C_n(f)| = |S|^{|S|^{n^d}}$ for all $n \in \mathbb{N}$. In [1], a concept called 'symmetry' is defined for one-dimensional subshifts: the symmetry of an SFT $X \subset S^{\mathbb{Z}}$ is defined as the limit superior of $\frac{1}{n} \log\log A(n)$, where $A(n)$ is the number of bijective CA on X which have neighborhood $[0, n-1]$. For $X = S^{\mathbb{Z}}$, this is 1 if logarithms are taken in base $|S|$, see [1]. We give a more general definition in the same vein, by taking the same limit for an arbitrary set of CA.

Definition 4. *Fix an alphabet S, and let F be a set of cellular automata on the full shift $S^{\mathbb{Z}^d}$ such that $f \in F$ implies $\sigma^{\boldsymbol{v}} \circ f \in F$ for all $\boldsymbol{v} \in \mathbb{Z}^d$. The* density *of F is defined as*

$$d(F) = \limsup_n \frac{1}{n^d} \log\log A([0, n-1]^d),$$

where $A(N)$ is the number of cellular automata in F with minimal neighborhood contained in N, and logarithms are taken in base $|S|$. If F is a set of cellular automata on a subshift $X \subset S^{\mathbb{Z}}$, we define F' by mapping illegal configurations to a fixed symbol, and let $d(F) = d(F')$.

It is easy to see that the density of the set of automorphisms of a one-dimensional SFT is equal to its symmetry (which in turn is equal to its entropy [1]), and that the density of the commutator of the identity map is 1. We summarize Proposition 3 by noting that the density of the commutator of any totally extremally permutive CA is 0. In [4], it was proved that if $f, g : S^{\mathbb{Z}} \to S^{\mathbb{Z}}$ are commuting radius-$\frac{1}{2}$ cellular automata and f is bipermutive, then there exist functions $\phi, \psi : S \to S$ such that $g_{\mathrm{loc}}(a, b) = f_{\mathrm{loc}}(\phi(a), \psi(b))$ (g is an *isotope* of f). From this one can compute the weaker upper bound of $\frac{1}{2}$ for the density of the commutator of a bipermutive CA.

6.2   Commutator of an Affine Totally Extremally Permutive CA

Next, we turn to affine totally extremally permutive cellular automata on $G^{\mathbb{Z}^d}$, where G is a finite group. By the next lemma, no generality is lost if we assume G to be abelian.

Lemma 5. *Let G be a finite group, and suppose there exists a totally extremally permutive and affine cellular automaton on $G^{\mathbb{Z}^d}$ with minimal neighborhood of size at least 2. Then, G is abelian.*

Proof. If there exists such an affine cellular automaton, then there must in particular exist a *homomorphism* f with minimal neighborhood of size at least 2. So, let $f : G^{\mathbb{Z}^d} \to G^{\mathbb{Z}^d}$ be such a homomorphism, and order the arguments of its local rule $f_{\mathrm{loc}} : G^n \to G$ so that it is permutive in its first two arguments. Let $g, h \in G$, and let $g', h' \in G$ such that $f_{\mathrm{loc}}(g', 1, 1, \ldots, 1) = g$ and $f_{\mathrm{loc}}(1, h', 1, \ldots, 1) = h$. Since f_{loc} is a homomorphism, we have

$$g \cdot h = f_{\mathrm{loc}}(g', 1, 1, \ldots, 1) \cdot f_{\mathrm{loc}}(1, h', 1, \ldots, 1) = f_{\mathrm{loc}}(g', h', 1, \ldots, 1)$$
$$= f_{\mathrm{loc}}(1, h', 1, \ldots, 1) \cdot f_{\mathrm{loc}}(g', 1, 1, \ldots, 1) = h \cdot g.$$

Thus G is abelian.   □

Lemma 6. *Let G, H be abelian groups, and let $g : G \to H$ be such that $g(a + b - c) = g(a) + g(b) - d$ holds for some $c \in G$ and $d \in H$, and all $a, b \in G$. Then, $g(a) = h(a) - g(2c) + 2d$ for a homomorphism $h : G \to H$. In particular, g is affine.*

Proof. We have

$$g(a + b) = g(a + (b + c) - c)$$
$$= g(a) + g(b + c) - d$$
$$= g(a) + g(b + 2c - c) - d$$
$$= g(a) + g(b) + g(2c) - 2d.$$

Denote $e = g(2c) - 2d$, and let $h(a) = g(a) + e$. Then

$$h(a + b) = g(a + b) + e$$
$$= g(a) + g(b) + 2e$$
$$= h(a) + h(b),$$

so h is a homomorphism and g is affine.   □

In [4] it was proved, using algebraic methods, that among CA with radius $1/2$, affine and bipermutive CA can only commute with affine CA. We show the small step required to generalize this result for our definition of commutator in one dimension:

Theorem 4. *Let $f : G^{\mathbb{Z}} \to G^{\mathbb{Z}}$ be bipermutive and affine (so that G is abelian), and let $g : G^{\mathbb{Z}} \to G^{\mathbb{Z}}$ commute with f. Then g is affine.*

Proof (Based on the results of [4]). By composing with shifts, we may assume f has neighborhood $[0, m_f]$ and g has neighborhood $[0, m_g]$. Then, since g commutes with f, it also commutes with f^k. Let k be large enough that $m_f \cdot k \geq m_g$. Then, the $m_f \cdot k$ blocking of f^k (the automaton obtained from f^k by joining blocks $m_f \cdot k$ consecutive cells into single symbols) is bipermutive and affine with radius $1/2$, and the corresponding blocking h of g has radius $1/2$. Thus, the result of [4] applies, and h is an affine self-map of $(G^{m_f \cdot k})^{\mathbb{Z}}$. But clearly g must then have been affine for $G^{\mathbb{Z}}$, because the blocking operation is a group isomorphism.

We can also prove this directly, using Lemma 1:

Proof (Using Lemma 1). First, we can assume that f has a unary fixed point $c(a)$ by taking powers of f, and we denote $g(c(a)) = c(b)$. Now, f also fixes $c(b)$. Without loss of generality, assume f has neighborhood $[0, m]$ and g has neighborhood $[0, n]$. Let $w \in G^{2n+1}$ and $e \in \{a, b\}$, and let $x \in G^{\mathbb{Z}}$ be the configuration with $x_{[-n,n]} = w$ and $x_i = e$ for $i \notin [-n, n]$. Denote $M = (|G|^{2n+1})!$ and apply Lemma 1, so that

$$f^M(x)_j = f^M(x)_{j-mM} = w_j \tag{2}$$

for all $j \in [-n, n]$.

Let then $w^1, w^2 \in G^{n+1}$, let $x \in G^{\mathbb{Z}}$ be the configuration with $x_j = w_j^1$ and $x_{j+mM} = w_j^2$ for all $j \in [0, n]$, and a everywhere else. By the affinity of f and (2), we have

$$f^M(x)_j = w_j^1 + w_j^2 - C$$

for all $j \in [0, n]$ and some constant $C \in G$. Thus we have $g(f^M(x))_0 = g_{\mathrm{loc}}(w^1 + w^2 - \underbrace{(C, \ldots, C)}_{n+1})$. On the other hand, we have $g(x)_j \neq b$ only when $j \in [-n, n]$ or $j - mM \in [-n, n]$, so using the affinity of f and (2), we see that $f^M(g(x))_0 = g_{\mathrm{loc}}(w^1) + g_{\mathrm{loc}}(w^2) - C$. Since f and g commute, these values are equal, and thus g is affine by Lemma 6 (setting $c = (C, \ldots, C)$ and $d = C$). $\qquad \square$

Now, let us reduce the multidimensional case to the one-dimensional case.

Theorem 5. *Let $f : G^{\mathbb{Z}^d} \to G^{\mathbb{Z}^d}$ be totally extremally permutive and affine (so that G is abelian), and let $g : G^{\mathbb{Z}^d} \to G^{\mathbb{Z}^d}$ commute with f. Then g is affine.*

Proof (Using Lemma 1). We only present a proof for $d = 2$. We first modify the neighborhoods of f and g. First, we compose with a shift so that the lexicographically minimal element in the neighborhood of f is $(0, 0)$. Then, we ensure that for the maximal element (m_1, m_2) of the neighborhood, we have $m_1 > 0$ by considering $\left(\begin{smallmatrix} 0 & 1 \\ -1 & 0 \end{smallmatrix} \right)(f)$ instead in the case $m_1 = 0$. We also make sure f has a pointy neighborhood by applying Lemma 2. These transformations amount to mapping $f \mapsto \sigma^v(A(f))$ for some $A \in SL_2(\mathbb{Z})$ and $v \in \mathbb{Z}^2$. Note that $f' = \sigma^v \circ A(f)$ and $g' = \sigma^{v'} \circ A(g)$ commute for all $v' \in \mathbb{Z}^2$, and f' is affine and totally extremally permutive.

Now, let the neighborhood of g' be contained in $[0, p-1]^2$ (by choosing v' appropriately), and consider the vertically periodic subshift X_p. The restrictions $f'|_{X_p}$ and $g'|_{X_p}$ simulate one-dimensional cellular automata on $(G^p)^{\mathbb{Z}}$ through the bijection ρ_p. By Lemma 3, the one-dimensional CA corresponding to $f'|_{X_p}$ is bipermutive, and it is clearly affine. Then, by Theorem 4, $g'|_{X_p}$ is affine. This implies that g' is affine as well, since g' has neighborhood $[0, p-1]^2$. Finally, also g is affine since transformations of $SL_d(\mathbb{Z})$ are group isomorphisms. $\qquad \square$

For the special case of totally extremally permutive *homomorphic* CA on a group of prime order, there is a very nice characterization for the commutator restricted to CA with quiescent state 0. This can be seen as a corollary of the previous results, but we present a very short direct proof based on Proposition 2 and Lemma 4.

Proposition 4. *Let $G = \mathbb{Z}_p$, let $f : G^{\mathbb{Z}^d} \to G^{\mathbb{Z}^d}$ be a totally extremally permutive homomorphism. Then $g : G^{\mathbb{Z}^d} \to G^{\mathbb{Z}^d}$ with $g(c(0)) = c(0)$ commutes with f if and only if g is homomorphic.*

Proof. Let g have radius r. Then $X^f = S^{\mathbb{Z}}$, where $X = \{0,1\}^{\mathbb{Z}^d} \cap Y$ and Y is the r-sparse shift, by Proposition 2. As $G = \mathbb{Z}_p$, all homomorphic automata commute, so in particular $h \circ f = f \circ h$ for the unique homomorphic automaton defined by $h|_X = g|_X$. Thus, $g = h$ by Lemma 4. $\qquad\square$

7   Conclusions

In this article, we have shown that a bipermutive one-dimensional cellular automaton topologically randomizes any sufficiently complicated mixing SFT, and that this is equivalent to the existence of a transitive point. We have also shown that if the CA is also a group homomorphism on a prime alphabet, then any nontrivial mixing SFT can be randomized. Next, we showed that this result partially generalizes to higher dimensions, in that an extremally permutive CA topologically randomizes all k-sparse shift, which are particular highly mixing SFTs. We used these results to obtain strong bounds on the size of the commutator of an extremally permutive automaton. Finally, we showed that the commutator of an extremally permutive affine cellular automaton consists of affine automata, solving the old open problem posed in [4].

Future directions for this line of research could include generalizing Theorem 1 and Proposition 1 by showing topological randomization for a larger and more natural class of subshifts. Question 1 is related to this problem. One could also try to combine the notions of topological randomization of subshifts and asymptotic randomization of measures, in the hope of generalizing Theorem 5.3 of [5] for measures of not necessarily full support. Also, if any cellular automaton topologically randomizes every k-sparse shift, Proposition 3 holds for it, so one could also try to extend Proposition 1 for other classes of automata in the hope of obtaining bounds for commutator sizes. Finally, it may be possible to generalize Theorem 5 for other algebraic structures than groups, or even for other natural classes of cellular automata, and this should be further investigated.

References

1. Boyle, M., Lind, D., Rudolph, D.: The automorphism group of a shift of finite type. Transactions of the American Mathematical Society 306(1), 71–114 (1988)
2. Hedlund, G.A.: Endomorphisms and automorphisms of the shift dynamical system. Math. Systems Theory 3, 320–375 (1969)
3. Lind, D., Marcus, B.: An introduction to symbolic dynamics and coding. Cambridge University Press, Cambridge (1995)
4. Moore, C., Boykett, T.: Commuting cellular automata. Complex Systems 11(1), 55–64 (1997)
5. Pivato, M.: The ergodic theory of cellular automata. Int. J. General Systems 41(6), 583–594 (2012)
6. Pivato, M., Yassawi, R.: Limit measures for affine cellular automata ii. Ergodic Theory and Dynamical Systems 24, 1961–1980 (2004)
7. Salo, V.: On Nilpotency and Asymptotic Nilpotency of Cellular Automata. ArXiv e-prints (May 2012)

On Polynomial Rings in Information Dynamics of Linear CA

Fritz von Haeseler[1],[*] and Hidenosuke Nishio[2]

[1] IFAT, Otto von Guericke Universität,
Universitätsplatz 2, 39106 Magdeburg, Germany
Friedrich.vonHaeseler@ovgu.de
[2] Kyoto University,
Iwakura Miyake-cho 204, Sakyo-ku, 606-0022, Kyoto, Japan
yra05762@nifty.com

Abstract. In this article we are considering linear cellular automata with states in the ring of maps from a finite field in itself. We are particularly interested in the structure of the subrings generated by the coefficients of powers of polynomials with coefficients in the above mentioned ring. We present results on the equality of these subrings together with an upper bound on the number of different subrings generated by this procedure.

1 Introduction

Information dynamics of cellular automata (CA) was introduced in [3,4]. The general question is the spreading of information by a cellular automaton. The information dynamics was concerned with CA whose cell states are polynomial rings in X over a finite field. For the benefit of the reader we briefly explain the basic ideas and fix some notation. Let R be a (finite) ring and $f : R^3 \to R$ a map, the local rule of the CA. Then f induces a map F, the global map, from $R^{\mathbb{Z}}$ to $R^{\mathbb{Z}}$, the set of bi-infinite sequences with values in R. For a configuration $\underline{c} \in R^{\mathbb{Z}}$ one defines a new sequence $F(\underline{c})$ by setting

$$F(\underline{c})(j) = f(\underline{c}(j-1), \underline{c}(j), \underline{c}(j+1))$$

for all $j \in \mathbb{Z}$. Iterating this global map F leads to a sequence of configurations $\underline{c}^t = F^t(\underline{c}), t \geq 0$.

In information dynamics one is interested in the following question; Assume that R is the ring of mappings from a finite field $\mathbf{GF}(q)$ to itself, then R can be described as the ring of polynomials in X of degree less than q. Now, given an initial configuration $\underline{c}$, defined as $\underline{c}(j) = a_j, j < 0$, $\underline{c}(0) = X$, and $\underline{c}(j) = b_j$ for $j > 0$, where a_j, b_j are constant polynomial functions and X stands for a variable or information, then X affects the cells of $\underline{c}^t(j)$, where $j = -t, \ldots, t$. The problem is to recover X by basic ring operations with the values of $\underline{c}^t$. In

---

[*] Corresponding author.

J. Kari, M. Kutrib, and A. Malcher (Eds.): AUTOMATA 2013, LNCS 8155, pp. 171–186, 2013.
© Springer-Verlag Berlin Heidelberg 2013

general, one associates to the configuration $\underline{c}^t$ a subring $\mathcal{C}^t \subseteq R$ which consists either of all $\mathbb{F}$-linear combinations of all finite sums and products of the $\underline{c}^t(j)$, or of all $\mathbb{F}$-linear combinations of finite sums and products of the $\underline{c}^t(j)$ and the elements of the field. Information dynamics is concerned with the sequence of subrings generated by a CA.

In [1] the author starts to investigate this problem for the ring of maps from a finite field into itself.

In this paper we continue this study for linear CA. A linear CA with states in a ring is best described as follows: The sequences $\underline{c} : \mathbb{Z} \to R$ are considered as formal Laurent series, $\underline{c}(Y)$, the local rule is a polynomial $P(Y)$ with coefficients in R and the global map is simply the multiplication of the formal Laurent series with the polynomial. One then has the nice description of $\underline{c}^t$ as $\underline{c}^t(Y) = P(Y)^t \underline{c}^0$.

In this article we consider linear CA with states in the ring of maps of a finite field to itself. For a local rule $P[Y]$ and the special initial configuration $\underline{c}^0 = X$ with $\underline{c}^0(j) = 0$ for $j \neq 0$ we associate a sequence of rings $\mathcal{P}(t)$ to the orbit $\underline{c}^t = P(Y)^t \underline{c}^0$, $t \geq 0$.

After the introduction of same basic facts and notions we present in Section 3 a precise definition of the subrings $\mathcal{P}(t)$ and their properties. We present necessary conditions for all subrings $\mathcal{P}(t)$ to be equal as well as an upper bound for the number of different subrings.

2   Some Basic Facts

With $\mathbb{F}$ we denote the finite field $\mathbf{GF}(q)$ with $q = p^s$ elements, where p is a prime, the characteristic of the field, and $s \in \mathbb{N} = \{1, 2, \ldots\}$. The set of all maps from $\mathbb{F}$ to $\mathbb{F}$ is denoted as $\overline{\mathbb{F}}[X]$ which can be thought of as residue class ring $\mathbb{F}[X]/(X^q - X)$. In other words, there is a one to one relation of maps from $\mathbb{F}$ to $\mathbb{F}$ and the polynomials $p(X)$ of degree less than q with coefficients in $\mathbb{F}$. For a subset M of $\overline{\mathbb{F}}[X]$ we define the *support* of M as

$$\text{supp}(M) = \{\xi \,|\, \text{there exists } f \in M \text{ with } f(\xi) \neq 0\}, \tag{1}$$

the *zero-set* of M is defined as

$$\mathcal{Z}(M) = \{\xi \,|\, f(\xi) = 0 \text{ for all } f \in M\}. \tag{2}$$

Moreover, two elements $\xi, \zeta \in \mathbb{F}$ are called *M-equivalent*, denoted as $\xi \equiv_M \zeta$, if $f(\xi) = f(\zeta)$ for all $f \in M$. If ξ and ζ are not M-equivalent, then ξ and ζ are called *M-separable*. Note that, if $\mathcal{Z}(M) \neq \emptyset$, then $\mathcal{Z}(M)$ is an M-equivalence class and all other M-equivalence classes belong to the support of M. The partition of $\mathbb{F}$ induced by the M-equivalence is denoted as $\mathbf{P}_M(\mathbb{F})$. With $\mathbf{P}_M(\text{supp}(M))$ we denote the partition of the support of M into M-equivalence classes. If $\mathcal{Z}(M) \neq \emptyset$, then

$$\mathbf{P}_M(\mathbb{F}) = \mathbf{P}_M(\text{supp}(M)) \cup \{\mathcal{Z}(M)\}.$$

The set $\overline{\mathbb{F}}[X]$ becomes a ring with pointwise addition and multiplication, i.e., $(f + g)(\xi) = f(\xi) + g(\xi)$ and $(fg)(\xi) = f(\xi)g(\xi)$ for $f, g \in \overline{\mathbb{F}}[X]$ and $\xi \in \mathbb{F}$.

Moreover, $\overline{\mathbb{F}}[X]$ is also an $\mathbb{F}$-vectorspace by setting

$$(r\,f)(x) = r\,f(x)$$

for $r \in \mathbb{F}$ and $f \in \overline{\mathbb{F}}[X]$. The dimension of the $\mathbb{F}$-vectorspace $\overline{\mathbb{F}}[X]$ is equal to $q = |\mathbb{F}|$.

Example 1. 1. The set of monomials $\{X^j \mid j = 0, 1, \ldots, q - 1\}$ forms a base of $\overline{\mathbb{F}}[X]$.

2. The above mentioned one to one correspondence of elements in $\overline{\mathbb{F}}$ and the polynomials in $\mathbb{F}[X]/(X^q - X)$ is now explained in detail.

Since $\mathbb{F}$ is a finite field with q elements, one has $\xi^{q-1} = 1$ for all $\xi \in \mathbb{F}^* = \mathbb{F} \setminus \{0\}$. For $\xi \in \mathbb{F}$ we define the polynomial

$$\delta_\xi(X) = 1 - (X - \xi)^{q-1},$$

which can be considered as an element of $\mathbb{F}[X]/(X^q - X)$. On the other hand, if we consider the map $\zeta \mapsto \delta_\xi(\zeta)$, then we see that δ_ξ is the characteristic function of ξ, i.e., $\delta_\xi(\zeta) = 1$ for $\zeta = \xi$ and zero otherwise. Obviously, the set $\{\delta_\xi(X) \mid \xi \in \mathbb{F}\}$ forms a base of $\overline{\mathbb{F}}[X]$. Moreover, the map from $\overline{\mathbb{F}}[X]$ to $\mathbb{F}[X]/(X^q - X)$ defined as

$$f \mapsto \sum_{\xi \in \mathbb{F}} f(\xi)\delta_\xi(X)$$

defines a ring isomorphism.

In connection with information dynamics of cellular automata we introduce the notion of a (sub)vectorspace-ring.

Definition 1. *A subset R of $\overline{\mathbb{F}}[X]$ is called a* (sub)vectorspace-ring *of $\overline{\mathbb{F}}[X]$ if*

1. *R is a subring of the ring $\overline{\mathbb{F}}[X]$*
2. *R is an $\mathbb{F}$-subvectorspace of the $\mathbb{F}$-vectorspace $\overline{\mathbb{F}}[X]$.*

From now on we call a (sub)vectorspace-ring R of $\overline{\mathbb{F}}[X]$ simply a vectorspace-ring. If $R \subseteq \overline{\mathbb{F}}[X]$ is a vectorspace-ring, then one has for all r, $s \in R$ and $\xi \in \mathbb{F}$ that $r \cdot s \in R$, $r + s \in R$ and $\xi r \in R$. The following examples show that there are subrings of $\overline{\mathbb{F}}[X]$ which are not vectorspaces and that there are subvectorspaces of $\overline{\mathbb{F}}[X]$ which are not subrings.

Example 2. 1. Let $\mathbb{F} = \mathbf{GF}(25)$ then the field $\mathbb{F}_5 = \mathbf{GF}(5)$ is a subfield of $\mathbb{F}$. Therefore the set of maps from $\mathbb{F}$ to $\mathbb{F}_5$ is a subring of $\overline{\mathbb{F}}[X]$. However, it is not a subvectorspace of $\overline{\mathbb{F}}[X]$.

2. If $\mathbb{F} = \mathbf{GF}(p)$, p a prime number, then every subring of $\overline{\mathbb{F}}[X]$ is also a subvectorspace.

3. The multiplicative group $\mathbb{F}^* = \mathbb{F} \setminus \{0\}$ is cyclic of order $q - 1$ with primitive element ρ, i.e., $\mathbb{F}^* = \{\rho^j \mid j = 0, \ldots, q-2\}$. For q odd we consider the identity map $\mathrm{id}_\mathbb{F}$. Clearly, the set $V = \{\xi \, \mathrm{id}_\mathbb{F} \mid r \in \mathbb{F}\}$ is a subvectorspace of $\overline{\mathbb{F}}[X]$, and each element of V is a bijection from $\mathbb{F}$ to $\mathbb{F}$. Since $1 = \rho^0 = \rho^{2(\frac{q-1}{2})}$ it follows that $\mathrm{id}_\mathbb{F}^2$ is not a bijection and hence not in V. This means that V is not a subring.

The following lemma links the dimension of a vectorpace-ring $R \subseteq \overline{\mathbb{F}}[X]$ with its support.

Lemma 1. *Let R be a vectorspace-ring of $\overline{\mathbb{F}}[X]$, then*

$$\dim(R) = |\operatorname{supp}(R)/ \equiv_R|$$

In other words, the dimension is equal to the number of R-equivalence classes which belong to the support of R. Note that Lemma 1 also applies to the trivial vectorspace-ring $R = \{0\}$, having dimension 0. Note also, that Lemma 1 applies only to vectorspace-rings of $\overline{\mathbb{F}}[X]$. I.e., if V is the vectorspace generated by the identity map on $\mathbb{F}$ with $q > 2$, then $\dim(V) = 1$. On the other hand, $|\operatorname{supp}(V)/ \equiv_V| = q - 1 > 1$.

As a consequence of the results in [1] we note

Corollary 1. *Let R be a non-trivial vectorspace-ring of $\overline{\mathbb{F}}[X]$, then the characteristic maps of the elements of the partition of $\operatorname{supp}(R)$, i.e., the maps $\chi_U : \mathbb{F} \to \mathbb{F}$ defined as*

$$\chi_U(\xi) = \begin{cases} 1 & \text{if } \xi \in U \\ 0 & \text{otherwise} \end{cases}$$

for $U \in \mathbf{P}_R(\operatorname{supp}(R))$, form a base of R.

Remark 1. If f and g are elements of the vectorspace-ring $R \neq \{0\}$ they can be written as

$$f = \sum_{U \in \mathbf{P}_R(\operatorname{supp}(R))} \alpha_U \chi_U \text{ and } g = \sum_{U \in \mathbf{P}_R(\operatorname{supp}(R))} \beta_U \chi_U,$$

where $\alpha_U, \beta_V \in \mathbb{F}$ correspond to the respective values of f and g on U. The sum of f and g is given as

$$(f + g) = \sum_{U \in \mathbf{P}_R(\operatorname{supp}(R))} (\alpha_U + \beta_U) \chi_U$$

and, as a consequence of the fact that $\chi_U \chi_V = 0$ if $U \cap V = \emptyset$, their product is

$$(f g) = \sum_{U \in \mathbf{P}_R(\operatorname{supp}(R))} \alpha_U \beta_U \chi_U.$$

Thus the maps χ_U, $U \in \mathbf{P}_R(\operatorname{supp}(R))$ form a base of the vectorspace-ring R

Further properties of subvector-rings are

Corollary 2. *1. Let V be a subvectorspace of $\overline{\mathbb{F}}[X]$, then*

$$|V| = q^{\dim(V)}$$

2. If R and R' are vectorspace-rings of $\overline{\mathbb{F}}[X]$ such that $|R| = |R'|$, then R and R' are isomorphic as vectorspace-rings.

3. *Let R and R' be vectorspace-rings of $\overline{\mathbb{F}}[X]$. The vectorspace-rings R and R' are equal if and only if*

$$\mathcal{Z}(R) = \mathcal{Z}(R')$$

and

$$\mathbf{P}_R(\mathrm{supp}(R)) = \mathbf{P}_{R'}(\mathrm{supp}(R'))$$

Proof. The proof of *1.* is clear. The proof of *2.* is as follows. If $|R| = |R'| = 0$, then $R = R' = \{0\}$ and the assertion holds. We therefore assume that $|R| = |R'| \geq 1$. By *1.* it follows that $\dim(R) = \dim(R')$ and Lemma 1, implies that $|\mathrm{supp}(R)/ \equiv R)| = |\mathrm{supp}(R'/ \equiv R')| = s$. With U_j, V_j, $j = 1, \ldots, s$ we denote the elements of $\mathbf{P}_R(\mathrm{supp}(R))$ and $\mathbf{P}_{R'}(\mathrm{supp}(R'))$, respectively. By Corollary 1, it follows that each $f \in R$ can be written as

$$f = \sum_{j=1}^{s} \alpha_j \chi_{U_j},$$

where $\alpha_j \in \mathbb{F}$ for $j = 1, \ldots, s$. The same holds for $g \in R'$ and the base χ_{V_j}, $j = 1, \ldots, s$. Due to the properties of the base, it is plain that $\Xi : R \to R'$ defined as

$$\Xi(f) = \Xi \left(\sum_{j=1}^{s} \alpha_j \chi_{U_j} \right) = \sum_{j=1}^{s} \alpha_j \chi_{V_j}$$

defines a vectorspace-ring isomorphism. This proves *2.*

Finally, assertion *3.* is a consequence of the proof of *2.* ∎

Remark 2. 1. The set $R = \{r \,|\, r \in \mathbb{F}\}$ of constant maps and the set $R' = \{r\delta_0(x) \,|\, r \in \mathbb{F}\}$ of maps with values equal to zero for all $\xi \neq 0$ are vectorspace-rings of dimension 1. Therefore they are vectorspace-ring isomorphic. However, as sets they are different.

2. Let R and R' be vectorspace-rings of $\overline{F}[X]$. Then $R' \subseteq R$ if and only if $\mathcal{Z}(R) \subseteq \mathcal{Z}(R')$ and the partition $\mathcal{P}_R(\mathbb{F})$ is finer than $\mathcal{P}_{R'}(\mathbb{F})$, i.e., every $U \in \mathcal{P}_R(\mathbb{F})$ is contained in a $V \in \mathcal{P}_{R'}(\mathbb{F})$, see [1].

3. If R is merely a subring of $\overline{\mathbb{F}}[X]$, then the cardinality of R is a power of p. As an example, consider $\mathbb{F} = \mathbf{GF}(4)$ and the set $R = \{0, 1 - X^3\} \subseteq \overline{\mathbb{F}}[X]$, i.e., R contains the zero map and the characteristic function $\delta_0(X)$ of 0 . Then R is a subring of $\overline{\mathbb{F}}[X]$ of cardinality 2.

Let $G = \{g_1, \ldots, g_n\} \subseteq \overline{\mathbb{F}}[X]$ be a subset of $\overline{\mathbb{F}}[X]$, with $\langle G \rangle$ we denote the smallest vectorspace-ring that contains G. With $\langle G \rangle_N$ we denote the smallest vectorspace-ring that contains G and the constant maps. The vectorspace-ring $\langle G \rangle$ consists of all finite $\mathbb{F}$-linear combinations of finite products of elements of G, and $\langle G \rangle_N = \langle G \cup \mathbf{C} \rangle$, where $\mathbf{C}$ denotes the constant maps in $\overline{\mathbb{F}}[X]$.

Example 3. 1. The polynomial X represents the identity map on $\mathbb{F}$ and one easily computes that

$$\langle \{X\} \rangle = \{ \sum_{j=1}^{q-1} r_j X^j \,|\, r_j \in \mathbb{F} \},$$

i.e., all maps from $\mathbb{F}$ to $\mathbb{F}$ with $f(0) = 0$, and that

$$\langle\{X\}\rangle_N = \{\sum_{j=0}^{q-1} r_j X^j \mid r_j \in \mathbb{F}\},$$

i.e., all maps from $\mathbb{F}$ to $\mathbb{F}$. Moreover, $\mathrm{supp}(\{X\}) = \mathrm{supp}(\langle\{X\}\rangle)$ and $\mathrm{supp}(\langle\{X\}\rangle_N) = \mathbb{F}$

2. Consider the field $\mathbb{F} = \mathbf{GF}(5)$ and the maps $f(X) = 3X + 2X^2 + 4X^3 + X^4$ and $g(X) = 1 + 4X + 4X^2 + 4X^3 + 3X^4$, which in a tabular form are given as

$\mathbb{F}$	0	1	2	3	4
f	0	0	2	1	1
g	1	1	0	0	0

Then one computes that $\langle\{f,g\}\rangle$ consists of all polynomials of the form

$$p(X) = a_1(1 + 4X + 4X^2 + 4X^3 + 3X^4) + a_2(2X + X^2 + 3X^3 + 4X^4)$$
$$+ a_3(4X + 3X^3 + 3X^4),$$

where $a_i \in \mathbb{F}$, $i = 1, 2, 3$. Using the base from Corollary 1 every element of $\langle\{f,g\}\rangle$ is a $\mathbb{F}$-linear combination of $\chi_{\{0,1\}}$, $\chi_{\{2\}}$ and $\chi_{\{3,4\}}$.
Note that $\xi \equiv_{\{f,g\}} \zeta$ if and only if $\xi \equiv_{\langle\{f,g\}\rangle} \zeta$.

The following Lemma 2 which is based on the results in [1] explains the above observations.

Lemma 2. *Let $G \subseteq \overline{\mathbb{F}}[X]$, then*

$$
\begin{array}{llll}
1) & \mathrm{supp}(G) & = & \mathrm{supp}(\langle G\rangle) \\
2) & \mathcal{Z}(G) & = & \mathcal{Z}(\langle G\rangle) \\
3) & \mathrm{supp}(\langle G\rangle_N) & = & \mathbb{F} \\
4) & \mathcal{Z}(\langle G\rangle_N) & = & \emptyset \\
5) & \xi \equiv_G \zeta & \Longleftrightarrow & \xi \equiv_{\langle G\rangle} \zeta \\
6) & \xi \equiv_G \zeta & \Longleftrightarrow & \xi \equiv_{\langle G\rangle_N} \zeta
\end{array}
$$

As a consequence we note

Lemma 3. *For a non-empty G subset of $\overline{\mathbb{F}}[X]$ the following holds*

1. *Any $f \in \langle G\rangle$ is of the form*

$$f = \sum_U \alpha_U \chi_U$$

where the sum is over $U \in \mathbf{P}_G(\mathrm{supp}(G))$ and $\alpha_U \in \mathbb{F}$.
2. *Any $f \in \langle G\rangle_N$ is of the form*

$$f = \sum_U \alpha_U \chi_U$$

where the sum is over $U \in \mathbf{P}_G(\mathbb{F})$ and $\alpha_U \in \mathbb{F}$.

Remark 3. If $f \in \overline{\mathbb{F}}[X]$ is bijective and $f(\xi) = 0$, then $\langle\{f\}\rangle$ consists of all maps with $f(\xi) = 0$, in particular $\dim\langle\{f\}\rangle = q - 1$. Furthermore, $\langle\{f\}\rangle_N$ is equal to $\mathbb{F}[X]$. This generalizes the above example for the identity map.

3   Cellular Automata

In this section we introduce one dimensional CA of radius 1 with states in $\overline{\mathbb{F}}[X]$. That means there exists a local rule $\mathbf{f} : \overline{\mathbb{F}}[X]^3 \to \overline{\mathbb{F}}[X]$ and its extension $\mathbf{F} : \overline{\mathbb{F}}[X]^{\mathbb{Z}} \to \overline{\mathbb{F}}[X]^{\mathbb{Z}}$ defined as

$$\mathbf{F}(\underline{c})(j) = f(\underline{c}(j-1), \underline{c}(j), \underline{c}(j+1)).$$

Then information dynamics is related to the following problem. Given the initial configuration $\underline{c} : \mathbb{Z} \to \overline{\mathbb{F}}[X]$ as $\underline{c}(0) = x$ and $\underline{c}(j) = 0$ otherwise, where x is the identity map on $\mathbb{F}$ and 0 the zero map on $\mathbb{F}$. If $\underline{c}^t$ denotes the configuration at time t how does the set of vectorspace-rings

$$\mathcal{P}(t) = \langle \{\underline{c}^t(j) \mid j \in \mathbb{Z}\} \rangle$$

or

$$\mathcal{P}_N(t) = \langle \{\underline{c}^t(j) \mid j \in \mathbb{Z}\} \rangle_N$$

evolve. What are possible relations between $\mathcal{P}(t)$ and $\mathcal{P}(0) = \langle \{x\} \rangle$ or $\mathcal{P}(t-1)$ and similarly for $\mathcal{P}_N(.)$.

Unfortunately, a general answer seems to be out of reach. It is therefore profitable to restrict our attention to a certain subclass of CA, namely, the linear, to be precise the $\overline{\mathbb{F}}[X]$-linear cellular automata. The linearity allows us to study local rules which depend on more than three cells.

The local rule of a linear CA is a linear map $\mathbf{f} : \overline{\mathbb{F}}[X]^{d+1} \to \overline{\mathbb{F}}[X]$ defined as

$$\mathbf{f}(f_1, \dots, f_{d+1}) = \sum_{i=0}^{d} g_i f_{i+1}, \tag{3}$$

where $g_i \in \overline{\mathbb{F}}[X]$ for $i = 0, \dots, d$. This yields a global map $\mathbf{F} : \overline{\mathbb{F}}[X]^{\mathbb{Z}} \to \overline{\mathbb{F}}[X]^{\mathbb{Z}}$ defined as

$$\mathbf{F}(\underline{c})(j) = \mathbf{f}(\underline{c}(j-d), \underline{c}(j-d+1), \dots, \underline{c}(j)),$$

for $j \in \mathbb{Z}$. If one denotes the elements of $\overline{\mathbb{F}}[X]^{\mathbb{Z}}$ as formal Laurent series, i.e. $\underline{c} = \sum_{j \in \mathbb{Z}} f_j Y^j$, with $f_j \in \overline{\mathbb{F}}[X]$, then $\mathbf{F}$ can be considered as the multiplication of a formal Laurent series with the polynomial

$$P(Y) = \sum_{j=0}^{d} g_j Y^j, \tag{4}$$

i.e., $\mathbf{F}(\underline{c}) = P(Y) \sum_{j \in \mathbb{Z}} f_j Y^j$. Note that $P(Y) \in \overline{\mathbb{F}}[X][Y]$, i.e., it is a polynomial with coefficients in $\overline{\mathbb{F}}[X]$. Given an initial configuration $\underline{c}_0$, then, due to the linearity one has that

$$\underline{c}^t = P(Y)^t \underline{c}_0.$$

For the t-th power of $P(Y)$ we denote by $\mathcal{P}(t)$ the vectorspace-ring generated by the coefficients of $P(Y)^t$, and $\mathcal{P}_N(t)$ is the vectorspace-ring generated by the coefficients of $P(Y)^t$ and the constant maps.

Example 4. 1. Consider the field $\mathbb{F} = \mathbf{GF}(2)$ and the polynomial $P(Y) = g_0 + g_1Y + g_2Y^2$. Then, since $f^2 = f$ and $2f = 0$ for all $f \in \overline{\mathbb{F}}[X]$, one obtains $\mathcal{P}(1) = \langle g_0, g_1, g_2 \rangle$, $\mathcal{P}(2) = \langle g_0, g_1, g_2 \rangle$, $\mathcal{P}(3) = \langle g_0, g_1, g_2 \rangle$, $\mathcal{P}(4) = \langle g_0, g_1, g_2 \rangle$. The extension of the list leads to the conjecture that $\mathcal{P}(t) = \mathcal{P}(1)$ holds for all $t \in \mathbb{N}$. This indeed is true, which follows from the obvious fact that the 0-th coefficient of $P(Y)^t$ is always equal to g_0 and the $2t$-th coefficient is equal to g_2 combined with the fact that the t-th coefficient of $P(Y)^t$ is equal to g_1. The last assertion follows from a simple induction argument and the equality $P(Y)^{2t} = P(Y^2)^t$.

2. Consider the field $\mathbb{F} = \mathbf{GF}(4) = \{0, 1, \zeta, 1 + \zeta\}$ with $1 + \zeta + \zeta^2 = 0$. The polynomial is $P(Y) = g_0 + g_1Y + g_2Y^2$, and the maps g_i, $i = 0, 1, 2$ are defined as

$\mathbb{F}$	0	1	ζ	$1+\zeta$
g_0	1	ζ	0	0
g_1	0	0	ζ	0
g_2	0	0	0	ζ

Due to the fact that $g_i g_j = 0$, whenever $i \neq j$ and due to the fact that $f^4 = f$ for all $f \in \overline{\mathbb{F}}[X]$ combined with characteristic of $\mathbb{F}$ is equal to two, one obtains that $\mathcal{P}(1) = \langle g_0, g_1, g_2 \rangle$, $\mathcal{P}(2) = \langle g_0^2, g_1^2, g_2^2 \rangle$, $\mathcal{P}(3) = \langle g_0^3, g_1^3, g_2^3 \rangle$, $\mathcal{P}(4) = \langle g_0, g_1, g_2 \rangle$. For the powers of the maps g_i we have

$\mathbb{F}$	0	1	ζ	$1+\zeta$
g_0^2	1	$1+\zeta$	0	0
g_1^2	0	0	$1+\zeta$	0
g_2^2	0	0	0	$1+\zeta$

$\mathbb{F}$	0	1	ζ	$1+\zeta$
g_0^3	1	1	0	0
g_1^3	0	0	1	0
g_2^3	0	0	0	1

By Lemma 2 one obtains that $\mathcal{P}(1) = \mathcal{P}(2) = \overline{\mathbb{F}}[X]$ and $\mathcal{P}(3) = \{f \mid f \in \overline{\mathbb{F}}[X] \text{ such that } f(0) = f(1)\}$. Moreover, by induction it is easy to show that $\mathcal{P}(3t + 1) = \mathcal{P}(3t + 2) = \overline{\mathbb{F}}[X]$ for $t = 0, 1, 2, \ldots$ and $\mathcal{P}(3t) = \{f \mid f \in \overline{\mathbb{F}}[X] \text{ such that } f(0) = f(1)\} = \mathcal{P}(1)$ for $t = 1, 2, 3, \ldots$.

Contrary to those examples, if $P(Y) = g_0 + g_1Y + g_2Y^2 + g_3Y^3$ or local rule of 4 cells, it is not at all clear what the relation between $\mathcal{P}(t)$ and $\mathcal{P}(1)$ is. The main part of this article is devoted to gain an understanding of the general situation with any $d \geq 0$ in Equation (3) and Equation (4).

A first general result is related to the property $\xi^q = \xi$ for all $\xi \in \mathbb{F}$.

Lemma 4. *Let $P(Y) \in \overline{\mathbb{F}}[X][Y]$, then one has $\mathcal{P}(qt) = \mathcal{P}(t)$ for all $t \in \mathbb{N}$.*

Proof. Since the field has the characteristic p, it follows that $P[Y]^{qt} = P[Y^q]^t$ which proves the assertion. ∎

For a polynomial $P(Y) \in \overline{\mathbb{F}}[X][Y]$ and $\xi \in \mathbb{F}$ we define the polynomial $P(Y)(\xi) \in \mathbb{F}[Y]$ as

$$P(Y)(\xi) = \sum_{i=0}^{d} g_i(\xi)Y^i.$$

Thus $P(Y)(\xi)$ is a polynomial with coefficients in $\mathbb{F}$. The coefficients of $P(Y)(\xi)$ are obtained by a simultaneous evaluation of g_i at ξ. Due to this description of $P(Y)(\xi)$ one has $(P(Y)(\xi))^t = (P(Y)^t)(\xi)$. Moreover, the elements of the zero set of $\mathcal{P}(1)$ are the values $\xi \in \mathbb{F}$ such that $P(Y)(\xi) = 0$, and ξ_1 and ξ_2 belong to the same $\mathcal{P}(1)$-equivalence class if and only if $P(Y)(\xi_1) = P(Y)(\xi_2)$.

Lemma 5. *Let* $P(Y) \in \overline{\mathbb{F}}[X][Y]$, *then* $\mathcal{P}(t) \subseteq \mathcal{P}(1)$ *and* $\mathrm{supp}(\mathcal{P}(t)) = \mathrm{supp}(\mathcal{P}(1))$ *for all* $t \in \mathbb{N}$.

Proof. The first assertion is obvious. For the second assertion let $\xi \in \mathcal{Z}(\mathcal{P}(1))$. Then $P(Y)(\xi) = 0$ and therefore $(P(Y)^t)(\xi) = (P(Y)(\xi))^t = 0$ which shows that $\xi \in \mathcal{Z}(\mathcal{P}(t))$. On the other hand, if $\xi \in \mathcal{Z}(\mathcal{P}(t))$, then $0 = (P(Y)^t)(\xi) = (P(Y)(\xi))^t$ yields $\xi \in \mathcal{Z}(\mathcal{P}(1))$. Thus $\mathcal{Z}(\mathcal{P}(1)) = \mathcal{Z}(\mathcal{P}(t))$ for all t, which implies the assertion. ∎

Based on the above Lemma and results in the Appendix we have the next result.

Theorem 1. *If* $P(Y) \in \overline{\mathbb{F}}[X][Y]$ *and if* $t \in \mathbb{N}$ *such that* $\gcd(t, q - 1) = 1$, *then*

$$P(t) = P(1).$$

Proof. By Lemma 5 we already know that $\mathrm{supp}(\mathcal{P}(t)) = \mathrm{supp}(\mathcal{P}(1))$, and it remains to show that the $\mathcal{P}(1)$-equivalence classes are the same as the $\mathcal{P}(t)$-equivalence classes. To this end let $\xi, \zeta \in \mathbb{F}$ be $\mathcal{P}(1)$-equivalent, this means

$$P(Y)(\xi) = P(Y)(\zeta),$$

and therefore

$$P(Y)^t(\xi) = P(Y)^t(\zeta),$$

i.e., ξ and ζ are $\mathcal{P}(t)$-equivalent. Now suppose that ξ and ζ are $\mathcal{P}(t)$-equivalent, i.e., $P(Y)^t(\xi) = P(Y)^t(\zeta)$. Since $\gcd(t, q - 1) = 1$, Lemma 10 applies and it follows that $P(Y)(\xi) = P(Y)(\zeta)$, i.e., ξ and ζ are $\mathcal{P}(1)$-equivalent. This proves the assertion. ∎

As Example 2 from above shows, it may happen that $\mathcal{P}(t) \neq \mathcal{P}(1)$, if $\gcd(t, q - 1) > 1$. In order to develop necessary and sufficient criteria for $\mathcal{P}(1) = \mathcal{P}(t)$ we introduce a stricter notion of separability.

Definition 2. ξ *and* $\zeta \in \mathbb{F}$ *are called* $(0, 1)$-*separable (relative to* $P(Y)$) *if there exists a coefficient* g_j *of* $P(Y)$ *such that either* $g_j(\xi) = 0$ *and* $g_j(\zeta) \neq 0$ *or* $g_j(\xi) \neq 0$ *and* $g_j(\zeta) = 0$.

The polynomial $P(Y)$ *is* $(0, 1)$-*separating if every pair* (ξ, ζ) *that is separable is* $(0, 1)$-*separable.*

Remark 4. If $P(Y) \in \overline{\mathbf{GF}(2)}[X][Y]$, i.e., the coefficients of P are maps $g : \{0, 1\} \to \{0, 1\}$, then every separable pair (ξ, ζ) is $(0, 1)$-separable.

As a consequence of $\xi^{q-1} = 1$ for all $\xi \in \mathbb{F}^*$ we have: ξ and ζ are $(0, 1)$-separable relative to $P(Y)$, if and only if there exists a coefficient g_j of $P(Y)$ such that

$$g_j(\xi)^{q-1} + g_j(\zeta)^{q-1} = 1.$$

The usefulness of the $(0,1)$-separability is demonstrated by the next result.

Theorem 2. *If $P(Y) \in \overline{\mathbb{F}}[X][Y]$ is $(0,1)$-separable, then*

$$\mathcal{P}(t) = \mathcal{P}(1)$$

for all $t \in \mathbb{N}$.

Proof. Let ξ and ζ be separable by $P(Y)$, i.e., there exist a g_j such that $g_j(\xi) \neq 0$ and $g_j(\zeta) = 0$ (or vice versa) and assume that ξ and ζ are not separable by $P(Y)^t$. Then we have $P(Y)(\xi)^t = P(Y)(\zeta)^t$. By Theorem 5 in the Appendix, there exists $\rho \in \mathbb{F}^*$ such that $P(Y)(\xi) = \rho\, P(Y)(\zeta)$. This is a contradiction to $g_j(\xi) \neq 0$ and $g_j(\zeta) = 0$. Therefore ξ and ζ are $P(Y)^t$-separable. ∎

The above result may suggest that the $(0,1)$-separabilty is preserved by the powers of $P(Y)$. However, as the following example shows, this is not true.

Example 5. Let $\mathbb{F} = \mathbf{GF}(3)$, i.e., $\mathbb{F} = \{0,1,2\}$ with addition and multiplication modulo 3. Let $P(Y) \in \overline{\mathbb{F}}[X]$ be given as

$$P(Y) = 1 + (1 + X^2)Y + (2X^2)Y^2 + Y^3 + Y^4$$

i.e., the maps g_i are given as

$\mathbb{F}$	0	1	2
g_0	1	1	1
g_1	1	2	2
g_2	0	2	2
g_3	1	1	1
g_4	1	1	1

Then 0 and 1 are $(0,1)$-separable relative to $P(Y)$ and they are not $(0,1)$-separable relative to $P(Y)^2$. Indeed, one computes

$$P(Y)^2 = 1 + (2 + 2X^2)Y + (1 + X^2)Y^2 + (2 + 2X^2)Y^3 + Y^4 + 2Y^5 + (1 + X^2)Y^6 + 2Y^7 + Y^8$$

and the coefficients of $P(Y)^2$ belong to the set $\{h_i \mid i = 1,2,3,4\}$ with

$\mathbb{F}$	0	1	2
h_0	1	1	1
h_1	2	1	1
h_2	1	2	2
h_3	2	2	2

Showing that 0 and 1 are separable by $P(Y)^2$ but not $(0,1)$-separable. Note also that 1 and 2 are not separable by $P(Y)^2$.

The next result provides a necessary and sufficient condition for two points ξ and ζ to be not $\mathcal{P}(t)$-separable, i.e., ξ and ζ are $\mathcal{P}(t)$-equivalent. As Theorem 1 and Example 4, 2. indicate, the only case where $\mathcal{P}(t) \subsetneq \mathcal{P}(1)$ is likely is the case that t is a divisor of $q - 1$. The following theorem provides necessary and sufficient conditions for $\mathcal{P}(t)$ to be a proper subset of $\mathcal{P}(1)$.

Theorem 3. *Let $\xi, \zeta \in \mathbb{F}$ be $\mathcal{P}(t)$-separable. For a divisor δ of $q-1$ the following holds: ξ and ζ are not $\mathcal{P}(\delta)$-separable if and only if there exists a $\rho \in \mathbb{F}^*$ such that $\rho^\delta = 1$ and $P(Y)(\xi) = \rho P(Y)(\zeta)$.*

Proof. The if-part of the proof is obvious. It remains to establish that $P[Y](\xi)^\delta = P[Y](\zeta)^\delta$ implies $P(Y)(\xi) = \rho P(Y)(\zeta)$. This is a consequence of Theorem 5. $\blacksquare$

Remark 5. Let δ and δ' be divisors of $q-1$ such that δ' divides δ. If ξ and ζ are not $\mathcal{P}(\delta')$-separable, then they are not $\mathcal{P}(\delta)$-separable.

Theorem 3 allows us to consider not only values of t which are a divisor of $q-1$.

Lemma 6. *If $t \in \mathbb{N}$ is such that $\gcd(t, q-1) = \delta$. Then ξ and ζ are not $\mathcal{P}(t)$-separable if and only if they are not $\mathcal{P}(\delta)$-separable.*

Proof. Since $t = \delta t'$, being not $\mathcal{P}(\delta)$-separable induces not being $\mathcal{P}(t)$-separable. This proofs the if part.

For the only-if part we write $t = \delta \delta' \bar{t}$ with $\delta = \gcd(t, q-1)$, $\gcd(\delta', \frac{q-1}{\delta}) = 1$ and $\gcd(\bar{t}, q-1) = 1$. By Theorem 5, there exists a $\rho \in \mathbb{F}^*$ such that $P(Y)(\xi) = \rho P(Y)(\zeta)$ and $\rho^t = 1$. Since $t = \delta\delta'\bar{t}$ and $\gcd(\bar{t}, q-1) = 1$ it follows $\rho^{\delta'\delta} = 1$. Since $\gcd(\delta', \frac{q-1}{\delta}) = 1$ it follows by Lemma 9 that $\rho^\delta = 1$. And therefore $P(Y)(\xi)^\delta = (\rho P(Y)(\zeta))^\delta = P(Y)(\zeta)^\delta$, which proves that ξ and ζ are not $\mathcal{P}(\delta)$-separable. $\blacksquare$

The above results allow to give an upper bound for the number of different vectorspace-rings of the form $\mathcal{P}(t)$.

Lemma 7. *Let $P(Y)$ be a polynomial with coefficients in $\overline{\mathbb{F}}[X]$. Then the number of different vectorspace-rings of the form $\mathcal{P}(t)$ is bounded by the number of divisors of $q-1$.*

Example 6. 1. For $\mathbb{F} = \mathbf{GF}(2)$, i.e., the field with 2 elements one has $\mathcal{P}(t) = \mathcal{P}(1)$ for all $t \in \mathbb{N}$. This follows from the fact that $\mathbb{F}^* = \{1\}$ has no proper subgroups.

2. Let $\mathbb{F} = \mathbf{GF}(3)$, i.e., $\mathbb{F} = \{0, 1, 2\}$ with addition and multiplication modulo 3. Then $q-1 = 3-1 = 2$ has only the divisors 1 and 2. Let $P[Y]$ be given as

$$P[x][Y] = (x + 2x^2) + (1 + x)Y + (2 + 2x)Y^2$$

i.e., the maps g_i, $i = 0, 1, 2$ are given as

$\mathbb{F}$	0	1	2
g_0	0	0	1
g_1	1	2	0
g_2	2	1	0

Since $P(Y)(0) = 2P(Y)(1)$, it follows that 0 and 1 are not $\mathcal{P}(2)$-separable. This is also established by the list of coefficients of $P[X]^2$, which is

$\mathbb{F}$	0 1 2
g_0^2	0 0 1
$2g_0g_1$	0 0 0
$g_1^2 + 2g_0g_2$	1 1 0
$2g_1g_2$	1 1 0
g_2^2	1 1 0

One sees that $\dim \mathcal{P}(1) = 3$ and $\dim \mathcal{P}(2) = 2$. Moreover, by Lemma 6 one has $\mathcal{P}(2t) = \mathcal{P}(2)$ and $\mathcal{P}(2t+1) = \mathcal{P}(1)$ for all $t \in \mathbb{N}$.

The next result gives a criterion for $\mathcal{P}(t) = \mathcal{P}(1)$ for all t.

Theorem 4. *Let $P(Y) = \sum_{j=0}^{d_1} g_j Y^j$ be a polynomial with coefficients in $\overline{\mathbb{F}}[X]$. Then the following holds: $\mathcal{P}(t) = \mathcal{P}(1)$ for all positive t if and only if for all ξ, $\zeta \in \mathbb{F}$, $\xi \neq \zeta$, and all $\rho \in \mathbb{F}^*$ one has $P(Y)(\xi) \neq \rho\, P(Y)(\zeta)$.*

In other words, if the coefficients of $P(Y)$ are written in matrixform, i.e., each row corresponds to a non-trivial coefficient of $P(Y)$, then $\mathcal{P}(t) = \mathcal{P}(1)$ for all t if and only if no column is a non-trivial, i.e., $\rho \in \mathbb{F}^* \setminus \{1\}$ multiple of another column.

Another inportant observation from the results above is that only the coefficients of $P(Y)$ determine $\mathcal{P}(t)$. If $Q(Y)$ is a polynomial with coefficients in $\overline{\mathbb{F}}[X]$, then $\mathcal{Q}(t)$ denotes the vectorspace-ring generated by the t-th power of $Q(Y)$. We then have

Lemma 8. *Let $P(Y) = \sum_{j=0}^{d_1} g_j Y^j$ and $Q(Y) = \sum_{j=0}^{d_2} h_j Y^j$ be polynomials with coefficients in $\overline{\mathbb{F}}[X]$. If the sets $\{g_j \mid j = 0, \ldots, d_1\}$ and $\{h_j \mid j = 0, \ldots, d_2\}$ are equal, then $\mathcal{P}(t) = \mathcal{Q}(t)$ for all positive t.*

The next example elucidates the above results.

Example 7. The finite field is $\mathbb{F} = \mathbf{GF}(7) = \{0, 1, \ldots, 6\}$ with addition and multiplication modulo 7. Then $\mathbb{F}^* = \{1, 2, 3, 4, 5, 6\}$ has order 6 and the divisors of 6 are 1, 2, 3, 6. If $P(Y) = \sum_{j=0}^{d} g_j Y^j$ is the linear rule for a CA, then by Lemma 7 there are at most 4 different vectorspace-rings of the form $\mathcal{P}(t)$. By Lemma 6, one has $\mathcal{P}(t) = \mathcal{P}(\delta)$ if $\delta = \gcd(t, 6)$. Thus it is sufficient to investigate $\mathcal{P}(t)$ for $t = 1, 2, 3, 6$.

Let the linear rule of a CA be given as

$$P(Y) = 1 + 3x + 2x^2 + 3x^3 + 6x^4 + x^5 +$$
$$(2 + 5x + 4x^2 + 4x^3 + 2x^4 + x^5)Y +$$
$$(3 + 6x^2 + 5x^3 + 5x^4 + x^5)Y^2 +$$
$$(4 + 2x + 3x^2 + x^3 + 2x^4 + x^5 + 2x^6)Y^3.$$

Writing the coefficients in matrix form one obtains

$$
\begin{array}{c|ccccccc}
\mathbb{F} & 0 & 1 & 2 & 3 & 4 & 5 & 6 \\
\hline
g_0 & 1 & 2 & 6 & 5 & 4 & 1 & 2 \\
g_1 & 2 & 4 & 5 & 6 & 2 & 4 & 5 \\
g_2 & 3 & 6 & 4 & 0 & 0 & 0 & 1 \\
g_3 & 4 & 1 & 3 & 2 & 3 & 6 & 0
\end{array}
$$

The rows represent the coefficents of $P(Y)$ and the columns represent the polynomials $P(Y)(\xi)$. From the matrix one easily deduces that $\operatorname{supp}(\mathcal{P}(1)) = \mathbb{F}$. By Theorem 1, it follows that $\operatorname{supp}(\mathcal{P}(t)) = \mathbb{F}$ for all t. Since the columns are mutually different it follows that different $\xi, \zeta \in \mathbb{F}$ are $\mathcal{P}(1)$-separable. This shows that

$$\mathcal{P}(1) = \overline{\mathbb{F}}[X].$$

An inspection of the columns reveals the folowing relations

$$
\begin{aligned}
P(Y)(1) &= 2P(Y)(0) \\
P(Y)(2) &= 6P(Y)(0) \\
P(Y)(4) &= 5P(Y)(3) \\
P(Y)(5) &= 3P(Y)(3) \\
P(Y)(5) &= 2P(Y)(4)
\end{aligned}
$$

Since $6^2 = 1$, it follows that 2 and 0 are not $\mathcal{P}(2)$-separable, see Theorem 3, and these are the only two elements which are not $\mathcal{P}(2)$-separable. It follows that

$$\mathcal{P}(2) = \{f : \mathbb{F} \to \mathbb{F} \mid f(0) = f(2)\},$$

or, equivalently, the partition of $\mathbb{F}$ induced by $\mathcal{P}(2)$ is $\mathbb{F} = \{0, 2\} \cup \{1\} \cup \{3\} \cup \{4\} \cup \{5\} \cup \{6\}$.

Since $2^3 = 1$, it follows that the pairs 0, 1 and 4, 5 are the only not $\mathcal{P}(3)$-separable pairs. Therefore

$$\mathcal{P}(3) = \{f : \mathbb{F} \to \mathbb{F} \mid f(0) = f(1) \text{ and } f(4) = f(5)\}$$

and the partition of $\mathbb{F}$ is given as $\mathbb{F} = \{0, 1\} \cup \{4, 5\} \cup \{2\} \cup \{3\} \cup \{6\}$.

Finally, since $\xi^6 = 1$ for all $\xi \in \mathbb{F}^*$, it follows that $P(Y)^3(0) = P(Y)^3(1) = P(Y)^3(2)$ and $P(Y)^3(3) = P(Y)^3(4) = P(Y)^3(5)$, therefore

$$\mathcal{P}(6) = \{f : \mathbb{F} \to \mathbb{F} \mid f(0) = f(1) = f(2) \text{ and } f(3) = f(4) = f(5)\}$$

and the partition of $\mathbb{F}$ is $\mathbb{F} = \{0, 1, 2\} \cup \{3, 4, 5\} \cup \{6\}$. To summarize we have 4 different vectorspace-rings of the form $\mathcal{P}(t)$, moreover

$$\mathcal{P}(t) = \mathcal{P}(\gcd(t, 6)).$$

We conclude with an observation which will be worthwhile to be investigated further. The divisors of $q - 1$ form a lattice as well as the vectorspace-rings generated by $P(Y)$. The partial order defined by this lattice is for the divisors $x \le y$ if x divides y and for the vectorspace-ring $V \le W$ if $V \subseteq W$. Figure 1 shows that the respective lattices are isomorphic.

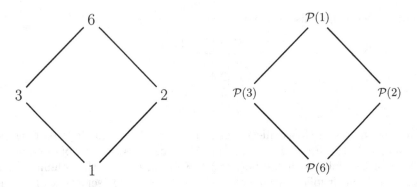

Fig. 1. The lattice structure of the divisors of 6 and the vectorspace-rings of $P(Y)$

4   Auxiliary Results

In this section we provide some necessary tools from the theory of finite fields, for more details see [2]. We also prove two auxiliary results needed several times throughout the text. Let $\mathbb{F}$ be a (finite) field. Then $\mathbb{F}^* = \mathbb{F} \setminus \{0\}$ equipped with the multiplication is a cyclic group of order $q-1$. Therefore there exists an $\epsilon \in \mathbb{F}^*$, a primitive element, such that $\mathbb{F}^* = \{\epsilon^s \mid s = 0, 1, \dots, q-2\}$ and $\epsilon^{q-1} = 1$. Since powers of elements of $\mathbb{F}$ as well powers of $\mathbb{F}[X]$ play an important rôle in the above, we denote two necessary results. The first is concerned with n-th powers in $\mathbb{F}^*$ and the second one deals with powers of polynomials.

Lemma 9. *For $n \in \mathbb{N}$ define $\pi_n : \mathbb{F}^* \to \mathbb{F}^*$ as $\pi_n(\xi) = \xi^n$. Then π_n is injective if and only if $\gcd(n, q-1) = 1$.*

Proof: Since $\mathbb{F}^*$ is a finite set, the injectivity of π_n implies the bijectivity, and vice versa. Since $\pi_n(\xi\,\zeta) = \pi_n(\xi)\,\pi_n(\zeta)$ the injectivity of π_n is equivalent to $\pi_n^{-1}(1) = \{1\}$. Since $\xi = \epsilon^s$ for $s \in \{0, \dots, q-2\}$ it follows that $\pi_n(\xi) = 1$ if and only if the equation $n\,s \equiv 0 \mod q-1$ has solutions $s \in \{0, \dots, q-2\}$. Note that $s = 0$ corresponds to the obvious solution $\xi = 1$. By Satz 3.1 in [5] the number of solutions is equal to $\gcd(n, q-1)$. This proves the assertion.   ∎

Theorem 5. *Let $p(Y), q(Y) \in \mathbb{F}[X]$ be polynomials different from 0 and let $n \in \mathbb{N}$ be greater than 0. Then the following holds: $p(Y)^n = q(Y)^n$ if and only if there exists $\rho \in \mathbb{F}^*$ such that $q(Y) = \rho p(Y)$ and $\rho^n = 1$.*

Proof: If $q(Y) = \rho p(Y)$ and $\rho^n = 1$, then $p(Y)^n = q(Y)^n$.
    Now let $p(Y)^n = q(Y)^n$. Let $\widehat{\mathbb{F}}$ be the splitting field of $p(Y)$, i.e.,

$$p(Y) = \alpha \prod_{j=1}^{d} (Y - \xi_j),$$

where $\alpha \in \mathbb{F}^* \subseteq \widehat{\mathbb{F}}$ and $\xi_j \in \widehat{\mathbb{F}}$, $j = 1, \ldots, d$. Since $q(Y)^n = p(Y)^n$, it follows that

$$q(Y)^n = \alpha^n \prod_{j=1}^{d} (Y - \xi_j)^n$$

over the field $\widehat{\mathbb{F}}$. We therefore conclude that $\widehat{\mathbb{F}}$ is the splitting field for $q(Y)$, i.e., there exists an $\beta \in \mathbb{F}^*$ such that

$$q(Y) = \beta \prod_{j=1}^{d} (Y - \xi_j)$$

and $\beta^n = \alpha^n$. For $\rho = \beta \alpha^{-1}$ we obtain $q(Y) = \rho p(Y)$. ∎

The next Lemma shows an application of the above two results

Lemma 10. *Let* $p(Y)$, $q(Y)$ *be polynomials with coefficients in the field* $\mathbb{F}$ *and let* n *be a positive natural number satisfying* $\gcd(n, q - 1) = 1$. *Then*

$$p(Y)^n = q(Y)^n$$

if and only if $p(Y) = q(Y)$.

Proof. If $p(Y) = q(Y)$, then the assertion is clear. Now assume that $p(Y)^n = q(Y)^n$. By Theorem 5 there exists a $\rho \in \mathbb{F}^*$ such that $q(Y) = \rho p(Y)$ and $\rho^n = 1$. Lemma 9 implies that $\rho = 1$. ∎

5   Concluding Remarks

In this article we have shown that the description of the subrings generated by a linear CA and with the special initial configuration $\underline{c}$ such that $\underline{c}(0) = 1$ and $\underline{c}(j) = 0, j \neq 0$ is fairly complete. The list of subrings can be computed alone from a knowledge of the coefficients of the polynomial $P(Y)$. As a next step towards a complete solution of the problem of information dynamics of (linear) CA is a description of the subrings generated by $P(Y)$ and a non-trivial initial configuration like $\underline{c}^0 = vxw$ where v and w are semi-infinite strings of constant maps as treated in [3].

The authors are grateful to Thomas Worsch for having interest and making discussions on this topics.

References

1. von Haeseler, F.: On a problem in information dynamics of cellular automata. J. Cell. Autom. 1(4), 377–393 (2006)
2. Lidl, R., Niederreiter, H.: Finite fields. In: Encyclopedia of Mathematics and its Applications, vol. 20, Addison-Wesley Publishing Company, Reading (1983)

3. Nishio, H., Saito, T.: Information dynamics of cellular automata. I. An algebraic study. Fund. Inform. 58(3-4), 399–420 (2003)
4. Nishio, H.: Completeness and degeneracy in information dynamics of cellular automata. In: Jedrzejowicz, J., Szepietowski, A. (eds.) MFCS 2005. LNCS, vol. 3618, pp. 699–707. Springer, Heidelberg (2005)
5. Schwarz, W.: Einführung in die Zahlentheorie. Die Mathematik: Einführungen in Gegenstand und Ergebnisse ihrer Teilgebiete und Nachbarwissenschaften. Wissenschaftliche Buchgesellschaft, Darmstadt (1975)

Author Index